History
for the IB Diploma

PAPER 3

The Soviet Union and Post-Soviet Russia (1924–2000)

SECOND EDITION

Allan Todd

CAMBRIDGE
UNIVERSITY PRESS

University Printing House, Cambridge CB2 8BS, United Kingdom

One Liberty Plaza, 20th Floor, New York, NY 10006, USA

477 Williamstown Road, Port Melbourne, VIC 3207, Australia

314–321, 3rd Floor, Plot 3, Splendor Forum, Jasola District Centre, New Delhi – 110025, India

79 Anson Road, #06–04/06, Singapore 079906

Cambridge University Press is part of the University of Cambridge.

It furthers the University's mission by disseminating knowledge in the pursuit of education, learning and research at the highest international levels of excellence.

www.cambridge.org
Information on this title: www.cambridge.org/9781316503690

First published 2012
Second edition 2016

20 19 18 17 16 15 14 13 12 11 10 9 8 7 6 5 4

Printed in Great Britain by CPI Group (UK) Ltd, Croydon CR0 4YY

A catalogue record for this publication is available from the British Library

ISBN 978-1-316-50369-0 Paperback

NOTICE TO TEACHERS IN THE UK
It is illegal to reproduce any part of this work in material form (including
photocopying and electronic storage) except under the following circumstances:
(i) where you are abiding by a licence granted to your school or institution by
the Copyright Licensing Agency;
(ii) where no such licence exists, or where you wish to exceed the terms of a licence,
and you have gained the written permission of Cambridge University Press;
(iii) where you are allowed to reproduce without permission under the provisions
of Chapter 3 of the Copyright, Designs and Patents Act 1988, which covers, for
example, the reproduction of short passages within certain types of educational
anthology and reproduction for the purposes of setting examination questions.

This material has been developed independently by the publisher and the content is in no
way connected with nor endorsed by the International Baccalaureate Organization.

Dedication
For our grandchildren, Alexander and Emilia

Contents

1   Introduction   5

2   Stalin's Rise to Power, 1924–29   21
    2.1 What was Stalin's position before 1924?   24
    2.2 How did Stalin win the struggle for power after 1924?   31
    2.3 Why was Stalin able to defeat his rivals?   41

3   Stalin's Revolution, 1929–41   47
    3.1 What were Stalin's main economic policies?   51
    3.2 How successful were Stalin's economic policies?   61
    3.3 What did Stalin do to consolidate his power?   64
    3.4 How did Stalin's foreign policy try to achieve security
        for the Soviet Union in the 1930s?   72

4   Stalin and the Soviet Union, 1941–53   86
    4.1 How did the Great Patriotic War, 1941–45, affect the
        Soviet Union?   90
    4.2 What were Stalin's main political and economic policies,
        1945–53?   97
    4.3 How did the emerging Cold War affect Stalin's foreign
        policy after 1945?   100

5   Khrushchev and De-Stalinisation, 1953–64   127
    5.1 What were Khrushchev's main political reforms?   130
    5.2 How did Khrushchev try to reform the Soviet
        economy?   137
    5.3 What were the main features of Khrushchev's
        foreign policy?   144

6   The Brezhnev Era: Stagnation and Drift, 1964–85   160
    6.1 What were the main political developments in
        the USSR, 1964–85?   163
    6.2 What were the main features of the
        Soviet economy, 1964–85?   172

6.3 How did Soviet foreign policy develop during
    this period?   182

7   Gorbachev and the Years of Reform, 1985–89   194

7.1 What were Gorbachev's main economic
    policies, 1985–89?   198

7.2 How did Gorbachev try to democratise the Soviet
    political system?   207

7.3 What were the main consequences of Gorbachev's foreign
    policy during the 1980s?   226

8   The Collapse of the Soviet Union, 1990–91   238

8.1 What happened with Gorbachev's economic
    policies, 1990–91?   241

8.2 What happened with Gorbachev's attempts to
    democratise the Soviet political system?   248

8.3 Why did the Soviet Union collapse in 1991?   256

9   Yeltsin and Post-Soviet Russia, 1992–2000   267

9.1 What were the main aspects of Yeltsin's rule
    in Russia, 1992–96?   270

9.2 How did Yeltsin maintain his rule from
    1996 to 2000?   284

9.3 Has the 'spectre of communism' been laid to rest?   292

10 Exam Practice   300

Index   319

Acknowledgements   328

Introduction

1

The Soviet Union and Post-Soviet Russia (1924–2000)

This book is designed to prepare students taking the Paper 3, Section 16 topic, *The Soviet Union and post-Soviet Russia 1924–2000* (in HL Option 4: History of Europe) in the IB History examination. It will begin by examining the history of the Soviet Union from the death of Lenin in 1924, before looking at Stalin's rise to power, and the consolidation and development of the Soviet state under his rule from 1924 to 1953. It will also touch on aspects relating to the impact of the Second World War and the Soviet Union's expansion from 1945 to 1953. It will then explore the major economic, political and social developments – as well as those relating to foreign relations – under the various Soviet leaders from 1953 to 1985. The reform period under Gorbachev after 1985 will also be considered: with special focus on the aims and impacts of his policies, and the eventual collapse of the Soviet Union in 1991. Finally, the main political and economic developments from 1992 to 2000 in post-Soviet Russia under Yeltsin will also be examined.

ACTIVITY

Carry out some research on the Bolshevik Revolution in Russia in November 1917, and the main developments in Russia from 1917 to 1921, including the Civil War. Then make some brief notes on these main issues. This will help you better understand the main arguments and events which took place after 1921.

Figure 1.1: The USSR and Eastern Europe, 1949–91.

Themes

To help you prepare for your IB History exams, this book will cover the main themes and aspects relating to *The Soviet Union and post-Soviet Russia 1924–2000* as set out in the IB *History Guide*. In particular, it will examine the USSR and post-Soviet Russia in the period 1924–2000 in terms of the major areas shown below:

- Stalin's rise and the nature of his rule, including the power struggle, his economic policies, the consolidation of his power, the purges and Great Terror, and the cult of personality
- the impact of the Great Patriotic War from 1941 to 1945, and the main political and economic developments in the Soviet Union from 1945 until Stalin's death in 1953
- the contribution of the emerging Cold War to the consolidation of the Soviet state, including the expansion of Soviet influence beyond its borders
- the economic and political policies pursued by Khrushchev in the period 1953–64, along with the most significant developments in foreign relations
- the main political, economic and foreign policies during Brezhnev's rule from 1964 to 1982, and the main developments in the USSR between 1982 and 1985
- the aims and impact of Gorbachev's political and economic policies on the Soviet Union, 1985–1991, and the foreign policy followed by Gorbachev after 1985
- the collapse of the Soviet Union in 1991 and the main political and economic developments in post-Soviet Russia under Yeltsin from 1992 to 2000.

Key Concepts

Each chapter will help you to focus on the main issues, and to compare and contrast the main developments that took place during the various periods of Soviet and post-Soviet history. In addition, at various points in the chapters, there will be questions and activities which will help you focus on the six key concepts – these are:

- change
- continuity
- causation
- consequence
- significance
- perspectives.

Theory of Knowledge

In addition to the broad key themes, the chapters contain Theory of Knowledge links, to get you thinking about aspects which relate to history, which is a Group 3 subject in the IB Diploma. The Soviet Union and post-Soviet Russia topic has several clear links to ideas about knowledge and history. The subject is highly political, as it concerns, among other things, aspects of ideology – namely a logically connected set of ideas which form the foundation of a relatively coherent system of political beliefs and/or political theory. As far as this book is concerned, the main ideologies which are relevant to your study are **communism** and **capitalism**.

At times, the extremely political nature of this topic has affected the historians writing about these states, the leaders involved, and the policies and actions taken. So questions relating to the selection of sources, and interpretations of them, by historians have clear links to the IB Theory of Knowledge course.

For example, when trying to explain aspects of the policies implemented by leaders, their motives, and their success or failure, historians must decide which evidence to select and use to make their case and which evidence to leave out. But to what extent do the historians' personal political views influence their decisions when they select what they consider to be the most important or relevant sources, and when they make judgements about the value and limitations of specific sources or sets of sources? Is there such a thing as objective 'historical truth'? Or is there just a range of subjective historical opinions and interpretations about the past which vary according to the political interests and leanings of individual historians?

It is also important to be aware that since 1985, and especially since 1991, many archives from the former Soviet Union have been opened up, which were not available to historians writing before those dates.

Therefore you are strongly advised to read a range of books giving different interpretations of the theory and practice, and of the various economic, political and social policies which were attempted during the period covered by this book, in order to gain a clear understanding of the relevant historiographies.

IB History and Paper 3 questions

Paper 3

In IB History, Paper 3 is taken only by Higher Level students. For this paper, IB History specifies that three sections of an Option should be selected for in-depth study. The examination paper will set two questions on each section – and you have to answer three questions. Unlike Paper 2, where there were regional restrictions, in Paper 3 you will be able to answer both questions from one section, with a third chosen from one of the other sections. These questions are essentially in-depth analytical essays. It is therefore important to ensure you study all the bullet points set out in the IB History Guide, if you wish to give yourself the widest possible choice of questions.

Exam skills

Throughout the main chapters of this book, there are activities and questions to help you develop the understanding and the exam skills needed for success in Paper 3. Your exam answers should show:

* factual knowledge and understanding
* awareness and understanding of historical interpretations
* structured, analytical and *balanced* arguments.

Before attempting the specific exam practice questions which come at the end of each main chapter, you might find it useful to refer first to

Chapter 10, the final Exam Practice chapter. This suggestion is based on the idea that if you know where you are supposed to be going (in this instance, gaining a good mark and grade), and how to get there, you stand a better chance of reaching your destination!

Questions and mark schemes

To ensure that you develop the necessary skills and understanding, each chapter contains comprehension questions and examination tips. For success in Paper 3, you need to produce essays which combine a number of features – in many ways, these require the same skills as the essays in Paper 2.

However, for the Higher Level Paper 3, examiners will be looking for greater evidence of *sustained* analysis and argument – linked closely to the demands of the question. They will also be seeking more depth and precision with regard to supporting knowledge. Finally they will be expecting a clear and well-organised answer, so it is vital to do a rough plan *before* you start to answer a question. Not only will this show you early on whether you know enough about the topic to answer the question, it will also help maintain a good structure for your answer.

So, it is particularly important to start by focusing *closely* on the wording of the question, so that you can identify its demands. If you simply take the view that a question is '*generally about this period/leader*', you will probably produce an answer which is essentially a narrative, with only vague links to the question. Even if your knowledge is detailed and accurate, it will only be broadly relevant – if you do this, you will get half-marks at the most.

The next important aspect of your answer is that you present a well-structured and analytical argument that is clearly linked to **all** the demands of the question. Each aspect of your argument/analysis/explanation then needs to be supported by carefully selected, precise and relevant own knowledge.

In addition, in order to access the highest bands and marks, you need to show, where appropriate, awareness and understanding of relevant historical debates and interpretations. This does not mean simply paraphrasing what different historians have said. Instead, try to *critically evaluate* particular interpretations: for example, are there any weaknesses in some arguments put forward by some historians? What strengths does a particular interpretation have?

Examiner's tips

To help you develop these skills, most chapters contain sample questions, with examiner tips about what – and what not – to do in order to achieve high marks. These chapters will focus on a specific skill, as follows:

- Skill 1 (Chapter 3) – understanding the wording of a question
- Skill 2 (Chapter 4) – planning an essay
- Skill 3 (Chapter 5) – writing an introductory paragraph
- Skill 4 (Chapter 6) – avoiding irrelevance
- Skill 5 (Chapter 7) – avoiding a narrative-based answer
- Skill 6 (Chapter 8) – using your own knowledge analytically and combining it with awareness of historical debate
- Skill 7 (Chapter 9) – writing a conclusion to your essay.

Some of these tips will contain parts of a student's answer to a particular question, with examiner comments, to help you understand what examiners are looking for.

This guidance is developed further in the Exam Practice chapter, where examiners' tips and comments will help you focus on the important aspects of questions and their answers. These will also help you to avoid the kind of simple mistakes and oversights which, every year, result in some otherwise-good students failing to gain the highest marks.

For additional help, a simplified Paper 3 mark scheme is provided in the Exam Practice chapter. This should make it easier to understand what examiners are looking for in examination answers. The actual Paper 3 IB History mark scheme can be found on the IB website.

The content covered by this book will provide you with the historical knowledge and understanding to help you answer all the specific content bullet points set out in the IB History Guide. Also, by the time you have worked through the various exercises, you should have the skills necessary to construct relevant, clear, well-argued and well-supported essays.

Background to the period – communism

In theory, communism is a social and economic system in which all significant aspects of a country's economy are socially owned and self-managed – either by the state or by local communities or cooperatives. Unlike in capitalist countries, where land, industries and banks are privately owned, social ownership is intended to result in a classless society. Such ideas came to prominence with the writings of **Karl Marx** and Friedrich Engels.

Karl Marx (1818–83):

He was a German philosopher and historian who developed the materialist concept of history (meaning that historians should look to social and economic aspects rather than 'ideas' as the main causal factors in history). He argued that class struggle and conflict were the most (but not the only) important factors behind social and economic – as well as intellectual and political – change. He also identified various stages in the development of human societies. He worked closely with his friend and collaborator, Friedrich Engels (1820–95), and together, in 1847, they wrote *The Communist Manifesto*. Marx then went on to write an in-depth study of the workings of capitalism, entitled *Capital* (*Das Kapital*). His ideas inspired many revolutionaries, including Lenin and Trotsky, who made the first attempt to put his ideas into practice in Russia, following the November 1917 Revolution. However, practice turned out to be very different from theory – and many have argued that communism has not yet been implemented anywhere.

Marx and Engels urged the industrial working classes in the developed capitalist countries (mainly Britain, Germany and the US at the time) to bring about socialist revolutions which would result in societies where – for the first time in human history – the ruling class would be the majority of the population. From this new form of human society, Marx believed it would be possible to move eventually to an even better one: communism. This would be a classless society but, because it would be based on the economic advances of industrial capitalism, it would be a society of plenty, not of scarcity. This would be based on greater freedom and abundance – and would eventually see a real decline in state power.

However, Marx did not write much about the political forms which would be adopted under socialism and communism. On these, he said only that, as the majority of the population would be in control, it would be more democratic and less repressive than previous societies. He argued that after the workers' revolution, measures should be adopted from day one to bring about the eventual 'withering away' of the state.

Marx did not believe that 'progression' through the stages of society that he had identified was inevitable. He also argued that, in special circumstances, a relatively backward society could 'jump' a stage – but only if that state was then aided by sympathetic advanced societies. He certainly did not believe that a poor agricultural society could move to socialism on its own, as socialism required an advanced industrial base.

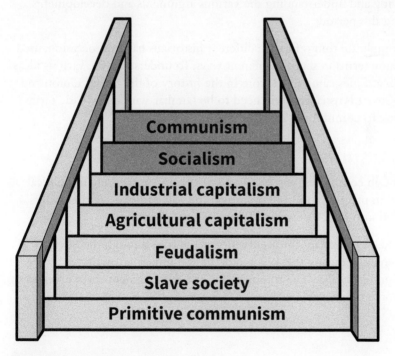

Figure 1.2: The stages of Marxist theory.

1

ACTIVITY

Before you begin to work your way through this book, try to find out a bit more about Marxism and its aims before Stalin came to power in the Soviet Union. When you have done so, write a couple of sentences to explain to what extent you think the aims of Marxism are: (a) achievable and (b) desirable.

Terminology and definitions

The history of the Soviet Union can often seem extremely complicated. In part, this is the result of the range of political terms involved in studying and understanding the various arguments and developments during this period.

To complicate things further, different historians have, on occasion, used the same terms in slightly different ways. To understand the various ideas which at times came to the fore in the history of the Soviet Union and post-Soviet Russia, you will need to be familiar with a few basic terms relating to communism and to capitalism.

Communism

Although communist parties are seen as being 'on the Left' in political terms, in practice communist parties – like all parties – are themselves divided into Left, Centre and Right wings or factions.

This helps to explain the arguments which tore through the Soviet Communists during the 1920s and 1930s – in particular, those surrounding Stalin's rise to power and the disagreements over economic and foreign policies.

Figure 1.3: The political spectrum: Left/Centre/Right.

Another difficult aspect to grasp is that 'communism' has meant – and still means – different things to different people, both to historians and to members and leaders of communist parties. The three main terms and distinctions you need to understand are:

- Leninism
- Marxism-Leninism
- Stalinism.

Leninism

Marx did not refer to himself as a 'Marxist'; he preferred the term 'communist'. However, his followers often preferred to call themselves 'Marxists' as well as communists. In this way they distinguished themselves from other groups which claimed to be 'communist', and emphasised that Marxism and its methods formed a distinct philosophy.

One such Marxist was the Russian revolutionary **Vladimir Ilyich Lenin**.

Lenin developed some of Marx's economic ideas, but his main contribution to Marxist theory related to political organisation. Lenin's main ideas, based on the extremely undemocratic political system operating in Tsarist Russia, were what became known as 'democratic centralism', and the need for a small 'vanguard' party (a leading group) of fully committed revolutionaries.

Vladimir Ilyich Lenin (1870–1924):

His real name was Vladimir Ilyich Ulyanov, and he had joined the Russian Social Democratic Party (RSDLP), a Marxist party when it was formed in 1898. He provoked a split in the RSDLP in 1903, and formed his own faction, known as the Bolsheviks. In exile until April 1917, he returned to Russia and immediately began to push for a revolution to overthrow the Provisional Government which had taken power following a revolution in February/March 1917. After the successful Bolshevik Revolution in October/November, he acted as prime minister until his death in 1924.

Leon Trotsky (1879–1940), a leading Russian Marxist, disagreed with Lenin. From 1903 to 1917, Trotsky argued that Lenin's system would allow an unscrupulous leader to become a dictator over the party. Nevertheless, both Lenin and Trotsky believed in the possibility of moving quickly to the socialist phase. This idea was similar to Marx's idea of 'permanent revolution', which argued that as soon as one revolutionary stage had been achieved, the struggle for the next would begin almost immediately.

Like Marx, both Lenin and Trotsky believed that Russia could not succeed in carrying through any 'uninterrupted revolution' without outside economic and technical assistance. When this assistance failed to materialise, despite earlier hopes of successful workers' revolutions in other European states after 1918, Lenin proved to be an extremely pragmatic – or opportunistic – ruler who was quite prepared to adopt policies which seemed in total conflict with communist goals and even with those of the 'lower' socialist stage. This is seen most clearly in relation to the New Economic Policy and the ban on factions and other parties (see 2.1, Lenin's 'Last Struggle', 1921–24). Yet Lenin argued that these were just adaptations to the prevailing circumstances and that, as soon as conditions allowed, there would be a return to 'socialist norms'.

Marxism-Leninism

The term Marxism-Leninism, invented by Stalin, was not used until after Lenin's death in 1924. It soon came to be used in Stalin's Soviet Union to refer to what he described as 'orthodox Marxism', which increasingly came to mean what Stalin himself had to say about political and economic issues. Essentially, Marxism-Leninism was the 'official' ideology of the Soviet state and all communist parties loyal to Stalin and his successors. However, many Marxists – and even members of the Communist Party itself – believed that Stalin's ideas and practices, such as 'socialism in one country' (see 2.2, The campaign against 'Trotskyism'), were almost total distortions of what Marx and Lenin had advocated and tried to achieve.

Stalinism

The term 'Stalinism' is used both by historians and by those politically opposed to Stalin to describe the views and practices associated with Stalin and his supporters. Historians and political scientists use it to mean a set of beliefs and a type of rule which are essentially deeply undemocratic and even dictatorial.

Marxist opponents of Stalin and post-Stalin rulers used the term in some of the ways used by historians. However, they were also determined to show that Stalinism was not an adaptation of Marxism but, on the contrary, a qualitative and fundamental aberration from both Lenin and Marx, and from revolutionary communism in general. In particular, they stress the way in which Stalin and his supporters rejected the goal of socialist democracy in favour of a permanent one-party state. They also emphasise how Stalinism in practice and in theory placed the national interests of the Soviet Union above the struggle to achieve world revolution.

Cold War

This term is used to describe the tension and rivalry between the USA and the USSR in the period 1945–91 – which finally ended when the Soviet Union collapsed at the end of 1991. The term 'Cold War' was originally used in the 14th century about the conflict between Christian and Islamic states, and refers to relations that, although hostile, do not build up into a 'hot war', that is, actual military conflict. The term was popularised in the years 1946–47 by US journalist Walter Lippmann,

and by US politician and businessman Bernard Baruch. The collapse of
the Soviet Union was hailed by some observers as the 'end of history',
which would usher in the global triumph of capitalism and neo-liberal
economics.

Capitalism

Essentially, capitalism is an ideology which is based on the belief that the
most important parts of a country's economy – such as banks, industries
and the land – should be owned and controlled by private individuals
and/or private companies. An important part of this belief is the view
that the state, or government, should not be involved in the economy. In
fact, in its early 'liberal' or 'classical' phase in the Industrial Revolution,
it was believed that, apart from providing an army and (grudgingly) a
police force, the government should not even provide social welfare.
This, it was argued, helped ensure 'freedom'. Although most capitalist
states eventually developed as liberal political democracies, this was not
always the case. Several capitalist states – such as Hitler's Germany in the
1930s and 1940s and Pinochet's Chile in the 1970s and 1980s – were
decidedly undemocratic.

Such a social and economic system is often called a 'free market' or 'free
enterprise economy'. In its early forms, capitalist firms and individuals
argued that prices, wages and employment should be determined by
'market forces' or 'supply and demand', not by government policies.
Yet at the same time, many industrialists pushed for laws which either
banned or restricted the formation of trade unions by employees.
However, during the second half of the 19th century and the first
half of the 20th century, these views were gradually modified in most
European countries, and states began to provide such public services as
education, old-age pensions, welfare benefits and a health service. After
1945, the term 'Keynesian economics' was often used to describe this
form of partially regulated capitalism. The term came from the theories
of British economist John Maynard Keynes in his book, *The General
Theory of Employment, Interest and Money*, published in 1936.

Neo-liberalism

Neo-liberalism is a more extreme version of capitalism which rejects
Keynesian economics and which, in several ways, harks back to the
early form of 'classical' unregulated capitalism. During the 1980s, the
'welfare capitalism', which had emerged by the mid-20th century, came

increasingly under attack in most Western states. In opposition to the welfare state, a return to 'liberal' capitalism was called for instead. These moves involved calls for a 'small' state – one which allowed private firms to take over the provision of various public utilities and welfare services; in which taxation of profits was reduced; and the rights of trade unions were restricted. At first, the economic policy associated with this 'rolling back' of the state was often called 'monetarism', and was quickly adopted by Reagan's governments in the US, and by Thatcher's in Britain.

Such policies were based on the ideas of Friedrich Hayek and Milton Friedman, and other theorists linked to the Chicago School of Economics, who increasingly argued for an unrestricted capitalism and the privatisation of most publicly owned social services. During the 1990s, these policies were applied in post-Soviet Russia (and in the former Eastern European states), and was often called economic 'shock therapy'. Most recently, these kinds of ideas and policies have usually been referred to as 'neo-liberalism', and have been associated with austerity and privatisation programmes in many Western states following the 2008 banking failures. These ideas have also been closely associated with the spread of economic globalisation.

Summary

By the time you have worked through this book, you should be able to:

- understand and explain how Stalin came to power, and how he maintained his position
- understand and account for the developments and policies during Stalin's rule, including the collectivisation of agriculture, the Five-Year Plans, the purges and the Great Terror, and Soviet foreign policy
- show an awareness of the impact and significance of the Second World War and the early stages of the Cold War on the USSR's economic and political development
- understand the significance of leaders such as Khrushchev and Brezhnev, and their key economic, political and foreign policies in the period 1953–85

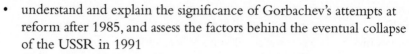

The Soviet Union and Post-Soviet Russia (1924–2000)

- understand and explain the significance of Gorbachev's attempts at reform after 1985, and assess the factors behind the eventual collapse of the USSR in 1991
- show a broad understanding of the main developments in post-Soviet Russia under Yeltsin in the period 1992–2000.

Stalin's Rise to Power, 1924–29

2

Introduction

Any study of the consolidation of the Soviet state from 1924 onwards involves a study of the policies and methods Stalin used to ensure its survival, development and expansion during his long leadership. Before examining these, however, it is necessary to understand how he rose to power, as many of the issues involved in the power struggle which broke out after 1924 formed the background to his later policies. This chapter, after providing some background on events 1917–24, will examine Stalin's rise, and the reasons why he was able to become the dominant leader of the Soviet Union – a position he held from 1928 until his death in 1953.

TIMELINE

1917 Oct/Nov: Bolshevik Revolution

1921 Mar: Kronstadt Rebellion; NEP adopted, factions and opposition parties banned

1922 Apr: Stalin becomes General-Secretary of the Communist Party

Dec: Lenin writes his last Testament; Triumvirate formed against Trotsky

1923 Jan: Lenin's Postscript recommends Stalin's dismissal

1924 Jan: Lenin dies; 13th Party Conference condemns Trotsky's views

May: Central Committee keeps Lenin's Testament secret and decides not to dismiss Stalin

1925 Apr: Party debate over 'permanent revolution' versus 'socialism in one country'

May: Start of the Leningrad Opposition

Dec: 14th Party Congress; the Leningrad Opposition is outvoted

1926 Jul: United Opposition formed; Zinoviev dismissed from the Politburo

1927 Oct: Stalin persuades the Central Committee to expel Trotsky and Zinoviev from the Central Committee

Nov: Trotsky and Zinoviev expelled from the Communist Party, and Kamenev from the Central Committee

Dec: 15th Party Congress: Zinoviev and Kamenev end the United Opposition

1928 Jul: Stalin and Bukharin clash over collectivisation

Aug: Bukharin tries to form an alliance with Trotsky

1929 Apr: Bukharin removed as editor of *Pravda*

Nov: Bukharin removed from Politburo

Note: The Russian calendar in use until 1918 was 13 days behind the calendar used in the rest of Europe. The revolutions of 1917 took place in February and October according to the old Russian calendar, but in March and November according to the Western calendar. This book therefore refers to the February/March Revolution and the October/November Revolution.

KEY QUESTIONS

- What was Stalin's position before 1924?
- How did Stalin win the struggle for power after 1924?
- Why was Stalin able to defeat his rivals?

Overview

- In November 1917, Lenin's Bolsheviks took power in a revolution which had the backing of large numbers of industrial workers and soldiers. After the revolution, the Bolsheviks (renamed the Russian Communist Party in 1918) formed a new revolutionary government.
- However, they faced violent opposition, and a civil war broke out which lasted until 1921. During this period, the constant turmoil led to serious political crises and economic collapse. These problems sparked growing disagreements among the Russian Communist Party (RCP) leaders about what policies to adopt after 1921.
- From 1922, Lenin had suffered a series of progressively serious strokes, which increasingly prevented him from taking an active part in politics. In December 1922, he wrote a Testament, outlining the strengths and weaknesses of the main leaders; in January 1923, worried by some of Stalin's actions, he added a Postscript, recommending Stalin be dismissed.

- Trotsky's main rivals, Zinoviev and Kamenev, made an alliance with Stalin, in order to prevent Trotsky replacing Lenin. Using his position as general-secretary, Stalin was able to control meetings and elections to conferences and congresses. Trotsky was soon isolated.
- With Trotsky defeated, Stalin then turned on Zinoviev and Kamenev, supported by Bukharin and the Right. Later, in 1928, having defeated the Left, Stalin turned on Bukharin and by 1929 had also defeated the Right of the Party.

Figure 2.1: Lenin (circled left) and Trotsky (circled right) with Red Army troops after the suppression of the Kronstadt Rebellion in 1921.

2.1 What was Stalin's position before 1924?

In early 1924, **Josef Stalin** seemed most unlikely to rise to the top. Yet, by 1929, he had politically defeated and neutralised all his main rivals – all of whom had seemed much more likely candidates for the leadership after Lenin's death.

Josef Stalin (1880–1953):

His real name was Josef Djugashvili; he joined the Russian Social
Democratic Labour Party and sided with Lenin in the 1903
split. Unlike most of the other communist leaders, he was not
an intellectual, and mainly undertook practical tasks (including
bank robberies and editing newspapers). In 1922, he took on
the role of General-Secretary of the Communist Party – a routine
administrative job which the other leaders did not want. He rarely
disagreed with Lenin and, after the latter's death in 1924, began to
use his position to make himself supreme ruler. He executed many
of his rivals in the purges of the 1930s, and remained head of the
USSR until his death in 1953.

Lenin's 'Last Struggle', 1921–24

During the final stages of the First World War, in February/March
1917, a revolution in Russia had overthrown the Tsar (emperor), and
an unelected provisional government had declared Russia to be a
democratic republic.

However, the Provisional Government failed to carry out land reform,
kept Russia in the war, and delayed holding promised elections.
Consequently, it became increasingly unpopular. In October/November,
a second revolution had taken place, at the insistence of Lenin. This
Bolshevik Revolution made Russia the world's first workers' state.

This new state – renamed the Russian Socialist Federal Soviet Republic
(RSFSR) – was then plunged into three years of civil war.

Though the Bolsheviks finally won power in 1921, the massive
economic and political problems all this turmoil and warfare had created
led to many sharp policy differences between the leading Bolsheviks.

A one-party state?

The most important disagreement was over economic policy. At the
start of the Civil War, an economic policy known as 'war communism'
had been adopted as an emergency measure. Grain had been
requisitioned from the peasants to ensure adequate supplies for the
Soviets' Red Army and the industrial centres; all private trade had been
banned; and all factories, mines and banks were nationalised (taken over
by the government). However, this policy – along with the damage

suffered as a consequence of the Civil War, and the restrictions on democracy during the war – had led to the Kronstadt Rising in March 1921, in which workers, sailors and soldiers had staged a serious revolt in protest.

Though this revolt had been ruthlessly crushed, Lenin persuaded the 10th Party Congress of 1921 to adopt a New Economic Policy (NEP) to replace War Communism – this introduced a partial step-back towards small-scale capitalism. This limited revival of capitalism, and the shock of the Kronstadt Rising, also led Lenin to introduce a ban on factions within the Communist Party – and a ban on opposition parties in the Soviets. Several communists opposed this ban, and later Lenin stated that it was a purely temporary measure, intended to cope with the acute political and economic crisis.

KEY CONCEPTS ACTIVITY

Significance: Find out more about War Communism, the Kronstadt Rising, and the NEP. Then explain why these policies and events, and the ban on factions and other parties, were so important for later political developments in the Soviet Union.

Stalin versus Trotsky

In May 1922, Lenin had the first of a series of strokes, which increasingly restricted his ability to take an active part in politics. Yet there were significant political differences over internal political democracy and what attitude to take about furthering world revolution. Leading communists began to consider what would happen if Lenin died. The most important communists after Lenin were the other members of the Politburo. The Politburo (short for 'Political Bureau') was the RCP's body responsible for making political decisions between Congresses. Though, in theory, the Politburo was responsible to the Central Committee (CC) which elected it, and to the Party Congress (which elected the CC), in practice, the Politburo soon came to dominate the other two bodies. In 1921, it comprised: Trotsky, Zinoviev, Kamenev, Bukharin, Rykov, Stalin and Tomsky. Of these, **Leon Trotsky** seemed the most likely to replace Lenin. After him, Zinoviev and Kamenev were strong political leaders (of the Petrograd and Moscow Communist Party branches, respectively) and had long been associated with Lenin – their weak spot was that they had been opposed to the

November Revolution at first. Bukharin, too, was a well-known and popular revolutionary leader. Stalin was not well known and seemed unlikely to emerge as a major leader. However, he had been appointed Commissar (minister) for the nationalities after the revolution and, in April 1922, had been appointed General-Secretary of the Communist Party; this position included appointing and dismissing communist officials.

Leon Trotsky (1879–1940):

His real name was Leon Bronstein. He had been a member of the RSDLP, but had opposed Lenin's ideas on party organisation. In August 1917, he joined the Bolsheviks, as both he and Lenin had now developed very similar outlooks. He was defeated by Stalin and his supporters, and expelled from the Soviet Union in 1929. In 1938, he set up the Trotskyist Fourth International, as he had become convinced by then that the Communist International (see 2.2, The campaign against 'Trotskyism') and its parties had become so 'Stalinist' and conservative that they were unreformable. He was assassinated in Mexico in 1940 by one of Stalin's agents.

QUESTION

What important position did Stalin take on in 1922? How did this help him become the ruler of the USSR?

Many of the leading communists resented Trotsky's rapid rise to the top of the party after August 1917. Zinoviev and Kamenev in particular believed they should take over from Lenin, and turned to Stalin for help to stop Trotsky succeeding – these three became known as the 'triumvirs' (a reference to Ancient Rome when, for a time, it was ruled by a government of three officials). As early as December 1922, they began moves to prevent Trotsky obtaining majority support. Though Lenin's strokes kept him from active involvement in politics, his awareness of these political and personal tensions caused him growing concern, and led him to propose to Trotsky that they should form a Joint Bloc for Democracy against growing signs of bureaucracy in the party and the state.

The Soviet Union and Post-Soviet Russia (1924–2000)

Lenin's Testament

Towards the end of December 1922, Lenin suffered a second stroke. Concerned about what might happen after his death, he dictated his initial thoughts for what he thought would be his last Testament, outlining the strengths and weaknesses of all the leading communists. He was particularly worried by Stalin's attitudes towards the non-Russian nationalities. After 1921, Lenin had come to favour a looser federation of autonomous states rather than a more centralised unitary state which Stalin was trying to push through.

Lenin was particularly concerned about Stalin's use of force against those in the Soviet republic of Georgia who were against his plans.

These concerns led Lenin to add a Postscript to his Testament in January 1923, recommending Stalin's removal from all his posts.

SOURCE 2.1

Files on the Georgian Affair were brought out for Lenin to examine. He had made his mind up about the verdict: Stalin and his associates were guilty of Great Russian chauvinism even though Stalin, Ordzhonikidze and Dzierzynski themselves were not Russians. Already at the end of the previous year, in an article on the national question, Lenin had acknowledged:

'I am, it seems, immensely guilty before the workers of Russia for not intervening sufficiently energetically and sufficiently sharply in the notorious question of autonomisation, officially known, it seems as the question of the union of soviet socialist republics.'

He also dictated an article on bureaucracy in the organs of party and government, making strong criticisms of the Workers' and Peasants' Inspectorate. It was obvious to informed observers that Stalin, who headed the Inspectorate, was his principal target... telling his secretaries to keep everything to themselves and to lock up his papers. This was how he plotted the downfall of an individual whom he considered the greatest danger to the Revolution...

Service, R., 2005, Stalin: a Biography, *London, Pan, p. 210.*

SOURCE 2.2

Since he became General Secretary, Comrade Stalin has concentrated in his hands immeasurable power, and I am not sure that he will always know how to use that power with sufficient caution. On the other hand Comrade Trotsky... is distinguished not only by his outstanding qualities (personally he is the most capable man in the present Central Committee) but also by his excess of self-confidence and a readiness to be carried away by the purely administrative side of affairs....

Stalin is too rude, and this fault, entirely supportable in relations amongst us Communists, becomes insupportable in the office of General Secretary. Therefore, I propose to the comrades to find a way of removing Stalin from that position and to appoint another man who in all respects differs from Stalin only in superiority; namely, more patient, more loyal, more polite, less capricious, and more attentive to comrades.

Extracts from Lenin's Testament and Postscript, 25 December 1922 and 4 January 1923. Quoted in Lynch, M., 1990, **Stalin and Khrushchev: The USSR 1924–64**, *London, Hodder & Stoughton, pp. 15–16.*

From then, until his death the following year, Lenin urged Trotsky on several occasions to launch a campaign against bureaucracy, and for the restoration of party and Soviet democracy.

QUESTION

Why did Lenin write a *Postscript* to his *Testament* in January 1923?

By January 1923, the triumvirs' alliance had been finalised. Soon a 'whispering campaign' was underway, concerning Trotsky's non-Bolshevik past, and his earlier disagreements with Lenin. However, Stalin appeared to be in serious trouble in March 1923 – his rudeness to Lenin's wife, **Nadezhda Krupskaya**, had led Lenin to send him a harsh letter, on 5 March, threatening to 'break relations' with him if he did not retract and apologise. Kamenev was aware of this, and of Lenin's intention to politically 'crush' Stalin: at this stage, it seemed that Stalin's ambitions were doomed to failure. But then Lenin suffered a third stroke, which left him paralysed and speechless for most of the time until his death in January 1924.

Nadezhda Krupskaya (1869–1939):

Often known as 'Nadya', she was a revolutionary and writer, and had married Lenin in 1898. She initially supported Stalin against Trotsky, but later, for a time, supported Zinoviev and Kamenev when they began to criticise Stalin. She was involved in education, acting as a deputy Commissar (minister) for Education in 1918 under Lenin, and again from 1929 to 1939. She also played a big role in establishing Komsomol (the Young Communist organisation).

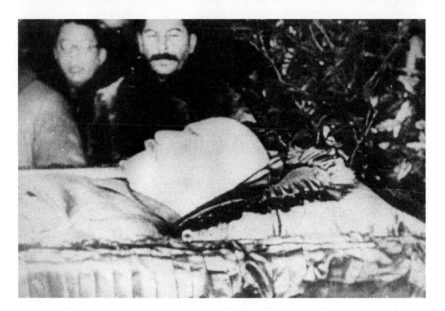

Figure 2.2: According to Boris Bazhanov (1900–83), Stalin's personal secretary from 1923 to 1925, Stalin was 'jubilant' over Lenin's death, though in public he put on a show of grief.

Most historians (such as Robert Service) accept the authenticity of Lenin's Testament and Postscript, and his letter of 5 March about Stalin's use of foul language against Krupskaya. However, these aspects are questioned by Hiroaki Kuromiya, who states, in his 2005 biography on Stalin, that all of these events have been the subject of recent scrutiny. In particular, he argues that there are 'too many documentary and evidential inconsistencies'.

ACTIVITY

See what you can find out about Lenin's Testament and Postscript, and Lenin's attitude towards Stalin in the period 1922–24. To help you get started, see Alan Woods' 1970s article called 'Lenin's Last Struggle' on the Marxist website. You could also refer to the book of the same name by Moshe Lewin, who for many years was Professor of History at the University of Pennsylvania. Then write a paragraph explaining which argument you think is most convincing regarding the authenticity of these two documents.

2.2 How did Stalin win the struggle for power after 1924?

Defeat of the Left, 1923–27

In April 1923, the 12th Congress opened with the customary greetings from party cells. All mentioned Lenin and Trotsky, several mentioned Zinoviev and Kamenev as well, while hardly any referred to Stalin. As far as the party's rank and file were concerned, it was clear who Lenin's successor was likely to be.

Formation of the Left Opposition, 1923

Nonetheless, with Lenin absent, Trotsky was isolated: the Congress re-elected Stalin as General-Secretary, and elected a new enlarged Central Committee – of the 40 members, only three were strong supporters of Trotsky. As General-Secretary, Stalin began to replace Trotsky's supporters with those loyal to him; by the end of 1923, Stalin had enough control of the party machine at local level to ensure that most of his nominees were elected as delegates to future congresses.

In October, 46 leading members of the Communist Party issued a statement criticising the leadership over economic policy and the lack of party democracy. Though Trotsky himself was not involved with this statement, several of his supporters were. The Central Committee censured Trotsky and the 46, and threatened them with expulsion if they circulated the Statement. It was at this point that Trotsky and the 46 joined forces to form what became known as the Left Opposition. Stalin now began to use his power to stifle criticisms and to isolate this Left Opposition, in preparation for the 13th Party Conference which was to debate these issues in January 1924.

The struggle in 1924

Stalin used his growing power over the party machine to ensure that as many supporters of the Left Opposition as possible were removed by the processes of indirect election of delegates to the Conference. The Conference condemned the views of Trotsky and the 46, and accused them of disloyalty to the Politburo. Only three delegates supported Trotsky – and more Oppositionists were demoted or dismissed from posts of responsibility. Then, on 21 January, Lenin died. Ten days later, the new constitution drafted by Stalin came into force, changing the RSFSR into the Union of Soviet Socialist Republics (USSR).

Just before the 13th Party Congress met in May 1924, Lenin's widow revealed his Testament to the Central Committee and senior Congress delegates. Its clear recommendation for Stalin's dismissal seemed guaranteed to prevent him ever succeeding Lenin as leader of the Communist Party. He was saved by Zinoviev and Kamenev who, thinking that Stalin was now seriously weakened, argued that the party needed to stick together. So, despite Krupskaya's protests, the Central Committee decided not to remove Stalin as General-Secretary and not to publish Lenin's Testament. Trotsky was then threatened with expulsion if he engaged in any further political controversy. His Left Opposition had been defeated, thus ending the first stage of the power struggle.

KEY CONCEPTS QUESTION

Causation and Consequence: What were the main reasons for the Central Committee's decision not to publish Lenin's Testament? What were the immediate consequences of this decision?

The campaign against 'Trotskyism'

In November 1924, the publication of Trotsky's speeches and writings of 1917, prefaced by his new article 'Lessons of October', sparked off another dispute. The introduction showed how close his views were to those of Lenin. It also revealed how Zinoviev and Kamenev had opposed Lenin on several important issues. As only Stalin seemed 'not guilty' of any offences against Lenin, Trotsky thus inadvertently strengthened Stalin's position. Trotsky believed in the theory of 'permanent revolution', which he had developed from Marx in 1906 and which was shared by most of the leading Bolsheviks by 1917, including Lenin. This argued that the revolution needed to be pushed forward in Russia, while communists should continue to encourage and help revolution in other countries – partly because an economically underdeveloped Russia needed the help of developed countries to progress to socialism.

In the autumn of 1924, Stalin first revealed his alternative: 'socialism in one country'. This stressed the need for peace and stability, and stated that, despite its backwardness and isolation, the new Soviet state could construct socialism on its own. This argument was supported by Nikolai Bukharin who, during 1924 and 1925, shifted to the right in the Communist Party. Stalin, for the Centre, and Bukharin, for the Right, argued that, with the failure of revolution in the rest of Europe, it was even more important to maintain the political and economic alliance (known as the *smychka*) which the NEP had established between the industrial workers and the peasantry. Stalin and his supporters also accused Trotsky of lack of faith in Russia and its people.

SOURCE 2.3

As early as 1914, Lenin's watchword was: The United Socialist States of Europe... He and his comrades knew that the emancipation of the workers could result only from the joint efforts of many nations; and that if the nation-state provided too narrow a framework even for modern capitalism, socialism was quite unthinkable within such a framework. This conviction permeated all Bolshevik thinking and activity until the end of the Lenin era.

Then, in the middle 1920s, the fact of Russia's isolation in the world struck home with a vengeance, and Stalin and Bukharin came forward to expound 'socialism in one country'.

Deutscher, I., 1975, **The Unfinished Revolution: Russia 1917–67,** *New York, Oxford University Press, pp. 66–67.*

The Soviet Union and Post-Soviet Russia (1924–2000)

What did Stalin mean by 'socialism in one country'? How did this differ from previous communist beliefs about achieving socialism?

In January 1925, Trotsky was removed from his position as Commissar of War, and was warned that any renewed controversy would result in his expulsion from the Politburo and the Central Committee. In May, he was given a new, relatively unimportant, post on the Supreme Council of the National Economy (Vesenkha). Soon – pointing out the threat he felt that US capitalism posed – he was arguing for moves towards socialist planning to strengthen the NEP. He also called for the Comintern (the Communist International, an organisation set up by the RCP in 1919, to help revolutionary movements in other countries, and so end Russia's isolation) to adopt a more revolutionary line.

Politburo divisions, 1925

By 1925, some communists were becoming aware that, though NEP had achieved some economic recovery, it was uneven. At the same time, some peasants were beginning to oppose the Soviet regime's attempts at centralisation: in some areas, Soviet officials were actually murdered.

By then, the party was clearly split into a Left, Centre and Right. The Left was now Zinoviev and Kamenev. In January, they tried to ease Stalin out of his post as General-Secretary, by proposing he take Trotsky's place as Commissar for War. From April, Zinoviev and Kamenev began to oppose socialism in one country as anti-Leninist. Bukharin and the Right supported Stalin and the Centre.

By the summer of 1925, these disagreements came into the open when Zinoviev attacked the growing dominance of Bukharin's rightist views. In September, Zinoviev and Kamenev launched a direct attack on the theory of socialism in one country. Then, in October, at the Central Committee which was to make preparations for the 14th Party Congress, Zinoviev and Kamenev were joined by Krupskaya in presenting a joint statement calling for a free debate on all issues. With the support of the Right, Stalin was able to defeat this call, and the Left was warned not to make any public criticisms of official policy.

Stalin then began to remove Kamenev's supporters from their positions in the Moscow party; however, he had little success with the Leningrad party where Zinoviev was still strong. All this time, Trotsky remained silent, even though Zinoviev and Kamenev were now advocating views very similar to those of his Left Opposition of 1923 to 1924. In addition, Zinoviev was still in a strong position – as well as controlling the Leningrad party and the Northern Commune, he was also President of the Comintern, and now had the support of Krupskaya.

The Congress met in December 1925, and there was a fierce debate between the differing groups; yet still Trotsky remained silent – even when Zinoviev referred to Lenin's Testament and his warnings about Stalin's abuse of power, and when Krupskaya expressed her opposition to the campaign against 'Trotskyism'. Despite the setback over the Leningrad delegates, Stalin had been able to ensure that the majority of those present supported him and Bukharin. The Congress then elected a new Central Committee with a majority of Stalin–Bukharin supporters. This in turn elected a new Politburo of nine, which also had a Centre-Right majority.

Regardless of this defeat, Zinoviev continued his campaign in Leningrad; and when the new Central Committee proposed disciplinary measures against Zinoviev and his supporters, these were opposed by Trotsky. Stalin therefore began a new campaign against Trotsky, while Zinoviev was now accused of Trotskyism. In early 1926, Zinoviev was forced to give over the leadership of the Leningrad party to Kirov, one of Stalin's supporters; while 'Zinovievists' were removed from their positions.

The United Opposition, 1926–27

In April 1926, Trotsky offered Zinoviev and Kamenev his support. In secret talks, they revealed their fears regarding Stalin's methods and policies. With some support from Krupskaya, and a few other prominent party members, Trotsky, Zinoviev and Kamenev formed a United (Joint Left) Opposition. This began the next stage in the power struggle.

Stalin launched his attack with criticisms of Trotsky's views, while Trotsky wrote to the Politburo, warning of the possible rule of an autocrat if the party wasn't reformed. A decisive contest took place over the next 18 months. The United Opposition formally declared its existence in July 1926, and described its position as the 'Bolshevik Left'. However, Stalin's control of the party enabled him to ban meetings and dismiss these Oppositionists.

2

The United Opposition then decided to appeal directly to the party rank and file – but again Stalin's control of the party machine meant they had little success. At the same time, Zinoviev, and especially Kamenev, became alarmed at calls from some Oppositionists to declare themselves as an independent party. These more radical views, and their growing isolation, led Zinoviev and Kamenev to fear expulsion from the only legal party: soon, they began to move away from Trotsky.

However, while plans were being made for the 15th Party Conference, one of Trotsky's supporters published the full text of Lenin's Testament in the *New York Times*. A Central Committee meeting condemned the United Opposition as a 'social democratic deviation' while Trotsky accused Stalin of being 'the grave-digger of the revolution'. Trotsky was expelled from the Politburo, while Zinoviev was removed from his position as President of the Comintern. During the Conference, Trotsky and Kamenev stuck to their guns, but Zinoviev tried to back-pedal. The Conference confirmed the expulsion of the three Opposition leaders from the Politburo, and threatened them with further actions if they re-opened the controversies.

Their obvious isolation led Krupskaya (who feared the Communist Party was in danger of splitting) to break away and make her peace with Stalin.

The newspapers continued their attacks on the United Opposition, and lesser members lost their jobs. Though Zinoviev and Kamenev decided to keep quiet, Trotsky decided to fight on – but many Oppositionists were then banished to isolated parts of the Soviet Union.

In June 1927, Stalin asked the Central Committee to expel Trotsky and Zinoviev. At first, Stalin was unable to get this action taken, and he had to postpone the 15th Party Congress, which was planned for November 1927 – he did not finally get his way until 23 October 1927. Meanwhile, the Opposition had prepared its Platform, thinking it would be discussed at the Congress. The opposition's attempts to address the crowds at the 10th anniversary celebrations of the November Revolution were broken up by Stalin's supporters and the police. Stalin then demanded that Trotsky and Zinoviev be expelled from the party. On 14 November, this was agreed; hundreds of expulsions of lesser Oppositionists followed.

Figure 2.3: An official cartoon of 1927, attacking the United Opposition, with Trotsky sitting at the table, and Zinoviev – depicted as a woman – standing; the smallest figure is Kamenev.

> QUESTION
>
> What is the message of the cartoon in Figure 2.3, and how does the artist try to put the message across?

When the Congress met, in December 1927, the United Opposition issued a statement signed by 121 of their leading members, asking for the expulsions to be annulled, but this was overwhelmingly rejected. Zinoviev and Kamenev – attracted by signs that Stalin was about to abandon NEP in favour of a programme of industrialisation and the collectivisation of agriculture – announced that, in order to stop the expulsions, and to prevent the formation of a second party, they would surrender and would make no more criticisms. Trotsky's supporters, however, refused to accept the decisions of this Congress: by 10 December 1927, therefore, the United Opposition was over.

Immediately after the Congress, another 1500 Oppositionists were expelled and 2500 signed statements of recantation. Meanwhile, Stalin was making plans to deport Trotsky and his unrepentant supporters; in January 1928, Trotsky was forcibly deported to Alma Ata in Turkestan, near the Chinese border. Other Oppositionists were deported elsewhere, in an attempt to isolate them and prevent them from communicating with each other.

Defeat of the Right, 1927–29

Stalin now turned his attention to defeating the Right. As early as the autumn of 1927, a crisis had been brewing in rural Russia. Despite three good harvests, there were bread shortages and high food prices all over Russia, as peasants refused to sell their produce at the prices fixed by the state. In many places, there had been riots, and forced grain collections had been made in some areas.

Bukharin and the NEP

Such events – and Stalin's consequent decision to adopt a new 'Left' course as regards industry and agriculture – began to produce a rift between the Bukharinists and the Stalinists. On 6 January 1928, the Politburo issued secret instructions to party organisations to be severe with those who obstructed grain collections, and the Communist Party newspaper *Pravda* (its name is Russian for 'Truth') began to carry articles attacking the *kulaks* (the wealthier peasants). In April, the Central Committee introduced emergency measures such as grain requisitioning. At the same time, those seen to have been too lenient with the *kulaks* (mainly Bukharinists) were removed from positions of power.

At first, Trotsky's supporters were pleased to see some of their policies being adopted, and now expected to be readmitted to the party. Some even thought perhaps they had been wrong about Stalin, and should now join him against Bukharin and the Right. Trotsky himself believed that Stalin and the Centre should be encouraged to break with the Right. In fact, since early 1927, Trotsky had seen Bukharin's faction as more of a danger to the gains of the November Revolution than Stalin's, as it was bigger and more right-wing. By May 1928, it was clear that Stalin was planning a 'second revolution' – and Trotsky's supporters began to split into 'conciliators' and 'irreconcilables'. Then, in June,

Zinoviev and Kamenev (and about 3000 other Oppositionists) were reinstated to the party.

During July, the food crisis became worse; temporarily, it seemed that Bukharin's faction was gaining the upper hand when he surprisingly won a vote in the Central Committee to slow Stalin's left turn. The emergency measures were stopped; but, by August, Stalin (having secured a majority in the Politburo) had renewed his 'leftward' course, and the breach with Bukharin was confirmed. Both factions then turned to the defeated Left Oppositionists for support.

A Trotsky-Bukharin bloc?

Bukharin used Kamenev as a go-between for an approach to Trotsky, arguing that the main issue facing the party was not economic policy but freedom of the party and the state, and claiming that Stalin was preparing to create a police state and take total power.

By September 1928, Trotsky was attracted by the idea of an alliance with Bukharin to restore full inner-party and Soviet democracy. However, the two leaders' respective supporters were extremely reluctant to cooperate with their former enemies. As a result, Stalin was able to defeat the Right without the formal support of the Left – Bukharin and the Right, now in panic, surrendered while the Left remained divided.

Nevertheless, support for Trotsky had started to grow in some party cells once Stalin had begun to adopt some of his ideas. Consequently, Stalin decided that Trotsky needed to be expelled entirely from Soviet Russia. This was partly because he feared a Left–Right alliance in the future, and partly because he suspected that some of his own faction still had some sympathy with the Opposition. On 16 December 1928, Trotsky was warned to stop all 'counter-revolutionary' activity. Finally, in January 1929, he was deported to Constantinople (present-day Istanbul).

SOURCE 2.4

Late in the summer of 1928 startling news,... reached Alma Ata [where Trotsky had been exiled]... reports from Moscow claimed that both the Bukharinists and the Stalinists mooted an alliance with the Left Opposition and that both were already vying for Trotskyist and Zinovievist support... shortly thereafter they [Stalin and Bukharin] were at loggerheads again; and Bukharin secretly met Kamenev in Sokolnikov's presence. He told Kamenev that both he and Stalin were going to be compelled to turn to the Left Opposition and try and make common cause with it... Of his meeting with Bukharin, Kamenev wrote a detailed account for Zinoviev... The Bukharin closeted with Kamenev and Sokolnikov was a very different man from the one who had only seven months earlier, at the fifteenth congress, helped to crush the Opposition... He arrived at Kamenev's home stealthily, terrified, pale, trembling, looking over his shoulders, and talking in whispers. He began by begging Kamenev to tell no one of their meeting... Without pronouncing Stalin's name he repeated obsessively: 'He will slay us'. 'He is the new Genghiz Khan'. 'He will strangle us'. On Kamenev, Bukharin already made 'the impression of a doomed man'.

Deutscher, I.,1970, **The Prophet Unarmed: Trotsky 1921–1929**, *Oxford, Oxford University Press, pp. 440–441.*

Stalin also moved against the Right, charging Bukharin, and other Rightist leaders with factionalism. In April 1929, Bukharin was removed from his posts as editor of *Pravda*, and political secretary of the Comintern. Those of the Right were then warned that further violations of party discipline would result in their expulsion from the Politburo. Then, in November 1929, Bukharin *was* removed from the Politburo. With his main rivals defeated, Stalin now appeared to have almost complete control of the Communist Party.

DISCUSSION POINT

On the basis of what you have studied so far regarding Stalin's rise to power, do you think anything could have been done before 1929 to prevent it? With a partner, try to work out some examples – with some relevant supporting facts – which show how his rise could *and* could not have been prevented.

2.3 Why was Stalin able to defeat his rivals?

Historians disagree on the reasons for Stalin's emergence and rise to power, as no single factor seems to offer a satisfactory explanation. In fact, the main historical approaches often overlap in several respects.

Power politics

Historians such as Robert Conquest see Stalin's rise as a deliberate manipulation of genuine political and ideological differences among the Bolshevik leaders, either simply to gain supreme power for himself by crushing all other factions or, as Robert C. Tucker suggests, to make himself into a revolutionary hero as important and famous as Lenin. His success is seen as depending not only on his political shrewdness and ruthlessness, but also on the weaknesses and mistakes of his rivals. For instance, E. H. Carr has portrayed Zinoviev and Kamenev as, respectively, careerist and weak-willed; while, according to Stephen Cohen, Bukharin's commitment to the NEP blinded him to the dangers posed by Stalin until it was too late. Lenin himself did not realise the threat from Stalin until 1922 – just two years before his death, during which time he was too ill to be politically active.

Figure 2.4: Lenin recuperating in Gorky, after his first stroke.

Stalin's main opponent, Trotsky, can be seen as having made several serious errors and miscalculations. In particular, Trotsky also either refused, or did not have the skill, to organise an effective faction of his own – though I. Deutscher argues that, without Lenin, he was virtually isolated at the top of the party from the beginning.

SOURCE 2.5

The decision [in 1923–24] to leave Stalin and his supporters in power indicates that at this fateful moment Trotsky understood neither Lenin nor Stalin. Known for his many brilliant analyses, historical and conjunctural, Trotsky was at the nadir [lowest point] of his political vigilance in 1923. Stalin had never been so vulnerable. A Leninist coalition, or a majority supporting Lenin's positions, was still possible. Revealing the whole of Lenin's testament to the Twelfth Congress and provoking a debate, rather than playing the game of 're-educating Stalin', was the last serious chance for a new course. But Trotsky let it slip, even though we know he soon moved into outright opposition to Stalin. The other two supposed Leninists in the Politburo, Zinoviev and Kamenev, were also deeply confused; deprived of Lenin's leadership, they lost their bearings... Was illness or extreme fatigue a factor in this massive failure of political acumen [skill] on Trotsky's part, of which there were to be further examples?

Lewin, M., 2005, **The Soviet Century,** *London, Verso, p. 29.*

ACTIVITY

Source 2.5 refers to illness and/or fatigue affecting Trotsky's political judgements. Carry out some additional research on this, and try to identify other examples. How much credit would you allocate to illness and fatigue in explaining Trotsky's mistakes with regard to Stalin?

Structuralist explanations

While there are several different structuralist explanations – so called because they are based on the economic and/or political structures of the past and present, rather than on individuals – they have one theme in common: that Stalin was a product of Russian history and the administrative system set up (often in a haphazard way) after 1917.

Some historians, such as S. S. Montefiore, see Stalin as essentially a ruler in the long Tsarist tradition of absolutist rule – the 'Red Tsar'. Others point to the impact of emergencies such as the Civil War which led to the development of appointment rather than election for party and state positions – what R. Daniels called a circular flow of power.

Socio-cultural explanations

S. Fitzpatrick suggests that social issues are closely linked to structuralist explanations, and emphasise the impact of the social structure on the politics and development of the Communist Party and the Soviet state. During the Civil War, for instance, the Bolsheviks attracted Russian patriots who resented the foreign intervention. Then, when it looked as if the Bolsheviks were winning, a large number of careerists (often former Tsarist bureaucrats) flocked to join the winning side in order to secure jobs. This became worse after 1921, when all opposition parties were banned. These new members were politically conservative, so were drawn to Stalin rather than the revolutionary views of Trotsky.

Ideological explanations

Several historians stress the genuine nature of the political differences among the communist leaders of the 1920s, especially over the NEP. The Left, basing itself on Marxism, stressed the danger inherent in the NEP, namely the stimulation of capitalist tendencies which might eventually lead to the restoration of capitalism if the state sector was not strengthened at the same time. These fears were strengthened by the socio-cultural developments referred to above, as many of the new groups (whether former Tsarist bureaucrats or former peasants) tended to favour capitalist rather than socialist policies.

The Right argued that, as the Soviet Union was overwhelmingly agricultural and economically underdeveloped, while industry was in crisis, the NEP was essential if the economy was to revive. However, the Right tended to overlook the conflicts which might arise between the 'Nepmen' (business men who benefitted from the NEP) and the *kulaks* on the one hand, and the workers' state on the other, and seemed to envisage a long period of a mixed economy.

Stalin's rise can be seen as a genuine political response by the Centre to steer a midway policy course. At the beginning, the Centre believed that the NEP was essential for recovery, and so opposed the Left which seemed to endanger it. But, later, the Centre came to see that a change was necessary – it became necessary to attack the policies of the Right which wished the NEP to continue virtually unchanged.

Stalin's policy of continuing the NEP and 'socialism in one country' seemed a safer bet than Trotsky's 'permanent revolution', as well as appealing to national pride. Stalin's dramatic change of course, beginning in 1927 and 1928, can be seen as a response to a real rural crisis, in which his switch to rapid collectivisation and industrialisation seemed entirely logical and correct. This was one reason why so many former Oppositionists moved to support him in 1928.

One version of the ideological explanation, which also combines elements of the socio-cultural theory, is that developed by Trotsky himself. Pointing to the failure of international revolution and the consequent isolation of the new Soviet state, he argued how Russian 'backwardness' and the growing political apathy of the working class, undermined the early Soviet democracy. This allowed conservative and reactionary elements to come to the fore, and eventually resulted in what he called 'bureaucratic degeneration'. By this, Trotsky meant that a new social and political elite of administrators (he rejected any claims that they were a new class), with increasing privileges, had emerged. At first this elite supported the Right but once the problems of the NEP exploded in 1927 and 1928 its members shifted its allegiance to Stalin and the Centre as the best hope for maintaining their positions. Thus Stalin's victory was the result not just of his opponents' mistakes but of unforeseen historical and cultural developments after 1917.

Theory of Knowledge

History and the individual

The historian A. J. P. Taylor (1906–90) claimed that *'The history of modern Europe can be written in terms of three titans: Napoleon, Bismarck and Lenin.'* This is an example of the 'great person' theory. Examination of events in Russia during 1917–29 involves studying the actions of people such as Lenin, Trotsky and Stalin. Do these events justify claims that such a theory of history is valid? Or are other factors more important?

Paper 3 exam practice

Summary activity

Copy the spider diagram below to show the main stages in Stalin's rise to power during the period 1922–29. Then, using the information from this chapter, and any other sources available to you, complete the diagram. Make sure you include, where relevant, brief comments about different historical debates / interpretations.

Figure 2.5: Stalin's rise to power, 1922–29.

Paper 3 practice questions

1 Evaluate the factors that led to Lenin opposing Stalin in the period 1922–24.

2 To what extent was the 1921 ban on factions and other political parties the main reason for Stalin's victory in the power struggle?

3 Examine the reasons why Stalin was able to remain in post after 1924, despite Lenin's Testament and Postscript.

4 'Stalin won the struggle for power after 1924 because his opponents were divided.' To what extent do you agree with this statement?

5 Discuss the reasons why Stalin was able to defeat all his opposition by 1929.

Stalin's Revolution, 1929–41

3

Introduction

You have seen how Stalin was able to defeat his rivals and gain control of the Communist Party and the Soviet Union. This chapter will examine the various policies and methods he used to ensure the survival, development and expansion of the Soviet state. The chapter will focus first on Stalin's economic policies for modernising and strengthening the Soviet Union. Secondly, it will examine how some of these policies led to criticisms of Stalin in the 1930s – and how he reacted, ruthlessly consolidating his own political power. Finally, the chapter will examine Stalin's foreign policy during the 1930s, which seems to have been intended to achieve and maintain Soviet security – this was also an important factor in his economic policies. In order to do this, he was prepared to play down the earlier Bolshevik commitment to revolutionary internationalism.

TIMELINE

1925 Dec: 14th Party Congress (the 'industrialisation congress')

1927 Dec: 15th Party Congress (the 'collectivisation congress')

1928 Jul: Bukharin wins Central Committee vote to slow down collectivisation

Oct: First Five-Year Plan starts

1929 Apr: 16th Party Conference (Right defeated over collectivisation; First Five-Year Plan approved); signs of some opposition to Stalin

Dec: Stalin calls for *Kulaks* to be 'liquidated as a class'

1930 Jan: Start of mass collectivisation

Dec: Syrtsov's 'bloc' expelled from Central Committee

1932 Sept: The Ryutin Affair

1933 Jan: Smirnov's 'anti-party group' charged with attempting to replace Stalin; Hitler becomes chancellor of Germany

1934 Jan–Feb: 17th Party Congress approves Second Five-Year Plan

Sept: Soviet Union joins League of Nations

Dec: Murder of Kirov; thousands arrested

1935 Jan: Mass arrests continue; secret trial of Zinoviev, Kamenev and 17 other members of a 'Moscow Centre'

May: Franco-Soviet Alliance

1936 Aug: First Show Trial (Trial of the Sixteen); start of the Great Purge

1937 Jan: Second Show Trial (Trial of the Seventeen)

Feb: Bukharin and Rykov expelled from the Party

May: Start of the purge of the Red Army

1938 Mar: Third Show Trial (Trial of the Twenty-one)

Sept: Sudetenland Crisis – USSR is not consulted

1939 Mar: 18th Party Congress approves Third Five-Year Plan; official end of the Great Purge; Germany invades the rest of Czechoslovakia

Aug: Nazi-Soviet Non-Aggression Pact

1940 Jul: The Baltic states are made part of the USSR

KEY QUESTIONS

- What were Stalin's main economic policies?
- How successful were Stalin's economic policies?
- What did Stalin do to consolidate his power?
- How did Stalin's foreign policy try to achieve security for the Soviet Union in the 1930s?

Overview

- During 1926 and 1927, insufficient grain was produced so, in 1928, Stalin considered ending the NEP by collectivising agriculture and pushing for more rapid industrialisation. This led to a clash with Bukharin and the Right.
- In 1928, the First Five-Year Plan for industrialisation concentrated on heavy industry, with high targets for increased productivity being set for each industry. In 1929, Stalin announced the forced collectivisation of agriculture.
- Early problems with forced collectivisation and the First Five-Year Plan led to criticisms of Stalin at the 16th Party Congress in June 1930. By 1932, the disruption of agriculture caused by

collectivisation led to famine in some parts of the USSR, as food production slumped.

- However, the results of the First Five Year Plan were more encouraging, and a Second Five-Year Plan was drawn up in 1933 which continued the emphasis on heavy industry.
- Nonetheless, the 17th Party Congress in February 1934 revealed continued criticism, and the growing popularity of Kirov. On 1 December, Kirov was killed in suspicious circumstances.
- Stalin then ordered a series of arrests and executions; after a secret trial, Zinoviev, Kamenev and other leading communists were given prison sentences.
- In August 1936, the Great Purge was launched by the first of the Show Trials. Soon, the Great Terror began and, in 1937, the NKVD (Narodny Komissariat Vnutrennih Del, People's Comissariat of Internal Affairs) spread its activities from the party to the officer corps of the armed forces.
- In 1938, with his political position secure, Stalin launched a Third Five-Year Plan, intended to concentrate on light industry and consumer goods; but, in 1940, it shifted to armaments production as fears of a Nazi invasion increased.
- Despite unrealistic targets and practical problems, industrial production increased. This later enabled the USSR to withstand the Nazi invasion of 1941.
- After 1933, when Hitler came to power in Germany, Soviet foreign policy was centred on trying to achieve an anti-fascist alliance with Britain and France.
- Such attempts failed and, in August 1939, the USSR made a Non-Aggression Pact with Nazi Germany. Poland was partitioned, and the USSR took over the Baltic republics.

Figure 3.1: Andrei Vyshinsky (centre), the prosecutor-general in the first Show Trial (against Zinoviev and Kamenev) in August 1936.

3.1 What were Stalin's main economic policies?

Stalin's turn to the Left

In the mid–1920s, when Trotsky and the Left Opposition were already arguing for a shift towards industrialisation, Stalin and his supporters had defended the maintenance of NEP as a Leninist policy. Bukharin in particular had dismissed the Left's arguments that NEP was now creating social classes which were threatening the socialist nature of the Soviet state, and warned against the dangers of creating 'a state of war with the peasantry'.

Causation: What were the main reasons for the opposition of Bukharin and the Right to call an end to NEP?

There is evidence, however, that as early as November 1925, Stalin was beginning to contemplate a new revolutionary shift, in order to make possible a transition from NEP to a socialist economy. By then, although production figures for heavy industry had virtually returned to pre-war levels, there was still unemployment, and many in the party began to think the state sector needed to be developed. As yet, however, with Zinoviev and Kamenev having formed the United Opposition with Trotsky (see 2.2, The United Opposition, 1926–27), he continued to work with Bukharin.

Industry and the Five-Year Plans

In December 1925, at the 14th Party Congress (later called the 'industrialisation congress'), the principle of economic modernisation was supported by the party and, at the 15th Party Conference in the autumn of 1926, Stalin called for the Soviet Union to catch up with and overtake the West as regards industrialisation. However, he still insisted that this had to be achieved by maintaining the worker-peasant alliance.

Meanwhile, Gosplan, the State General Planning Commission (set up in 1921), was busily involved in economic planning, producing its first economic plan in August 1925. Its second plan, in 1926, included an outline Five-Year Plan, with specific plans for each year. At the same time, Vesenkha, the Supreme Council of the National Economy (which operated from 1917 to 1932, and was responsible for state industry), was drafting schemes for the development of the Soviet economy.

There was great rivalry between Vesenkha and Gosplan; and there were also divisions within these organisations between non-party specialists (who were more conservative about short-term possibilities), and the party specialists (who believed rapid industrialisation was possible, and that the NEP was now hindering this). In addition, by 1927, there were fears of imminent war, so many came to believe that rapid industrialisation was now necessary if the Soviet Union was to be able to meet any invasion.

ACTIVITY

Carry out some research on the war scares of 1927. What impact do you think these had on developments within the Soviet Union?

By 1927, the United Opposition had been defeated, so Stalin felt able to adopt (albeit in a crude and distorted form) some of its economic policies. Of these, the main ones were:

- to modernise agriculture (via voluntary collectivisation) to provide extra food and workers for industrialisation
- to step up the industrialisation of the USSR
- to take action to curb the growing influence of pro-capitalist forces emerging from the NEP.

At the 15th Party Congress in December 1927, Stalin stressed the foreign threats and the need to develop heavy industry. At this stage, there were no general agreements on growth targets – both Vesenkha and Gosplan actually produced rival plans – and the Congress still spoke of maintaining the basic elements of the NEP.

However, the 'grain crisis' in agriculture which developed in 1927 and 1928 (see 3.1, Collectivisation of agriculture) persuaded Stalin that the NEP should be abandoned in favour of rapid industrialisation. This led to a serious split between Stalin and Bukharin in July 1928. By the end of 1928, with the Right virtually defeated (see 2.2, Defeat of the Right, 1927–29), Stalin pushed for higher production targets from Vesenkha and Gosplan, and non-party specialists were purged.

The First Five-Year Plan, 1928–32

The First Five-Year Plan began on 1 October 1928, and concentrated mainly on heavy industry (coal, iron, steel, oil and machine-production); overall, industrial production was planned to increase by 300%. Light industry, too, was to double its output; and, in order to ensure that sufficient energy was available, electricity production was to increase by 600%.

Soon, reports (mostly unreliable) began to arrive in Moscow of how targets were being exceeded. Talk then began in 1929 of fulfilling the plan in four years instead of five; Stalin officially gave his backing to this approach in June 1930.

The Soviet Union and Post-Soviet Russia (1924–2000)

There were significant achievements, which fundamentally transformed the Soviet economy. Hundreds of new factories and mines were set up in many regions – some of which had not had any industry before 1928. New industrial complexes, such as Magnitogorsk, were built, and new rail links and hydro-electric schemes were established.

QUESTION

What can you learn from the First Five-Year Plan about:
a   the perceived need for rapid industrialisation
b   continuing opposition to Stalin?

Subsequent Five-Year Plans

In December 1932, when Stalin announced that the First Five-Year Plan had been fulfilled, this was an exaggeration – despite tremendous growth, no major targets had actually been met. Implementation costs had been much greater than allowed for by Gosplan, and the great increases in coal, iron and industrial goods proved too much for the railway system to cope with. During 1932 and 1933, as urban populations rapidly expanded, there were housing shortages, while the effects of forced collectivisation in the countryside (see 3.1, Collectivisation of agriculture) led to food shortages and rationing.

The Second Five-Year Plan

Nonetheless, Gosplan drew up the Second Five-Year Plan. This was intended to create a fully socialist economy from 1933 to 1937, although nothing was finally approved until the 17th Party Congress in January 1934. The final draft simply called for increased production and improved living standards, and the need to build on the achievements of the first plan.

From 1934 to 1936, there were many successes. In particular, machine-production and iron and steel output grew rapidly, making the Soviet Union practically self-sufficient in these areas. Many schemes began producing, while nearly 5000 new enterprises opened (compared with almost 2000 under the first plan).

Figure 3.2: Miners in the 1930s, photographed looking happy and determined – like their role model, Alexei Stakhanov.

One reason for the success of the Second Five-Year Plan was the big increase in labour productivity. Following the success of Alexei Stakhanov, a miner in the Donbas region, in digging out 102 tonnes of coal in one shift (the normal figure was 7 tonnes) in August 1935, work-norms were greatly increased. Soon, most industries had their own model workers, who received higher bonuses and other material advantages (such as new flats) as well as being given medals as 'Heroes of Socialist Labour'. At the same time, the worst effects of forced collectivisation were over, allowing rationing to be abandoned in 1935.

KEY CONCEPTS QUESTION

Significance: Who was Stakhanov, and what was his significance for Stalin's industrialisation programme?

The Soviet Union and Post-Soviet Russia (1924–2000)

Despite significant achievements and successes under the second plan, the industrialisation programme was hit by problems in 1937: the winter of 1937–38 was severe; the Purges saw thousands of managers and experts either imprisoned or executed (see 3.3, The Great Terror, 1937–38); while the worsening international situation increasingly resulted in funds being diverted to defence (see 4.2, Economic reconstruction).

The Third Five-Year Plan

Planning for the Third Plan had begun in February 1936, but the purging of Gosplan specialists created confusion and delays, and the Third Plan was not formally approved until the 18th Party Congress in March 1939. By then, earlier proposals to develop light industry and increase the production of consumer goods were already being undermined by a new emphasis on heavy industry and defence. Nonetheless, huge increases in production were planned, and **Molotov** claimed that, because the first two plans had laid the foundation for a socialist economy, this third plan would complete the process and enable the Soviet Union to begin the transition to communism. The Third Five-Year Plan, however, was totally disrupted in June 1941, when Nazi Germany launched its invasion (see 4.1).

Vyacheslav Molotov (1890–1986):

He was a great supporter of Stalin, becoming a member of the Politburo in 1926. He backed Stalin's economic policies (as well as the Great Purge). From 1939 to 1949, he was Commissar for Foreign Affairs. He continued to hold high office after Stalin's death, but was removed from the Central Committee in 1957.

Theory of Knowledge

History and economics

Historians are not just concerned with describing what happened in the past, they are also involved in attempts to explain it. One theory of history, known as 'economic determinism' – and closely associated with Karl Marx – sees economic factors as crucial. How far does a study of Stalin's economic policies in the 1930s show that economic needs are the main engine or driving force of history?

Collectivisation of agriculture

From 1924 to 1926, the NEP had led to a gradual increase in agricultural production; however, despite a good harvest in 1926, state collections were 50% of what had been expected. This was mainly because, as peasants prospered, they consumed more of their produce – in addition, as there were insufficient consumer goods being produced by industry, there was less incentive to sell their surplus. As a consequence, only about 13% of the grain harvest found its way into the towns. Emergency measures were taken in some areas against *kulak* 'speculators' and 'Nepmen', including the seizure of grain and increasing the taxes on *kulaks* to force them to sell more grain but, in 1927, deliveries declined further. Many communists believed it was because the *kulaks* were deliberately withholding grain – this not only threatened hunger in the expanding towns, it also undermined the possibility of stepping up industrialisation.

Thus, by the time of the 15th Party Congress in December 1927 (later known as the 'collectivisation congress'), many communists were beginning to see continuation of the NEP as blocking both agricultural and industrial development. However, at this Congress, Stalin argued that the problems could be overcome by strengthening cooperative farms, increasing mechanisation and by supporting the voluntary collectivisation of farms (*kolkhozes*). These voluntary cooperative or collective farms were intended to result in bigger farms and higher yields. At this stage, there was no mention of forced collectivisation or of destroying the *kulaks* as a class.

In 1928, however, the problem of insufficient grain purchases continued. In Siberia, Stalin instructed local officials to increase state grain procurements. Their response was to seize more grain and to close markets – those who resisted were arrested as *kulaks* under Article 107 of the Criminal Code (passed in 1927 to deal with speculation). After the 1928 harvest, these actions (which became known as the Urals-Siberian method) began to result in serious unrest in rural areas, and in bread shortages, as grain was hidden to avoid requisitioning or to await higher prices.

In July 1928, Bukharin was able to get through an increase in the price of grain and an end to the forcible measures. Stalin, though, was determined that industrial development should not be disrupted by any diversion of money to the *kulaks* – and, soon after, ordered that emergency actions should continue.

SOURCE 3.1

...The socialisation or collectivisation of agriculture pre-supposed a strong industrial base for the mechanisation of large, collective agriculture. Stalin had naturally taken the grain crisis seriously because it threatened to jeopardise industrialisation: 'We cannot allow our industry to be dependent on the caprice of the kulaks.' It was evident to both him and his supporters that agriculture had to serve the industrialisation drive. They never doubted the primacy of industrial interests over those of agriculture. The Soviet Union had to be industrialised and modernised, if only to survive in a hostile international climate.

Kuromiya, H., 2005, **Stalin,** *Harlow, Pearson Longman, p. 85.*

This provoked Bukharin, in September 1928, into implicitly criticising Stalin's actions by publishing a defence of the NEP. By the end of 1928, a combination of a fall in sales of grain to the state, and a crop failure in the central and south-eastern regions of the USSR, led to dramatic increases in free-market prices, a further slump in grain deliveries to the state and the introduction of rationing during the winter of 1928–29. During 1929, the forcible Urals–Siberian method was carried out in most of the Soviet Union, and the NEP and the *smychka* were destroyed in all but name. From November 1929, Stalin launched a programme of collectivisation and called for the *kulaks* to be 'liquidated as a class'.

Collectivisation

By the end of 1929, with the fear of an impending attack by capitalist powers and an extremely ambitious Five-Year Plan, Stalin was determined that the crisis in agriculture be resolved before the spring sowing for the 1930 harvest. As a first emergency measure, a massive grain procurement campaign was launched, with extremely high quotas. Officials, determined to avoid punishment for failure (as had happened in 1928) used their power to arrest, deport and confiscate the property of any peasant who failed to hand over their quota. In all, some 16 million tons were collected – in some areas, over 30% of the entire crop was taken.

The grain procurement campaign of 1929–30 was a short-term emergency measure, similar in principle if not in degree to earlier ones in 1927 and 1928. Action against *kulaks* was stepped up after

January 1930 when urban brigades of workers and Komsomol (Young Communist League) members, with the support of police and Red Army soldiers, went into the countryside to organise the setting up of collectives. Initially, persuasion was the main method, but Stalin pressed for rapid results, and violence was increasingly used.

Richer peasants often destroyed their crops and livestock rather than hand them over to the local *kolkhoz*, or raided the *kolkhozes* to retake their property. Local parties were given targets for how many households should be collectivised – officials (ambitious for promotion or fearing to be denounced as Rightists) increasingly resorted to force. Many were imprisoned or executed for their resistance, and around 150000 were forcibly migrated to poorer land in the north and east.

By March 1930, it was reported that 58% of peasant households had been collectivised – but the process provoked serious resistance, including arson, riots and armed rebellions. This chaos and violence worried the Politburo, and Stalin was pressurised by other communist leaders into calling a halt. Official policy returned to voluntary collectivisation, and many peasants had their property restored. By October 1930, only about 20% of households were still collectivised.

However, once the 1930 harvest had been secured, collectivisation resumed in earnest; by 1937, the official figure for households in collective farms was 90%. Each collective was headed by a farm manager who took control of the harvest and ensured all taxes were duly paid to the government. Machine-Tractor Stations (MTS) were established to supply seed and to hire out machinery to local *kolkhozes* (payment was made by grain). Between 1929 and 1932, over 2500 Machine-Tractor Stations were built.

Behind these statistics, however, there was great upheaval and confusion which resulted in a dreadful famine in the years 1932 and 1933. The first sign of problems appeared in October 1931 and grew into the most severe famine in Russia's history. Though the worst was over by 1933, some areas were still affected by serious food shortages in 1934. Despite increasing warning signs of this rural catastrophe, Stalin persisted with forced collectivisation, and high state grain procurements.

After 1933, agriculture did revive, though grain production only increased slowly. In 1935, it finally surpassed pre-collectivisation figures (75 million tons); by 1937, production reached 97.4 million tons. Livestock numbers increased even more slowly, and in fact did not exceed pre-collectivisation levels until 1953. However, the drive towards collectivisation continued, and state procurement quotas were constantly raised. As a result, life on the collectives remained very hard for most of the 1930s.

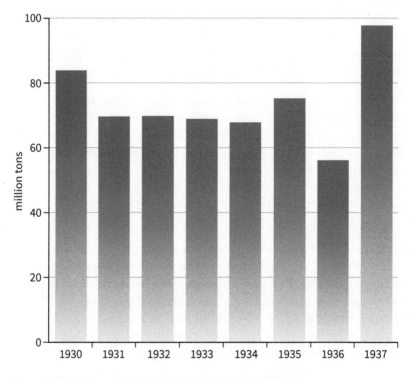

Figure 3.3: Grain production in the Soviet Union, 1930–37.

DISCUSSION POINT

Do you think that Stalin's industrial and agricultural programmes were justified, despite the heavy human and social costs? Do you think the agricultural and industrial revolutions which took place in several Western European states in the period 1750–1850 were significantly different in their human costs?

3.2 How successful were Stalin's economic policies?

Many historians have suggested that Stalin did not have a 'master plan' which he decided to implement in 1928. They believe that changes came about in both agriculture and industry because of unforeseen problems arising from the NEP. In addition, Stalin's constant interference – especially by increasing targets – prevented the plans from being coherently and successfully implemented.

'Revolution from above'?

Such historians see Stalin's initial response to the grain crisis as an emergency short-term measure which triggered off a sequence of developments that led to more and more radical decisions being taken. M. Lewin, for example, argues that Stalin did not really know where his policies might take the Soviet Union.

Others, such as R. Tucker, argue that Stalin clearly intended to modernise the Soviet Union, and adopted deliberate agricultural and industrial policies to do so, once he had defeated his opponents. Others go on to argue that Stalin was deliberately attempting to complete the Bolshevik Revolution of 1917, and thus consciously launched his own 'second revolution, from above'. This would enable him to take his place alongside Lenin as a hugely significant leader and revolutionary.

Industrial production and official statistics

Official statistics, produced during and after Stalin's rule, about the increases in productivity achieved by the five year plans, are highly suspect: for the period 1928–40, the official figure for increased industrial production is 852%. Similar doubts apply to figures relating to specific industries. However, though applying stricter criteria, most historians, such as A. Nove, accept that there were tremendous increases, especially in heavy industry.

Figure 3.4: In this 1933 Soviet cartoon, a foreign capitalist mocks the First Five-Year Plan as 'Fantasy, raving, utopia'; four years later, he weeps to see that the plan has been successful and he has been proved wrong.

One problem with these official statistics is that many factory managers, fearful of being punished for non-fulfilment of targets, either deliberately underestimated production capacity or claimed production figures higher than those actually achieved.

QUESTION
Why are there problems for historians when trying to establish the results of the Five-Year Plans?

An associated problem was the lack of skill of many of the industrial workers in state enterprises. Many were former peasants: around 9 million joined the ranks of industrial workers under the First Five-Year Plan alone. Nor was production helped by 'storming', which involved workers, and machines, working for 24 hours or more at a time, in order to meet or surpass targets. Machines frequently broke down, so disrupting production.

The impact of collectivisation on agriculture

The move towards collectivisation, announced in 1929, had been intended to solve a serious shortfall in the amount of grain needed to feed the urban population. However, the destructive resistance to collectivisation by *kulaks*, and the disruption caused by deporting about 2.5 million people to the Gulag in the years 1930 and 1931, led to a serious and sudden drop in food production generally by 1931. This led to a famine in 1932 and 1933, especially in Ukraine and the north Caucasus, during which millions died. Historians disagree on the total number of deaths, with estimates varying from S. Wheatcroft's 3.5 million to R. Conquest's 7 million. However, the famine was only one cause of the deaths that can be attributed to the process of collectivisation in general. Again, historians are divided, with total estimates (including deaths caused by the famine) ranging from S. Wheatcroft's 6 million to S. Rosenfield's 20 million.

The economic results of collectivisation – and especially its relation to the success of the Five-Year Plans – are also areas of controversy. Historians such as M. Ellman have argued that after 1928 grain deliveries to the state did increase, so allowing rapid industrialisation to succeed; while others – such as S. Wheatcroft, R. W. Davies, and J. Cooper – have argued that if NEP had continued, industrial growth rates would have been much lower than those achieved by the Five-Year Plans. These historians thus see collectivisation as facilitating industrialisation in various ways.

However, other historians such as A. Barsov, J. Millar and H. Hunter, offer a revisionist argument, claiming that collectivisation was an economic disaster which consequently made little contribution to the industrialisation programme. In particular, Millar, in 1974, put forward the view that, in fact, peasants *received* rather than surrendered resources – this was based on the argument that industrial inputs into agriculture during the period of collectivisation outweighed the value of farm produce provided by the farms. Although A. Nove, in his book *An Economic History of the USSR* (1989), criticises some of Barsov's figures, he tends to avoid taking sides in this debate, and thus provides a useful summary of the main arguments.

3.3 What did Stalin do to consolidate his power?

Continued opposition, 1929–35

Though Stalin had defeated his main opponents by 1929, he was not totally dominant. In the late 1920s, his calls for stricter action against defeated opponents were not always supported by members of the Politburo, and Stalin had to accept compromises. Furthermore, though removed from high office, Bukharin and other leading Rightists still had sympathisers and supporters in the party.

The early problems arising from mass collectivisation and rapid industrialisation began to create doubts and political divisions even within the Politburo, where only Molotov and Kaganovitch were uncritical supporters of Stalin. In December 1930, Syrtsov and others were expelled from the Central Committee for criticising the excesses being committed under collectivisation – significantly, they had previously supported Stalin in the struggle against Bukharin and the Right.

A more serious indication of opposition came in 1932 when Ryutin, a Rightist, wrote a document calling for the end of forced collectivisation, the rehabilitation of the defeated Oppositionists, and the dismissal of Stalin. In September, Ryutin, Zinoviev, Kamenev and 17 others were put on trial and then expelled from the Central Committee. Stalin had wanted Ryutin executed, but the Politburo refused – showing Stalin did not yet have complete control.

Purges, 1933–35

In December 1932, a party purge was ordered. There had been previous purges before 1933. These had involved checking the personal qualities and behaviour (such as drunkenness or political inactivity) of Communist Party members – those found wanting had had their party cards taken away.

Violence was not involved, and disgraced members were later allowed to rejoin if their behaviour improved. From 1933 to 1935, nearly 1 million – about 20% of party members – were expelled, including many party officials, as 'Ryutinites'. Despite these expulsions, however, opposition to Stalin continued after the Ryutin Affair: in January 1933, Smirnov (another leading communist) was expelled for forming an 'anti-party group' in order to remove Stalin.

> QUESTION
>
> How do the Syrtsov, Ryutin and Smirnov affairs show that Stalin was still not in complete control of the Communist Party by 1933?

A major turning point seems to have been the 17th Party Congress (the Congress of Victors) which took place in February 1934 – the economic chaos and the unrest generated by collectivisation and industrialisation meant no Congress had been called between 1930 and 1934. Evidence suggests that **Kirov** might have been asked by some leading local officials to replace Stalin, but that he refused. However, this Congress did abolish the post of General-Secretary. Thus, in principle, Stalin was now no more important than the three other secretaries of the Communist Party – including Kirov – who were elected after the Congress. Although it is possible that Stalin himself desired this, in order to share responsibility for the economic crisis, the Central Committee elected by the Congress gave an indication that not all in the Communist Party approved of Stalin's leadership – Kirov received votes from almost all the 1225 delegates who voted, while about 300 did not vote for Stalin.

> **Sergei Kirov (1888–1934):**
>
> He joined the Bolsheviks in 1904, and was elected to the Politburo in 1930. He was head of the Leningrad Communist Party, and was popular. He was also a party moderate, and had opposed some of Stalin's more extreme economic and repressive measures. He was assassinated in 1934 and his death was immediately followed by the start of the Great Purge.

Kirov was known to have doubts about the pace of industrialisation and Stalin's methods of disciplining the Party. In December 1934, under suspicious circumstances, Kirov was assassinated. Stalin immediately claimed this was part of a plot to overthrow him and the rule of the Communist Party, supposedly organised by a 'Leningrad Opposition Centre' which had links with Trotsky's Left Opposition and the United Opposition. The recently reorganised NKVD, which had absorbed the OGPU (the Unified State Political Directorate) in July 1934, was given sweeping powers of arrest, trial and execution.

ACTIVITY

See what additional information you can find out about Kirov's popularity and his subsequent murder. What evidence is there to make you think that Stalin was closely involved?

In the next few weeks, over 100 party members were shot, and thousands of Trotskyists and Zinovievists were arrested, including Zinoviev and Kamenev. In January 1935, Zinoviev and Kamenev, and 17 others, were tried and imprisoned for five to ten years.

The Great Purge and the Great Terror

During the power struggle of the 1920s, many of Stalin's Left and Right opponents had lost senior posts or had even been expelled from the party. These purges were not violent, nor were they as extensive as those of the 1930s. By mid-1935, these purges had begun to come to a halt – partly, no doubt, because of the improving economic situation. However, a new purge began in the summer of 1936, involving the first Show Trial, and signalling the start of what became known as the Great Purge.

The Show Trials

These were public trials from 1936 to 1938, in which leading communists were accused of plotting against Stalin and the Soviet Union. The interrogation methods of the NKVD – and the belief of many communists in the 1930s that Stalin, despite his many faults, was all that stood between the gains of the November Revolution and the restoration of capitalism – led to many bizarre 'confessions'.

The NKVD claimed to have uncovered a Trotskyist-Zinovievist counter-revolutionary conspiracy, which was said to be in league with capitalist states, former Civil War White Guards and *kulaks*. In the Trial of the Sixteen, in August 1936, Zinoviev, Kamenev, Smirnov, Syrtsov, and 12 others were accused of organising this conspiracy and plotting to kill Stalin and other Politburo members. NKVD interrogations (based on the 'conveyor system' of sleep deprivation, continued questioning and beatings) resulted in 14 of them admitting their 'guilt'. All 16 were found guilty and then executed.

SOURCE 3.2

...The recantations of the men in the dock are far less surprising than they might have been otherwise... Throughout they had been oppressed by the insoluble conflict between their horror of Stalin's methods of government and their basic solidarity with the social regime which had become identified with Stalin's rule... They were preyed on by their own scruples and remorse; but they were also terrorized by Stalin's terror. The stories that they were hypnotized or given mysterious drugs may be safely dismissed. But it cannot be doubted that they were subjected to physical and moral torture of the sort that is used in third-degree interrogation in Russia – and elsewhere. In addition, the political police... had been given the right to take the defendants' relatives as hostages... Even the most indomitable, those most ready to sacrifice their own persons for their cause, cannot feel that they have the right to sacrifice their parents or children in the same way.

Deutscher, I., 1966, **Stalin: A Political Biography**, *Harmondsworth, Penguin, p. 371.*

Some of the 'confessions' implicated the former Right Opposition leaders. These, and others, were questioned but were not arrested, and these investigations were dropped: possibly because Bukharin refused to confess, and possibly because of disagreements within the Politburo. Stalin then appointed **Ezhov**, as head of the NKVD.

Nikolai Ezhov (1895–1940):

He joined the Bolsheviks in 1917 and played an active part in the November Revolution and the Civil War. He helped to organise the collectivisation of agriculture, and his career was aided by Kaganovitch's support. He helped develop the idea of a Trotskyist-Zinovievist conspiracy and, as head of the NKVD from 1937 to 1938, he organised the Show Trials against the Old Bolsheviks, and the purge of the armed forces. He was removed in 1938, and executed in 1940.

A second Show Trial, the Trial of the Seventeen, took place in January 1937, involving 17 communist leaders accused of plotting with Trotsky to carry out assassinations, terrorist activities, sabotage of industry and spying. Once again, NKVD interrogations produced 'confessions'. This time, 13 were sentenced to death. Following this second Show Trial, the Central Committee met during February and March 1937 – its main business was to consider stepping up the exposure and destruction of the 'Trotskyist Conspiracy'. Ezhov took the cue from Stalin and, at one of the meetings, accused Bukharin of having known of Trotsky's plans.

Figure 3.5: 'The Murderer's Hygiene', a 1937 Soviet cartoon that portrays Trotsky as an executioner, finishing his day's work and 'washing his hands in fear'.

Bukharin refused to 'confess' to this, and a special sub-committee expelled him from the party – he was then immediately arrested. In early March, Bukharin, along with several other Rightists, was charged with having links with Trotsky and his supporters.

The last, and biggest of the Show Trials was the Trial of the Twenty-One, in March 1938. It focused on Bukharin, and 20 others, accused of membership of a 'Trotskyist-Rightist bloc'. Once again, most of the accused 'confessed' to their 'crimes', though not Bukharin. The court returned the desired verdict, and Bukharin and 17 others were shot.

ACTIVITY

Try to put yourself in a similar position to those accused in the Show Trials of 1936–38. Assuming you had a genuine commitment to a particular political or religious ideology, which factor would be the most important to you in deciding whether to make a false 'confession': avoiding pain or death; saving your family; loyalty to your beliefs or cause? Then write a couple of sentences to explain your choice.

The Great Terror, 1937–38

By the time of the last important Show Trial, the Great Purge had transformed into the Great Terror – or *Ezhovshchina* ('the time of Ezhov' – 1937–38, the height of the Great Terror) – as the number of denunciations, expulsions, trials, imprisonments and executions multiplied. Initially, the purges had mainly affected party members; by mid-1937 they had widened to include large numbers of administrators and specialists, including engineers and railway workers. Many ended up in the Gulag, while others were simply executed by the NKVD.

It also spread to the Red Army. Some officers or former officers had been implicated in the first or second Show Trials in 1936 and 1937. Then, in May 1937, Marshal Tukhachevsky (Chief of General Staff and a Deputy Commissar for Defence) and Gamarnik (head of the Red Army's Political Commissars and also a Deputy Commissar for Defence) were arrested and accused of plotting with Trotsky and foreign enemies to assassinate Soviet leaders. On 12 June 1937, Tukhachevsky and some other leading commanders were executed. This Great Terror then spread down to the lower ranks of the Red Army so that, by the end of 1938, the list of those executed included three out of the five Red Army marshals, 14 out of the 16 top commanders, all eight admirals and 60 of the 67 Corps Commanders.

Also badly hit were the air force officers and the military intelligence service. In all, about 35 000 of the entire officer corps (about 50%) were either executed or imprisoned.

The Great Terror also began to affect large numbers of ordinary people. Many, keen to avoid suspicion falling on themselves, tried to prove their loyalty to Stalin by denouncing others. Some also saw it as a way of settling scores, or securing the jobs of those who had been purged. By the end of 1938, most Russians were living in a state of terror, reluctant to talk openly to anyone. At that point, however, the Great Terror began to diminish.

> QUESTION
>
> **How did the Great Purge affect the Red Army, and Soviet society in general?**

As early as October 1937, Stalin raised doubts about the purging of industrial workers and, in January 1938, the Central Committee decided a party recruitment drive was necessary to replace those purged as a result of false denunciations.

In December 1938, **Beria** replaced Ezhov as General Commissar for State Security and, at the 18th Party Congress in March 1939, Stalin and Zhdanov announced that 'mass cleansings' were no longer needed and even admitted that 'mistakes' had been made. As a result, mass arrests ended, several thousand Gulag prisoners were released and many more who had been expelled from the party and had lost their jobs were rehabilitated.

> **Lavrenti Beria (1899–1953):**
>
> He was an early supporter of Stalin. In 1938, he replaced Ezhov as head of the NKVD and was responsible for the elimination of Ezhov and several other NKVD officials at the end of the Great Terror. When Zhdanov died in 1948, it was thought Beria would succeed Stalin as ruler of the Soviet Union; but, when Stalin died in 1953, Beria was quickly arrested and executed.

SOURCE 3.3

One thing is sure: it was Stalin who instigated the carnage of 1937–8, although there was a current of popular opinion in the USSR that it was not essentially his fault. Supposedly his associates and advisers had persuaded him that only the most extreme measures would save the state from destruction; and in later decades this notion continued to commend itself to a handful of writers. But this was self-delusion. Stalin started and maintained the movement towards the Great Terror. He did not need to be pushed by others. He and nobody else was the engineer of imprisonment, torture, penal labour and shooting.

Service, R., 2005, **Stalin: A Biography,** *London, Pan, p. 347.*

KEY CONCEPTS ACTIVITY

Perspectives: There is considerable debate about the Great Terror. Carry out some additional research, and make notes, on the various historical arguments about:

- the numbers affected
- the possible reasons for it
- the extent of Stalin's responsibility.

Historians and the Great Terror

There has been considerable debate about the impact of the Great Purge and the Great Terror, the reasons behind them, and Stalin's responsibility for them.

Before Gorbachev came to power in 1985, estimates of the total number of victims varied from 5 million to 18 million. However, in 1990, as part of *glasnost*, KGB archives were opened to the public (see 7.2, *Glasnost*) – according to their figures, the total number of victims imprisoned or executed was 2 million. These lower figures are now taken as fairly reliable by many historians – and support the lower estimates given before 1990 by such historians as J. F. Hough and M. Fainsod, and by T. H. Rigby. However, some more recent evidence has reopened the debate, with some historians now favouring an upward revision of the number of victims. This 'numbers' issue is complicated by the difficulty in separating out deaths due to collectivisation and the famine.

As regards debate about the causes for the Great Terror, orthodox views focus on Stalin's role and his position as dictator of the Soviet Union. Some historians, such as R. Tucker, have argued that Stalin launched the purges because he was suffering from some sort of mental illness or, at least, paranoia, which resulted in irrational and extreme action. Opposed to this, other historians, such as I. Deutscher, have argued that the policies were a 'rational' response – either to the existence of real opposition within the USSR, or to the increasingly threatening international situation following Hitler's rise to power in 1933. R. Medvedev, for instance, has linked Stalin's actions to the huge support given to Kirov at the 1934 Party Congress; while J. Arch Getty has suggested that Stalin's references to a Trotskyist-Zinovievist plot were in part based on fact. In particular, there is evidence that in the period 1930–32, several middle-ranking communist officials contacted Trotsky about forming a new opposition bloc.

However, other historians have presented revisionist and structuralist explanations which try to shift the focus away from Stalin, and on to other factors. G. Rittersporn, for example, has argued that although Stalin made crucial appointments at the centre (such as replacing Yagoda with Ezhov as head of the NKVD), the NKVD and local party bosses were often out of control in the chaos of the 1930s, and frequently took matters well beyond Stalin's initial intentions.

3.4 How did Stalin's foreign policy try to achieve security for the Soviet Union in the 1930s?

Stalin's main foreign policy concern seems to have been achieving and maintaining Soviet security – also an important factor in his economic policies. In order to do this, he was prepared to play down the earlier Bolshevik commitment to revolutionary internationalism. At times, though, his actions seemed to be a continuation of Tsarist-style Russian imperialism.

To understand Stalin's foreign policy in the 1930s, it is necessary to have some idea of the Soviet Union's situation in the 1920s. Immediately after the Bolshevik Revolution of 1917, the leaders did not expect the new Soviet state to survive. However they did hope to inspire workers' revolutions in more economically advanced countries – this was especially important as the main foreign powers intervened against Lenin's government in the Civil War which lasted from 1918 to 1921. To begin with, the Communists hoped that the Comintern would help revolutionary socialist uprisings in Germany, Hungary and Italy – and future ones – to succeed. Soviet isolation would then be ended by the appearance of other workers' states, which would help economic recovery and growth in Russia. However, by 1921, these attempted revolutions had been defeated.

After 1921, the West attempted to create a 'cordon sanitaire' to isolate Soviet Russia – mainly by economic and trade embargoes to restrict Bolshevik attempts to rebuild the Russian economy. According to Winston Churchill (a determinedly anti-Communist politician), such measures were intended to 'strangle infant Bolshevism in its cradle'. Furthermore, the Bolshevik government – which had been excluded from the peace settlements – was also excluded from 1920s' diplomacy. All of this had underlined Soviet weakness and isolation – Stalin and other Soviet leaders who negotiated with the West after 1945 had lived through these developments.

SOURCE 3.4

...Politicians such as Wilson, Lloyd George and Clemenceau made peace after the First World War in a context coloured by the Bolshevik seizure of power... As well as punishing Germany for the war, the West also sought to isolate the new USSR. They chose not to moderate the harsh terms of the Treaty of Brest-Litovsk that Germany had imposed on Trotsky and the Soviet leadership in 1918 (which had involved the loss of much territory). They also intervened in support of anti-Bolshevik forces.

Sewell, M., 2002, **The Cold War***, Cambridge, Cambridge University Press, p. 16.*

Shunned by the US, the Western European democracies and the increasingly authoritarian regimes in Central and Eastern Europe, Soviet Russia turned to the other outcast in Europe – Germany. In 1922, the two countries signed the Treaty of Rapallo – in return for allowing secret German military training and arms manufacture in Russia, Germany provided economic assistance and established trade links. In 1930, three years before Hitler became chancellor of Germany, the Treaty of Berlin continued and developed these arrangements. By then, the Soviet Union had diplomatic links with all major states, except the USA, which remained extremely anti-communist.

Stalin's concerns in the 1930s

As the major capitalist states were hit by the Great Depression in the early 1930s, Stalin's fears about a possible war increased – communists believed that capitalist states solved serious economic crises by war.

By 1932, with Germany moving increasingly to the right – under the impact of the Depression – France started to see that the Soviet Union's Red Army might be a powerful block in the east to rising German militarism. Consequently, in November 1932, a Franco-Soviet non-aggression pact was finally concluded. By then, Soviet Russia had already signed similar pacts with Poland, Finland and the three Baltic republics (Estonia, Latvia and Lithuania), in an attempt to safeguard its western borders from any German expansionism.

QUESTION

With which countries did Stalin sign a series of pacts in the early 1930s? What were his main reasons for doing so?

Soviet fears increased in 1933, when Hitler and the Nazis came to power in Germany, as Nazi ideology was violently anti-communist and Hitler's stated aims included the desire to take 'Living Space' in the east, especially from the USSR. Relations with Germany deteriorated; Stalin cancelled all military cooperation with Germany, and took up French offers of joint military discussions and assistance. In November 1933, the US – which was becoming alarmed at Japanese aggression in Asia (first shown by Japan's invasion of Manchuria in 1931) – finally asked the Soviet Union to establish diplomatic relations. However, this improved relationship was fragile.

The search for an anti-fascist alliance

In December 1933, Litvinov, the Soviet Commissar for Foreign Affairs, argued that, because of the threats from Japan and, especially, Germany, the Soviet Union's best defence lay in an alliance with Britain, France and the US, to uphold the peace settlements of 1919–20. In 1934, the Soviet Union and France began to draft a treaty by which the Soviet Union would help guarantee France's borders with Germany in return for French military help if Germany attacked the Soviet Union. However, proposals to guarantee Germany's eastern frontiers foundered.

Soviet fears also led Stalin to apply for membership of the League of Nations, and this was granted in 1934. The Soviet Union then made efforts to strengthen the League's 'collective security' role, by which members of the League were meant to act together to prevent war by applying economic sanctions or, in the last instance, taking military action against aggressors. However, events in 1935 and 1936 soon led Stalin to return to direct diplomacy as the best way of securing the defence of the USSR.

ACTIVITY

Carry out some further research on Soviet foreign policy in the 1930s. Do you think the evidence points to a genuine desire to work with the League of Nations? Or was Stalin's main aim to achieve security for the Soviet Union?

In May 1935, France signed a new treaty with the Soviet Union which included mutual protection of Czechoslovakia from any attack by Nazi Germany – but France specifically avoided making any definite military commitment. Then, in October 1935, Italy invaded Abyssinia (modern-day Ethiopia), and Stalin noted the lack of any effective response from the League. He was further unsettled by the League's weakness over Hitler's reoccupation of the Rhineland (a demilitarised zone established by the peace treaties, 1919–20) in March 1936 and, later in the year, over German and Italian involvement in the Spanish Civil War. Stalin's concerns were increased in October, when Hitler and Mussolini signed the Rome-Berlin Axis. In November, Hitler signed an Anti-Comintern Pact with Japan; in October 1937, Italy joined this alliance.

Although Stalin kept his options open (attempts were made, periodically, to achieve non-aggression agreements with both Germany and Japan), the main thrust of Soviet policy in 1936 was still towards achieving an anti-Nazi alliance with Britain and France. However, Britain's 'National' (but essentially Conservative) government was strongly anti-communist and, at that time, saw Nazi Germany as a useful block against the spread of communism. In addition, many believed that aspects of the Versailles settlement should be 'revised' to take account of Germany's 'legitimate' grievances. Thus, Britain saw 'appeasement' of Nazi Germany as preferable to strengthening the League – or forming an alliance with the USSR.

Stalin's concerns about Britain's refusal – until too late – to accept his repeated offers after 1933 of an alliance against the threat posed by Nazi Germany, were increased by the support Western states gave, before 1939, to right-wing regimes and groups. For instance, Britain and France gave political and military backing to Pilsudski's undemocratic and anti-Semitic regime in Poland; while during the Spanish Civil War, many US companies – with the tacit approval of the US government – gave significant economic assistance to Franco's semi-fascist Nationalists.

Japan's invasion of Manchuria worried Stalin, so he tried to reach an accommodation with the Japanese. However, Japan's foreign policy was still undecided: one faction favoured expansion at the expense of the Soviet Union, the other wanted to expand in the Pacific and South East Asia. In July 1937, when Japan launched a full-scale invasion of China, Stalin feared the USSR might have to face a two-front attack from Nazi Germany and Japan. Consequently, under a new treaty with China, signed in August 1937, the Soviet Union sent military aid to the nationalist government and, in August 1939, the Red Army inflicted a serious defeat on Japan's forces, which had crossed into Soviet territory, at the Battle of Khalkin-Gol.

The Nazi-Soviet Non-Aggression Pact

While events were unfolding in Asia, the Soviet Union's diplomatic approach to Western European states began to falter.

In March 1938, neither Britain nor France opposed Hitler's *Anschluss* (union) with Austria, though this was forbidden by the Treaty of Versailles. More worrying for the USSR was the growing crisis over the Sudetenland in Czechoslovakia. The Soviet Union offered to act on the Franco-Soviet Pact of 1935, designed to protect Czechoslovakia. France, however, was not prepared to act without Britain – and Britain refused.

In addition, Poland refused to give permission for the Red Army to cross Polish territory. Then, on 29 September 1938, Britain, France and Italy agreed, in Munich, that Czechoslovakia should hand over the Sudetenland to Germany.

Figure 3.6: A Soviet cartoon about the Munich Agreement of 1938. The signpost says 'Western Europe' and 'USSR' – Britain and France are shown directing the Nazis to the USSR.

QUESTION

What is the message of the cartoon in Figure 3.6?

3 The Soviet Union and Post-Soviet Russia (1924–2000)

In March 1939, Nazi Germany invaded the rest of Czechoslovakia. Once again, Britain and France took no action. This was despite the fact that, from September 1938, Stalin continued to urge Britain and France to join the USSR in taking military steps to stop Hitler's aggressive foreign policy. However, Britain finally decided that Poland, Hitler's next likely target, should be protected and, in April, Britain initiated some talks with the Soviet Union about the possibility of joint action to 'guarantee' Poland against Nazi aggression – but the talks faltered.

SOURCE 3.5

Stalin had always expected war to break out again in Europe... The second premise [of Soviet foreign policy] was the need to avoid unnecessary entanglement in an inter-imperialistic war. Stalin had always aimed to avoid risks with the USSR's security, and this preference became even stronger at the outbreak of the Spanish Civil War in mid-1936. The dream of Maksim Litvinov... of the creation of a system of 'collective security' in Europe was dissipated when Britain and France refused to prevent Germany and Italy from aiding the spread of fascism to Spain. But what could Stalin do?... If he dealt with the victor powers of the Great War, what trust could he place in their promises of political and military co-operation? If he attempted to approach Hitler, would he not be rebuffed? And, whatever he chose to do, how could he maintain that degree of independence from either side in Europe's disputes he thought necessary for the good of... the USSR?

Service, R., 1997, A History of Twentieth-Century Russia, London, Allen Lane/Penguin, p. 254.

By May 1939, Stalin – increasingly suspicious of the real motives behind British and French foreign policy – decided that, in order to avoid war, more serious approaches should be made to Germany and Japan for the signing of non-aggression pacts. Evidence released since the collapse of the Soviet Union in 1991 suggests that a military alliance with Britain and France was Stalin's favoured option. Britain, however, was still dragging out negotiations when, on 23 August 1939, it was announced that the USSR and Nazi Germany had signed a Non-Aggression Pact.

This cynical decision was in order to buy time for the USSR to prepare for the expected German attack. The pact, which was supposed to last ten years, did not make the two countries allies, but stated that they would stay neutral in any war in which the other was involved. Secret clauses divided Poland and large parts of Eastern Europe between the two signatories – Germany was to have western Poland, while the USSR had eastern Poland, Finland, the three Baltic republics, and part of Romania (Bessarabia) which previously had been part of tsarist Russia.

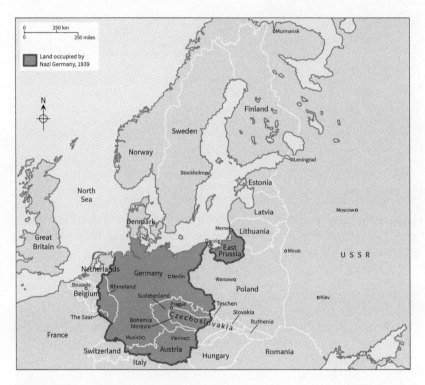

Figure 3.7a: Soviet security concerns on its western border in 1938–39 (see also Figure 3.7b for Soviet security concerns on its eastern border in 1938–39). Before 1941, the USSR thus faced a potential two-front war.

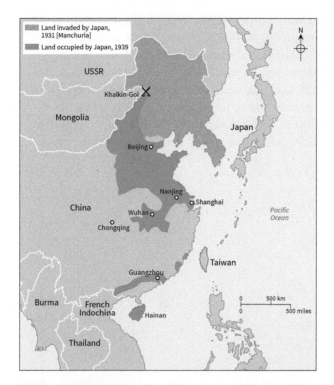

Figure 3.7b: Soviet security concerns on its eastern border in 1938–39 (see also Figure 3.7a for Soviet security concerns on its western border in 1938–39). Before 1941, the USSR thus faced a potential two-front war.

QUESTION

In what ways do the maps in Figure 3.7 support the view that, in 1938 and 1939, Stalin had reason to fear a two-front war against the Soviet Union?

Thus the USSR regained territory taken from it by Poland in 1921 – and obtained a 'buffer zone' between it and Nazi Germany. Shortly afterwards, on 1 September 1939, Germany invaded 'its' part of Poland and, on 3 September – to both Hitler's and Stalin's surprise – Britain and France declared war on Germany. In accordance with the pact, the USSR stayed neutral.

QUESTION
What were the main terms of the Nazi-Soviet Non-Aggression
Pact of 1939? How valid is the argument that this agreement was
evidence of Soviet imperialism?

The debate about Soviet foreign policy

Historians are divided as to the real aims and motives of Soviet foreign
policy in the 1930s. Some 'collective security' historians, such as A.
J. P. Taylor and, more recently, G. Roberts, have argued that Stalin's
policy – as pursued by Litvinov – was genuine. They point out that
even after the Munich Crisis of September 1938, Stalin still hoped for
an alliance with Britain and France. Only when he became convinced
that these countries were in fact encouraging Hitler to 'go east' did he
decide to try making a short-term deal with Hitler, to avoid war while
Soviet defences were built up. Even then, it is argued, he still continued
negotiations with Britain in the hope that an anti-Nazi alliance might
be reached at the last moment.

However, these views are opposed by 'Germanist' historians – such as
R. Tucker, who argue that Stalin's approaches to the West were a screen
behind which the USSR continued with its policy of close relations
with Germany, which had begun with the Treaty of Rapallo in 1922.
Such historians see Stalin's contacts with Britain and France as ploys to
put pressure on Germany to sign a non-aggression agreement with the
Soviet Union.

A third group of historians stress the importance of 'internal politics' in
understanding Soviet foreign policy in the 1930s. For example, J. Haslam
and C. Kennedy-Pipe have both stressed the genuine policy differences
which existed between the pro-Western Litvinov, and Molotov, who
placed greater faith in the independent strength of the Soviet Union.
Such historians see Stalin as wavering between these two options.

However, G. Roberts has pointed out that Soviet archives released
since 1991 have shown that the infrequent Soviet contacts with Nazi
Germany from 1935 to 1939 were made only in response to German
approaches. Furthermore, he sees any internal policy differences among
Soviet leaders over Soviet security as being quite limited – more
important in changing Stalin's course was the persistent reluctance of

France and, especially Britain, to conduct serious negotiations with
the Soviet Union. In the end, this undermined the 'western, collective
security' option and left the isolationist policy of making a temporary
insurance deal with Nazi Germany as the only viable option.

ACTIVITY

Carry out some additional research on Soviet foreign policy in
the 1920s and 1930s. To what extent do you think what you have
discovered shows that Stalin was a real threat to the West?

Theory of Knowledge

History and ethics

The comedian Groucho Marx (1890–1977) once said:
*'These are my principles and if you don't like them
– I have others!'* History often involves examination
of politicians and states making what are known as
'realpolitik' decisions – meaning decisions based on
pragmatic considerations (such as strategic or material
needs) rather than on political principles (such as ideology
or morality). This often entails being prepared to do deals
with enemies in order to gain some short-term advantage
– the Nazi-Soviet Non-Aggression Pact of August 1939 is
one example of this approach. Working with a partner,
develop arguments for and against such an approach. Can
you think of any 21st century examples of realpolitik? Do
you think an ethical foreign policy is (a) desirable and (b)
achievable?

DISCUSSION POINT

Do you think that Britain and France, by not joining with the
Soviet Union to enforce collective security in the years 1935–38,
missed a real chance of stopping Hitler's aggression? Or do you
think the Second World War was inevitable?

Paper 3 exam practice

Question

Evaluate the **successes and failures** of **Stalin's economic policies** during the period **1928–41. [15 marks]**

Skill

Understanding the wording of a question

Examiner's tips

The first step in producing a high-scoring essay is to look *closely* at the wording of the question. Every year, students throw away marks by not paying sufficient attention to the demands of the question.

It is therefore important to start by identifying the **key or 'command' words** in the question. With this one the key words are as follows:
• evaluate
• successes and failures
• Stalin's economic policies
• 1928–41.

Key words are intended to give you clear instructions about what you need to cover in your essay – hence they are sometimes called 'command' words. If you ignore them, you will not score high marks, no matter how precise and accurate your knowledge of the period.

For this question, you will need to cover the following aspects:
• **evaluate:** requires an analytical and structured argument which assesses the overall outcomes of Stalin's economic policies. This will involve, where relevant, consideration and evaluation of different historical interpretations / perspectives.
• **successes and failures:** both the positive and the negative aspects of Stalin's industrial and agricultural policies will need to be considered. An answer which considers only successes *or* failures will not score more than half marks, even if the argument and knowledge is excellent.
• **Stalin's economic policies:** the focus here must be on the state of the Soviet economy in 1928, Stalin's aims, and the outcomes of

aspects such as the Five-Year Plans and the forced collectivisation of agriculture.
* **1928–41:** the period from 1928 to 1941 is the focus here. Be careful to focus on the time period specified in the question – don't go beyond 1941.

Common mistakes

Under exam pressure, two types of mistakes are particularly common.

One is to begin by giving some pre-1928 context, but then to continue giving a detailed account of Lenin's rule from 1917 to 1924, and then economic and political developments from 1924 to 1928. It is true that a brief reference to the situation just before 1928 will be relevant for putting your answer into context. However, the period before 1928 must not be any *significant* part of your answer. As the question is focused on Stalin's economic policies from 1928 to 1941, such an answer would only score the very lowest marks, no matter how detailed and accurate your knowledge of Lenin's economic policies might be.

The other – more common – mistake is to focus *entirely* on the dates. This is almost certainly likely to end in the production of a general and descriptive account of the economic policies during this period. Such a narrative-based account will not score highly, as it will not explicitly offer a considered evaluation of successes and failures, which is a central part of the question.

Both of these mistakes can be avoided if you focus carefully on the wording of the question. For more on how to avoid irrelevant and narrative answers, see Chapter 6.

Activity

In this chapter, the focus is on understanding the question and producing a brief essay plan. So, look again at the question and the tips, and then the simplified mark scheme in Chapter 10. Now, using the information from this chapter, and any other sources of information available to you, draw up an essay plan – perhaps a spider diagram – which has all the necessary headings for a well-focused and clearly structured response to the question.

Paper 3 practice questions

1 To what extent was Stalin's economic 'revolution from above' planned in advance?

2 Discuss the reasons for, and the effects of, Stalin's attempt to modernise the Soviet economy in the period 1928–41.

3 'Stalin's turn to the left as regards economic policy in 1928 was mainly to do with his desire to secure absolute political power within the Communist Party.' To what extent do you agree with this statement?

4 Evaluate the reasons for the launching and course of the Great Purge and the Great Terror.

5 Examine the nature of the methods Stalin used after 1929 to establish his power in the Soviet Union.

6 'Stalin's collective security line in the 1930s was no more than a feint designed to fool the West and obtain offers from Nazi Germany.' To what extent do you agree with this statement?

4 Stalin and the Soviet Union, 1941–53

Introduction

Stalin's main aim during the 1930s seems to have been to ensure the survival and growth of the Soviet Union. This quest for Soviet security continued in the period 1941–53, as shown by both his economic and foreign policies. The 'Great Patriotic War' – which began with Nazi Germany's invasion of the Soviet Union in June 1941 – had a great impact on the Soviet Union. This impact – and the emerging Cold War after the end of the Second World War – led Stalin to conclude that Soviet security required, among other things, the expansion of the Soviet Union beyond its borders. At times, his foreign policy seemed, to many observers, to be a continuation of tsarist–style Russian imperialism.

TIMELINE

1941 June: Operation Barbarossa (German invasion of the Soviet Union) begins

Dec: Zhukov's counter-offensive; US attacked by Japan

1942 Sept: Start of the Siege of Stalingrad

1943 Feb: Sixth Army surrenders

Jul: Battle of Kursk

Nov: Tehran Conference

1944 Jun: D-Day (start of the second front in Europe)

Oct: Moscow Conference

1945 Feb: Yalta Conference

Apr: Death of Roosevelt; Vice-President Truman takes over

May: Red Army occupies Berlin; Lend-Lease programme to USSR ended by US

Jul: Potsdam Conference

Aug: US A-bombs dropped on Hiroshima and Nagasaki

1946 Mar: Fourth Five-Year Plan; Churchill's 'Iron Curtain' speech

Oct: Rigged elections in Bulgaria

Nov: Rigged elections in Romania

1947 Jan: Rigged elections in Poland; formation of Bizonia

Mar: Truman Doctrine

Jun: Marshall Plan

Aug: Rigged elections in Hungary

Sept: Formation of Cominform; 'two camps' doctrine

1948 **May:** Rigged elections in Czechoslovakia

Jun: Yugoslavia expelled from Cominform; formation of Trizonia; new currency for Western zones of Germany; start of Berlin Blockade

1949 **Jan:** Formation of Comecon

Apr: Formation of NATO

May: End of Berlin Blockade

Aug: Soviet A-bomb tested

Sept: Formation of West Germany

Oct: Formation of East Germany

1951 **Mar:** Fifth Five-Year Plan

1952 **Oct:** 19th Party Congress

1953 **Mar:** Death of Stalin

KEY QUESTIONS
- How did the Great Patriotic War, 1941–45, affect the Soviet Union?
- What were Stalin's main political and economic policies, 1945–53?
- How did the emerging Cold War affect Stalin's foreign policy after 1945?

Overview

- From 1939 to 1941, the Soviet Union stayed neutral in the Second World War, and concentrated on building up its defences. However, in 1940, with Britain undefeated, Soviet defensive measures were scaled down. Operation Barbarossa, the massive German invasion of the Soviet Union which began on 22 June 1941, took Stalin completely by surprise.
- When Japan attacked the US in December 1941, Britain, the USSR and the US formed a Grand Alliance to defeat Germany and Japan – despite their mutual distrust.
- But tensions in the Grand Alliance began to emerge. In 1943, at the Tehran Conference, Stalin was concerned about the delay in opening

a second front in the west, and there were disagreements over the post-war futures of Germany and Poland.

- In 1945, in the closing stages of the Second World War, these differences deepened at the Yalta and Potsdam Conferences – especially when Truman became president of the USA, following Roosevelt's death.
- Despite having won the war, Stalin remained very concerned about Soviet security. He also remained deeply suspicious of potential rivals. The army commanders were very popular by 1945, and many hoped for a relaxation of Stalinist rule.
- At home, Stalin used the party machine to reassert control over the military – Stavka (military high command) and GKO (defence committee) were abolished, and several top commanders (including Zhukov) were demoted.
- Stalin then virtually ignored leading party bodies such as the Politburo and the Central Committee. During the years 1945–53, occasional purges took place – but not on the scale of the 1930s.
- Stalin launched the reconstruction of the Soviet Union via the Fourth and Fifth Five-Year Plans. Industry soon revived, but agriculture continued to present problems of under-production.
- In foreign affairs, relations between the Soviet Union and the other Grand Alliance partners (the US and Britain) began to deteriorate badly into what was soon called the 'Cold War'.
- Stalin's chief policy aims were to obtain reparations from Germany; to secure the weakening of Germany; and to establish a buffer zone of Eastern European states along its western borders.
- With the US taking a more hardline approach under Truman, Stalin's objectives were frequently blocked. He was particularly concerned by developments in 1947, when the US announced the Truman Doctrine and the Marshall Plan.
- The Soviet Union increased its control of eastern Europe during the period 1947–49; this included setting up Cominform in 1947, and Comecon in 1949.

QUESTION

What does the source in Figure 4.1 suggest about conditions in the USSR by the end of the Second World War? How might this have contributed to Stalin's sense of insecurity?

Figure 4.1: Russian refugees return to their devastated home town in 1944; the destruction wrought on the USSR during the war made the country vulnerable in Stalin's eyes.

4.1 How did the Great Patriotic War, 1941–45, affect the Soviet Union?

After Britain and France declared war on Germany in September 1939, Stalin believed the danger of an imminent German attack had passed. Until Britain and France had been defeated in the west, he did not believe Hitler would attack and so risk a two-front war. Thus the attack launched by Nazi Germany in June 1941 took Stalin by surprise.

Early stages

In the 1939–41 interval before the Nazi attack on the Soviet Union, Stalin did order some military action. Though some historians see these conflicts and occupations as being essentially a continuation of

Tsarist imperialism, or proof of Soviet intentions to 'export' revolution by conquest, many (such as C. Ward) view them as essentially defensive steps, taken in the light of western inaction over the open aggression displayed by Nazi Germany and Imperial Japan.

Despite declaring war on Germany for its invasion of Poland, Britain and France at first did nothing (the so-called 'Phoney War' period), confirming Stalin's suspicions about their real intentions. So, on 17 September, the Red Army invaded 'their' half of Poland.

Secondly, Stalin, wishing to obtain better protection for Leningrad (where there were important armaments factories) and Murmansk (the USSR's only northern ice-free port), tried to negotiate with Finland for exchanges of territory and the lease of some strategic islands. When Finland – which had good relations with Nazi Germany – refused, he ordered an invasion at the end of November 1939. The Red Army, still adversely affected by the loss of senior commanders during the Great Purge, did badly in what became known as the 'Winter War', which ended in March 1940.

Stalin also signed military agreements with the Baltic states in 1939, allowing Soviet troops to be stationed in their territories. Then, in June 1940, Lithuania was taken over; in July, all three Baltic states became republics of the USSR.

By the summer of 1940, therefore, the Soviet Union had extended its frontiers in the west and south. Any German attack would now be resisted by the Red Army on non-Russian territory. Although France had already been defeated in May 1940, Britain had not – thus Stalin felt confident that Germany would not attack in the near future.

KEY CONCEPTS QUESTION

Causation: What were the reasons for Stalin's decision to slow down the USSR's military preparations in 1940?

Operation *Barbarossa*, June 1941

When Germany lost the Battle of Britain, military preparations in the Soviet Union were slowed down. Yet, since December 1940, Hitler had begun preparing for an invasion of the USSR. In the lead up to the invasion, there were massive German military preparations along its eastern frontiers, plus several Luftwaffe incursions over the Soviet borders. Stalin, and several senior NKVD officials, dismissed reports from NKVD agents that an invasion was imminent – instead, it was believed they were just manoeuvres to extract some concessions.

The German invasion (codenamed Operation Barbarossa – 'Red Beard') on 22 June 1941 was massive and swift. It began what Soviet citizens later came to know as the 'Great Patriotic War'. Over 4 million troops from Germany and its Axis allies were involved, along with over 3000 tanks, 50 000 pieces of artillery and 5000 war planes. The invasion forces advanced quickly and deeply into western Russia. Within a week, the Red Army's defences had been smashed, vast quantities of equipment and supplies had been destroyed or captured and a third of the air force had been destroyed before it could even take off; while over 500 000 people had been taken prisoner.

SOURCE 4.1

[Stalin's] 'pact diplomacy' with Nazi Germany might have been unavoidable. He was not ready for war, and the prospect of a war on two fronts (including against Japan) was a nightmare, which he actually avoided (as Hitler fell into the trap). But the way Stalin played his game with Germany was lamentable... Suffice it to say here that his stubborn refusal to allow the military units on the frontiers, in the rear, or anywhere else, to take the slightest precautions to get ready for the imminent attack... makes for very depressing reading. His self-serving confidence... was probably the reason for the state of shock and paralysis of will that struck him for about a week at the beginning of the war when he realised that... the Germans were already conquering enormous territories of Russia.

Lewin, M., 1997, 'Stalin in the mirror of others', in Kershaw, I. and Lewin, M., eds, **Stalinism and Nazism: Dictatorships in Comparison,** *Cambridge, Cambridge University Press, pp. 126–7.*

Stalin lost his nerve, and it was Molotov who took effective charge of the country. The system of military command was altered. Stavka (the Soviet Military High Command), chaired by Stalin, was set up to take charge of all land, air and sea operations; while the State Committee of Defence (GKO) was established a few days later. This latter body was to oversee not just the military but also the political and economic aspects of the war.

On 3 July, Stalin, back in charge, announced that, because of the tremendous German advances, a 'scorched earth' policy was to be adopted. This meant that where the Red Army was forced to retreat, troops and Soviet citizens had to remove everything (machinery, food, livestock) to the east. What could not be moved (such as unharvested crops or houses), had to be destroyed, in order to leave nothing for the advancing enemy. At the same time, partisan and sabotage units, mainly controlled by the NKVD, were to be set up to operate behind enemy lines.

By August, the Baltic republics had been lost and much of the important agricultural areas of Belorussia and Ukraine were occupied. However, the German army was soon bogged down by heavy rain and mud.

In September, the Germans launched a massive attack on Moscow which took Stavka by surprise. Stalin considered the possibility of seeking peace terms (similar to the Treaty of Brest-Litovsk of 1918), while many government offices were moved from Moscow to Kuibyshev in the east. In the end, however, he decided to stay and fight.

Moscow – and the Soviet Union – were saved by a combination of factors. Firstly, the serious defeats suffered by the Red Army led to Marshal Zhukov taking over command of the whole Western Front on 19 October 1941. Zhukov's forces were strengthened by Siberian troops moved from the Far East – a move made possible because Soviet spies had discovered that the Japanese army had decided to expand in the Pacific rather than attacking the Soviet Union.

Secondly, the Russian weather began to hit German troops and equipment, neither of which had been prepared for a winter war. There was also a lack of food owing to Stalin's 'scorched earth' policy. As the German advance slowed, Zhukov launched a counter-offensive in December 1941 – this was successful, and was followed by further counter-offensives. The Germans suffered high casualties and were pushed back several hundred kilometres in places.

Nonetheless, by the end of 1941, the Soviet Union's position seemed desperate – about 4 million soldiers were dead or captured, and the Red Army had also lost huge amounts of equipment.

The war from 1942 to 1945

In early 1942, Stalin planned a new offensive, as the Red Army had been strengthened by equipment (mostly jeeps and lorries) from the US, which in November 1941, had made a Lend-Lease agreement with the Soviet Union. This provided for some US military equipment to be sent to the USSR. After the US had declared war on Germany in December 1941, the flow of equipment increased, though Soviet requests for troops were ignored.

In August 1942, the Germans began their attempt to take Stalingrad – at times, the Germans held most of Stalingrad, but there was incredible Soviet resistance. Zhukov's counter-offensive – Operation Uranus – began in September and, by November, the German Sixth Army was surrounded; in February 1943, the remnants surrendered.

The battle for Stalingrad proved an important turning point in the war – according to Churchill, the Soviet victory there 'tore the guts out of the German army'. The Soviet Union had faced the bulk of the German forces on its own – at least 75% of all German troops and military equipment had been sent to the Russian front.

Figure 4.2: Soviet troops street-fighting in Stalingrad.

and Russia (1924-2000)

> **QUESTION**
>
> Why was the battle for Stalingrad such an important turning point in the war in Europe?

During 1943, the Red Army slowly pushed the German army westwards, but its losses continued to be heavy. In July 1943, however, the Germans found themselves surrounded and suffered heavy losses at Kursk – the biggest tank battle in history. From September 1943, the Soviet offensive was stepped up. By the end of the year, over 60% of the territory lost since 1941 had been recaptured. In January 1944, the long siege of Leningrad – begun in September 1941 – was ended; by August 1944, all German forces had been expelled from the Soviet Union. The Red Army then began to invade Germany's Axis partners in Eastern Europe; in early January 1945, the Red Army crossed into Germany, reached the River Elbe in April and, in May, entered Berlin.

The debate about the Soviet victory

Ever since the end of the war, historians have argued about the reasons for the Soviet victory, and have considered a variety of military, political and economic factors. According to C. Ward, there are two main interpretations: the negative argument and the positive argument.

The negative argument – favoured, for instance, by R. Medvedev – is that, because of Stalin's mistakes (such as trusting Hitler after the 1939 pact, and the slowing down of defence preparations after 1940), the Soviet Union was almost on the point of total defeat. What saved it was a combination of German mistakes and good luck.

The positive argument stresses the expertise of the Soviet military leaders, and the underlying strengths of the Soviet system – in particular, the ability of its administrative and economic systems to maintain and even increase production during a devastating war. R. Overy, for example, has noted that, despite its bureaucratic image, the Soviet system showed real flexibility (for instance, in using partisan groups and guerrilla warfare in conjunction with Red Army offences) and organisational power.

The impact of the Great Patriotic War

Despite having survived and – perhaps surprisingly – won the war, the Soviet Union was in a terrible state by 1945.

Overall, the Second World War resulted in some 50–60 million deaths – of these, about 25 million were Soviet citizens. Some estimates of Soviet deaths put the figure as high as 28 million, but it is impossible to be exact, as there were no published censuses in the 20 years from 1939 to 1959. Of these deaths, about 9 million were Soviet military personnel – approximately half of these died after being captured, from various causes, including hunger, exposure, disease, forced labour and execution. Civilians suffered even more – at least 15 million Soviet civilians also died, from bombing, hunger, exposure, forced labour, reprisals for partisan actions, and from 'special actions' carried out by Nazi SS units (often aided by regular German army forces).

The war was also immensely economically destructive. Between what was destroyed (or looted and sent back to Germany) by the Germans, and what the Russians themselves destroyed by their 'scorched earth' policy, many of the gains of the Five-Year Plans had been wiped out. In all, about 25% of pre-war capital stock had been lost – in some of the occupied areas, the percentage was more than double this.

In view of the dreadful destruction suffered by the USSR, Stalin saw economic reconstruction as a priority. From mid-1944, as Soviet forces took back Soviet territory previously occupied by German forces, Stalin had become increasingly aware of how damaged and weakened the Soviet Union was – he was thus determined to extract reparations from Germany.

QUESTION

How do you think the human and economic destruction suffered by the Soviet Union during 1941–45 was likely to affect Stalin's aims after 1945 in relation to Germany?

4.2 What were Stalin's main political and economic policies, 1945–53?

Against all expectations, Stalin – and the Soviet Union – had survived the Great Patriotic War. Those who had survived the war felt proud of their system, which they believed had saved not only the Soviet Union, but also the rest of Europe, from Nazi domination. Many Soviet citizens hoped for some political relaxation now that the war was over. Such hopes were quickly dashed as Stalin, fearing the growing antagonism building up between the Soviet Union and the Western powers, determined to re-establish his position after the upheaval of war by maintaining tight political control, and to reconstruct the Soviet economy as quickly as possible.

Re-establishing political control

During the war, massive areas of the USSR had been beyond the control of Moscow, while the prestige of Red Army generals had been tremendously increased by their recent victories over Nazi Germany. Stalin was determined to reassert political control over both the armed forces and the Communist Party after the war.

In September 1945, Stalin abolished Stavka and then the GKO; and in June 1946, Marshal Zhukov was demoted, while other high-ranking officers also lost influence and positions. In August 1946, the system of political commissars in the army was reintroduced, in order to reassert party control of the military. From 1945 to 1953, there were virtually no promotions to the higher ranks in the armed forces. Meanwhile, Stalin ensured his cult of personality was continued.

Once the military had been sufficiently controlled, Stalin decided to exclude leading party members from the decision-making processes. He dispensed with both the Politburo and the Central Committee, neither of which met between 1947 and 1952. Instead, Stalin met with small sub-committees composed of those he trusted at any particular time. Soon, Stalin had resorted to the methods of the 1930s, including purges.

The Soviet Union and Post-Soviet Russia (1924–2000)

From 1946 to 1948 the Soviet Union went through another period of repression, when there was a push for 'ideological purity' in all parts of Soviet life, including science, literature, the arts and the media. This was supervised by **Zhdanov** (who, along with Molotov and **Malenkov**, was one of Stalin's main advisers), hence this period is known as the *Zhdanovshchina* – 'the time of Zhdanov'.

Andrei Zhdanov (1896–1948):

Promoted to the Politburo in 1935, he became one of Stalin's closest advisers. From 1934 to 1945, he headed the Leningrad party; in 1946, he launched a campaign based on the idea of the world (and hence science, literature and the arts) being divided into 'two camps': the bourgeois (capitalist) and the socialist. This process continued until 1953.

Georgi Malenkov (1902–1988):

He had been a political officer in the Red Army during the Civil War and became one of Stalin's close advisers during the 1920s and 1930s. In 1941, he was elected to the Central Committee, and served on the State Defence Committee during the war. He became deputy prime minister, and joined the Politburo, in 1946. On Stalin's death in 1953, with Beria's support, he became prime minister of the Soviet Union and party leader.

The Communist Party also suffered during this period: in June 1948, there was trouble with Yugoslavia (see 4.3, Yugoslavia); then, in August, Zhdanov died. Stalin used these events to begin a purge – from July 1949, over a thousand leading party and administrative officials were arrested, and many were executed in what became known as the 'Leningrad Affair'.

The 19th Party Congress, delayed for five years until October 1952, was significant. As Stalin was too ill to make his usual Central Committee report, Malenkov and **Khrushchev** began to emerge as potential successors. While Malenkov gave the Central Committee report, Khrushchev announced that a new top body, called the Presidium (twice the size of the old Politburo) was to be set up.

This Congress also voted to change the name of the party from the All-Russian Communist Party (Bolsheviks) to the Communist Party of the Soviet Union – the title it retained until the collapse of the Soviet Union in 1991.

> **Nikita Khrushchev (1894–1971):**
>
> He joined the Communist Party in 1918 and was elected to the Central Committee in 1934. He was party secretary of Ukraine, and was elected to the Politburo in 1939. He acted as a senior political commissar on the Stalingrad front during the Second World War. One of Stalin's close advisers after 1945, he went on to rule the Soviet Union from 1955 to 1964 (see Chapter 6). In 1956, at the party's 20th Congress, he made a speech attacking Stalin for his crimes. He was overthrown by Brezhnev in 1964.

Economic reconstruction

The economy was a top priority for the Soviet government after the war: nearly 100 000 *kolkhozes* and 2000 *sovkhozes* had been partially or completely destroyed; railways, roads and bridges had been ruined in large quantities; and retreating German armies had systematically stripped the occupied areas of all the industrial equipment and agricultural produce they could, and had destroyed the rest. With the withdrawal of the US Lend-Lease programme in 1945 and the refusal of the US and Britain to honour earlier agreements on massive reparations from Germany, it was clear that the Soviet Union would have to rely on its own resources.

In industry, Stalin outlined a 15-year programme for long-term recovery, and a Fourth Five-Year Plan was announced in March 1946. As with the earlier plans, most emphasis was placed on rebuilding heavy industry and on reviving agriculture. Once the surviving mines and factories had been reopened, and the war industries switched back to industrial production, industry began to revive.

By 1950, Stalin was claiming that production levels were equal to or higher than those for 1940. Although these claims were exaggerations, a surprisingly rapid and extensive recovery was made. A Fifth Five-Year Plan ran from 1951 to 1955, and set relatively lower targets. However, the Cold War between the West and the Soviet Union, which had started in 1946 to 1947 (see 4.3, below), resulted in increasing amounts of state funds going to the defence industry.

The revival of agriculture was less successful. Even before 1941, agricultural production had been insufficient, but the effects of war had been disastrous. In many areas, the collective system had totally collapsed, and many peasants had grabbed land to work as private plots. In September 1946, Stalin announced that all previously collectivised land would be reclaimed. After 1946, things began to improve: state meat procurements were just about back to 1940 levels by 1950, though the 1950 harvest was still about 15% below the figure for 1940.

4.3 How did the emerging Cold War affect Stalin's foreign policy after 1945?

When the USSR was attacked by Germany in June 1941, and then the US by Japan in December 1941, the USA and Britain soon joined with the Soviet Union in a Grand Alliance to defeat Germany and Japan, as they now saw Hitler as a more serious and immediate threat than Stalin. However, many of the tensions which had existed before the Grand Alliance was formed continued after 1941 and, during the war, new ones arose. The foreign policy Stalin pursued after 1945, including his approach to eastern Europe, arose from various factors. These included:

- the tremendous destruction the Soviet Union had suffered during the war
- the threat of the USA's nuclear monopoly after 1945
- Stalin's determination to establish the security of the USSR in the new post-war world.

Tensions within the Grand Alliance, 1939–44

There had been tensions between the Soviet Union and the Western powers before the formation of the Grand Alliance; others arose during the course of the war. These various tensions eventually led to the collapse of the Grand Alliance and, quite rapidly, to the emergence of what became known as the Cold War. This had a significant influence on the foreign policy pursued by Stalin after 1945.

Roosevelt, the president of the USA, saw Nazi Germany as more expansionist than the USSR, and thought a weakened Soviet Union, at the end of the war, could be persuaded to drop the idea of world communism, in return for security guarantees and help in economic reconstruction – the latter would also help the US economy. Roosevelt initially felt this was preferable to the continued existence of world blocs, an arms race, and the threat of future wars – though, in his last months, there is evidence that his attitude to the demands of the USSR began to harden.

However, the foreign policy developments of the 1930s, following Hitler's rise to power in 1933, played a big role in making the USSR and the states opposed to Communism mutually suspicious. Stalin saw the refusal of Britain and France to join an anti-Nazi alliance, and the Munich Agreement, as encouragement for Nazi Germany to attack the USSR; while the West saw Soviet foreign policy between 1939 and 1941 as evidence of Soviet expansionism. These mutual suspicions remained even after the formation of the Grand Alliance.

New problems soon began to emerge within the Grand Alliance. The Soviet Union had not helped Britain in the years 1939 to 1941, while the US had done little to assist the USSR until it found itself at war with both Japan and Nazi Germany. As well as seeing Allied aid as inadequate, Stalin had even feared the Allies would make a compromise peace with Hitler, and then launch a joint attack against the USSR.

As early as July 1941, Stalin urgently requested that Britain open up a second front in German-occupied Western Europe to take pressure off the Soviet Union. Instead, there were repeated delays, and when the US and Britain were finally ready to attack, they decided to invade Italy first; it was not until June 1944 that France was finally invaded. The repeated delays made Stalin suspicious about his Allies' motives – indeed he feared that these arose from a deliberate plan to ensure that the USSR was seriously weakened.

Despite these tensions, relations between the three Allies still seemed good in 1943. However, during a series of conferences, differences increasingly began to emerge.

By November 1943, when the 'Big Three' met at the Tehran Conference to discuss the post-war settlement of Europe, the victories of Stalingrad and Kursk made it clear that the Red Army was now already winning on the eastern front, even without Allied assistance in the west of Europe. This time, Stalin at last received assurances of an Allied invasion of France, to take place in the spring of 1944.

With the war continuing, the Big Three managed to maintain the alliance: there was initial outline agreement that the Soviet Union (invaded three times via Poland since 1900) could have its 1918 border with Poland restored, while Poland's western border would move further west, at the expense of Germany. There was also agreement that no Central European alliance would be allowed against the Soviet Union.

In October 1944, Churchill (Britain's prime minister) flew to Moscow to meet Stalin. Here, they reached initial outline agreement on respective spheres of influence in south-eastern and eastern Europe after the war. This informal agreement was known as the 'Percentages Agreement'. The percentage ratios, for Britain and the USSR respectively, in the Eastern European states were to be as follows:

Country	% of British influence	% of Soviet influence
Romania	10	90
Greece	90	10
Bulgaria	25	75
Hungary	25	75
Yugoslavia	50	50

Table 4.1: The respective 'spheres of influence' of Britain and the Soviet Union, according to the 'Percentages Agreement' of October 1944.

Significantly, no agreement was reached over Poland, which was therefore not mentioned in this agreement.

QUESTION

What was the 'Percentages Agreement'? What events in the period 1919–41 led Stalin to see this as an important agreement for post-war Soviet security?

Although Roosevelt was not present at the meeting, he made no objections when informed about what had been agreed.

The Yalta Conference, February 1945

In early 1945, with the war clearly coming to an end, differences between the Allies began to emerge – at first, over what to do with Germany and Eastern Europe. These formed the important items on the agenda of the two Allied conferences of 1945.

Germany soon became one of the major factors in the worsening relations between the US and the USSR. After 1945, it was clear that Germany would be fundamental to the European (and even global) balance of power – and thus of tremendous importance to Soviet security concerns. As the tensions grew into the Cold War, both sides feared Germany becoming part of the opposing camp.

Figure 4.3: Left to right: Churchill, Roosevelt and Stalin at the Yalta Conference in February 1945.

The Yalta Conference of February 1945 agreed, quite amicably, to temporarily divide Germany into four zones of occupation, with outline agreement on compensation (reparations) for the damage done by Nazi Germany, especially to the USSR. Despite wanting huge reparations from Germany, Stalin was against the idea of permanently splitting Germany into two – France was alone in wanting a permanent division. Instead, Stalin hoped reparations would both weaken Germany sufficiently to prevent it becoming a potential future threat, and allow the USSR to rebuild following the destruction suffered at the hands of the German armed forces. However, the US and Britain believed his demands were too high.

> QUESTION
>
> Did Stalin want Germany to be divided permanently after the Second World War? Did any of the other Allies desire this?

Stalin was also dismayed by Roosevelt's suggestion at Yalta that the issues raised in the 'Percentages Agreement' should be decided by the planned United Nations Organisation, after the war was over. Roosevelt thus seemed to be backing away from the idea of a Soviet 'sphere of influence' in Eastern Europe. Yet Stalin felt such a sphere – which he believed had been agreed in the Moscow 'Percentages Agreement' – was essential for Soviet security.

SOURCE 4.2

At the conferences of Tehran and Yalta... some kind of loose agreement was reached among the 'Big Three'... It was understood that the Soviet Union had a legitimate interest in ensuring that the countries along her western and south-western borders should not only come within the USSR's 'sphere of influence', but also be governed by regimes which would be politically at least well-disposed to their eastern neighbour... [but] the explicitly hostile declarations of some western politicians, as well as Russia's long experience of vulnerability to invasion from the west, made Stalin unwaveringly determined that the military security of the USSR should have absolute priority over the political independence of those countries, some of which had in any case recently fought alongside Hitler.

Wood, A., 1997, **Stalin and Stalinism***, London, Routledge, pp. 53–4.*

These growing tensions increased, in April 1945, when Roosevelt died and was succeeded by Vice-President **Truman** who took a much more hardline approach to the Soviet Union. Tension increased in May, when the Lend–Lease scheme was ended without notice.

Harry S. Truman (1884–1972):

He became a leading Democrat politician, and was Roosevelt's Vice-President following the 1944 election. He had little experience of foreign affairs, but became President of the USA in 1945, following Roosevelt's death. It was Truman who authorised the use of atomic weapons against Japan, and was responsible for the Truman Doctrine and the Marshall Plan – all of which were key factors in the early years of the Cold War.

105

Theory of Knowledge

History and bias

Truman's policies towards Stalin and the Soviet Union after 1945 were affected by his anti-communist attitudes. However, bias is also a problem for historians – and many people think history is more prone to bias than the natural sciences. 'Topic choice' is one area in which bias can affect the writing of history. What are the other two main areas in which bias might be a potential problem?

The Potsdam Conference, July–August 1945

At the Potsdam Conference, held in July and August 1945, it was clear that the differences between the USSR and the West regarding Germany had become greater. In particular, it was decided that each country could only take reparations from its own zone of occupation. This was a blow to Stalin. He had placed great emphasis on reparations from Germany, and at Yalta, it had been agreed that $10 billion would be a starting point for negotiation.

Now, Truman went back on earlier agreements, and said the US would only agree to the Soviet Union having reparations from the eastern zone of Germany – which was mainly agricultural and therefore poorer – along with 25% of the machinery from the three western zones, *if* the USSR in return sent 60% of the value of goods received from the west, in the form of goods and raw materials. Then, in August 1945, a Soviet request for a loan of $1000 billion was 'lost' by the US State Department. So Stalin decided to increase reparations from its own 'sphere of influence', necessitating increased Soviet control of Eastern Europe.

QUESTION

Why was Stalin so determined to obtain massive reparations from Germany after 1945?

SOURCE 4.3

Stalin's postwar goals were security for himself, his regime, his country, and his ideology, in precisely that order. He sought to make sure that... no external threats would ever again place his country at risk. The interests of communists elsewhere in the world, admirable though those might be, would never outweigh the priorities of the Soviet state as he had determined them.

Gaddis, J. L., 2005, **The Cold War***, London, Penguin, p. 11.*

The Potsdam Conference was also affected by the USA's decision to drop nuclear bombs on the Japanese cities of Hiroshima and Nagasaki. Although Stalin was aware that the US had developed this weapon, the US decision not to share the technology of this new weapon – something favoured by several US advisers – increased his sense of insecurity. This was further increased by the US insistence on its right to use such weapons.

ACTIVITY

Identify and explain the main reasons for the disintegration of the Grand Alliance in the period 1941–45 – including the main areas of disagreement at the Yalta and Potsdam Conferences. Then try to put them in order of importance, writing a short paragraph to justify your first choice.

QUESTION

Why might a photograph such as Figure 4.4 have led to increased security fears in the Soviet Union in the period 1945–49?

4

Figure 4.4: The Japanese city of Hiroshima after it was flattened and devastated on 6 August 1945 by the first atomic bomb to be used in warfare; the bomb was dropped by the USA and it killed over 75 000 people.

Growing Soviet influence in Eastern Europe

Though orthodox historians have seen Stalin's actions in Eastern Europe as resulting from long-term expansionist aims, some revisionist historians have argued that the Soviet Union only acted defensively after 1945 in response to what was perceived by Stalin as real threats from the West, and that the non–nuclear USSR was too weak after the war to entertain the prospect of even European, let alone global, domination.

According to this school of thought, all the Soviet Union desired in 1945 was compensation from Germany in order to rebuild its economy, and a buffer-zone of friendly states along its borders in the west. Historians such as C. Kennedy-Pipe have argued that Stalin's main fear was of a revived Germany, and that Soviet policy in Europe in 1945 was aimed at preventing this, either by cooperation with the West or, failing that, through protecting its western borders by controlling the newly liberated states of Eastern and Central Europe.

Stalin's security concerns

Stalin and other Soviet statesmen were acutely aware of Russia's long-term vulnerability, given past experiences of invasions via the states of Eastern Europe. As early as 1944, as Soviet troops pushed the German army out of Eastern Europe, Stalin attempted to control these states as a kind of 'buffer zone' against future invasions.

For the USSR, security meant three main aims:

- economic reconstruction which was, in part, to come via compensation from Germany and the other nations which had caused such destruction on Soviet territory after 1941
- ensuring Germany would never again become a military threat
- the establishment of 'friendly' states on its western borders.

Despite emerging from the Second World War in 1945 as one of the victorious great powers, the Soviet Union was weaker, both militarily and economically, than Britain or the US realised. As a consequence, Soviet foreign policy during Stalin's last years – despite being opportunistic and expansionist – remained largely defensive and conservative.

SOURCE 4.4

Stalin's political strategy in postwar Germany was a variation of his more general project for a people's democratic Europe. The hope was that postwar Germany would evolve into a left-wing, democratic and anti-fascist state ruled by a coalition including Stalin's communist allies. While Stalin was optimistic that the people's democratic project could succeed in Germany, he could not guarantee that the politics of a future German state would be to his liking. But he could control developments in his own zone where the Soviet occupation authorities, in alliance with East German communists, pursued people's democracy with the aim of extending this model to the rest of Germany when reunification took place. Stalin's economic aim in relation to Germany was the implementation of the Yalta and Potsdam decisions on the payment of $10 billion worth of reparations to the Soviet Union, which was vital to Russia's postwar reconstruction.

Roberts, G., 2006, **Stalin's Wars: From World War to Cold War, 1939–1953**, *New Haven, Yale University Press, pp. 350–2.*

The Soviet Union and Post-Soviet Russia (1924–2000)

The tremendous destruction suffered by the USSR led to a great feeling of vulnerability, and played an important part in Stalin's desire to keep Germany weak – and to control Eastern Europe.

Soviet foreign policy in Eastern Europe post-1945 was in part coloured by the US refusal to share the technology of its nuclear weapons.

Truman insisted that concessions would only be forthcoming if the Soviet Union accepted that the US should be the strongest power, based on its nuclear monopoly. These disagreements and suspicions soon developed into a nuclear arms race between the two superpowers, which became an important element of the Cold War.

The Soviet Union then turned to the pursuit of security via tight control over Eastern Europe and the development of its own atomic weapons. At first, the US believed that it could win the emerging Cold War by stimulating massive economic growth in the West which could then 'win' the Eastern European states away from the Soviet Union.

Figure 4.5: A Soviet cartoon showing Nazi aggression 'hatching out' again, while the USA, France and Britain look on.

QUESTION

What is the message of the cartoon in Figure 4.5, and how does the artist put his point across? To what extent do you think this cartoon is a reflection of genuine Soviet security fears over recent developments concerning Germany?

Theory of Knowledge

History and 'inevitability'

Some historians see the breakdown of the Grand Alliance – and Soviet takeover of Eastern Europe – as inevitable, given the long-standing conflict which had existed since 1917. Yet many historians stress the events of 1946–48 as crucial in understanding Soviet actions. They argue that, before then, the Soviet takeover (like the start of the Cold War) was not 'inevitable'. Instead, they point to the actions, attitudes and mistakes of leaders such as Truman and Stalin; or the fact that, after 1945, both were attempting to create their own empires for economic or security reasons. To what extent do you think the very concept of 'inevitability' is invalid, whatever aspect of history is being studied?

After 1945, Stalin was determined that the Soviet Union would never again suffer invasion. Before the war, with the exception of Czechoslovakia, the Eastern European states had all been ruled by undemocratic, right-wing anti-communist regimes; of these, Hungary and Romania had become allies of Nazi Germany. Thus it was seen as vital to Soviet interests that these countries should be ruled by governments which would not be hostile to the USSR.

The US shift away from accepting a Soviet 'sphere of influence', which Stalin believed had been agreed under the 'Percentages Agreement' (see 4.3, Tensions within the Grand Alliance, 1939–44), persuaded him to begin taking practical measures to ensure Soviet security interests in Eastern Europe. As the Cold War began, it soon became clear that Stalin intended to impose Soviet political control (and later Soviet-style economic and social systems) on these countries.

Establishing the Iron Curtain

Stalin's initial desires were for friendly governments in the Eastern European states, and for a steady flow of industrial and agricultural produce to help speed up the USSR's reconstruction. During the period 1944–46, he opposed any social revolution in these countries – despite the often strong wishes of local communist parties. Such revolutionary transformations, Stalin believed, might jeopardise his aims, by alienating the US and Britain who, at first, had seemed to acquiesce to Eastern Europe being mainly under Soviet influence.

As the Soviet Union established its control over the countries of Eastern Europe – behind what Churchill described as an 'Iron Curtain' – the Red Army, which had remained in these countries after driving out the Axis forces, began to dismantle some of the industries in those countries, in particular in Germany's former Axis partners Hungary and Romania; raw materials were also commandeered. This was all sent back to the Soviet Union as reparations, in an attempt to help restore its war-devastated economy.

The Soviet takeover

Once the Red Army was in control of the Eastern European states, anti-fascist coalition governments were set up – with Stalin insisting that local communist parties be given a significant role. As tensions between the 'Big Three' heightened during 1945–48, the Soviet Union insisted on an even greater share of power for these various local communist parties. Soon, opposition parties were increasingly restricted, and elections were frequently rigged; later, these communist-dominated governments began to nationalise industry and land.

The first country to experience growing Soviet control was Poland. There, a coalition government initially took over, and was recognised by the West in July 1945. However, Stanislaw Mikolajczyk, the new deputy prime minister and leader of the important Peasants' Party, was uncooperative with Stalin's attempts to increase Soviet influence and, as a result, the elections due in February 1946 were postponed until January 1947. Communist manipulation and vote rigging ensured a communist victory in the elections, with Mikolajczyk's party wining only a handful of seats. The coalition government was eventually replaced by a communist government.

While events in Poland unfolded, Soviet control was also being established in Romania. By late 1944, the Red Army had defeated all Axis forces in Romania, and a coalition government dominated by communists was set up. In February 1945, Stalin insisted on his choice becoming prime minister of the new Romanian government which, after the inclusion of representatives of the National Peasants and the Liberals, had been recognised by the West. However, the government was increasingly bypassed and, by mid-1945, the communists were clearly in control. After a stormy election campaign (and vote rigging) in November 1946, the communists and their allies had won almost all the seats. During 1947, all three main opposition parties were closed down and later, on 30 December 1947, the king abdicated: the new Peoples' Republic of Romania was then declared.

The Red Army had defeated all Axis forces in Bulgaria by late 1944. Bulgaria had a small but strong Communist Party. The communist-dominated Fatherland Front ignored earlier Soviet agreements about allowing representatives of the opposition to have a role in government. Rigged elections were held in November 1945, 'won' by the Fatherland Front and, in September 1946, the monarchy was abolished. After the October 1946 elections, the communists were mainly in control and, during 1947, the activities of the main opposition party were increasingly restricted.

Stalin was initially less worried about the kind of government which might rule in Hungary. Free elections were held in November 1945, with the non-communist peasant-based Smallholders Party (KGP) becoming the largest single party and so forming a government. This faced a Left Bloc, made up of Communists, Social Democrats and National Peasants and, on 5 March 1946, a coalition government was set up. But demonstrations against the government forced the resignation of right-wing KGP deputies. Further moves, taken by the security forces (controlled by a communist minister) culminated in the arrest of KGP deputies on counter-revolutionary charges. As the Cold War developed, Stalin's line changed and, in August 1947, the elections were rigged. In November 1947, the new communist government banned all parties which were not pro-communist.

The final developments in the growing Soviet domination of Eastern Europe came in Czechoslovakia. Before 1939, Czechoslovakia – unlike the other Eastern European states – had been a parliamentary democracy; while support for the Czech Communist Party, and the

Soviet Union, was quite strong. In elections held on 26 May 1946, which were free and fair, the communists won 38% of the vote. A coalition government of communists and non-communists was formed. However, in mid-1947 a serious industrial and agricultural crisis developed. When the Communist Minister of the Interior began to appoint 'trusted comrades' to important police posts and to prepare show trials, most non-communist ministers resigned in protest on 20 February 1948. The communists organised huge demonstrations, and then called a general strike on 24 February. All remaining non-communist ministers then resigned. A new government, with the communist Klement Gottwald as prime minister, was then formed; he replaced those who had resigned with supporters of the Communist Party. New elections in May 1948 were rigged, with the Communist Party and its allies winning over 66% of the seats.

Figure 4.6: A British cartoon, dated 1948, commenting on Stalin's takeover of Eastern Europe; Stalin (seated) 'switches' Eastern European countries, while Molotov (standing) spins the globe.

Russia 1924-2000

> ACTIVITY
>
> Try to find several other examples of Western cartoons published in the period 1945–49 about the Soviet takeover of Eastern Europe. Then try to assess (a) their reliability and (b) their usefulness for trying to understand Soviet actions during this period.

Stalin and Eastern Europe, 1947–48

During the summer of 1947, following the Truman Doctrine and the Marshall Plan, Stalin had come to see Europe as being divided into two antagonistic camps and believed that strengthened control of Eastern Europe was now essential for Soviet security.

During 1947, Stalin made a series of treaties – with both economic and military terms – with these Eastern European states, linking them to the Soviet Union. Increasingly dominated by the USSR, these Eastern European states became known as 'satellite states' – meaning 'client' or 'subordinate' states.

Then, on 22 September 1947, Soviet control was taken a step further when the communist parties of these states met in Poland. Stalin set up the Communist Information Bureau (Cominform). In some ways this was a successor to the Comintern (which Stalin had abolished in 1943). Its main function was to keep the communist parties ruling Eastern Europe under Moscow's tight control, and coordinate the activities of their governments.

At its first conference, under Zhdanov's influence, the Truman Doctrine and the Marshall Plan were condemned as extending US power prior to launching a new world war. Zhdanov, in his opening speech, spoke of the world being divided into two opposing camps: the Soviet-led anti-imperialist and democratic camp; and the US-led imperialist and anti-democratic camp. According to Zhdanov, the US was trying to dominate Europe and the world. Only the Soviet bloc was preventing this and trying to preserve world peace.

The formation of Cominform marked the end of Stalin's flexible foreign policy in relation to US actions – even after rejecting the Marshall Plan, the Soviet Union had at first been undecided on what steps to take next. The Truman Doctrine, the Marshall Plan and the decision to allow German reconstruction thus proved to be important turning points.

Yugoslavia

One exception to the Soviet takeover of Eastern Europe was Yugoslavia where, before the Second World War had ended, Josip Tito had already established a communist government, despite Stalin's 'Percentages Agreement' with Churchill (see 4.3, Tensions within the Grand Alliance, 1939–44), and had begun a socialist transformation of Yugoslavia.

In January 1948, along with Dimitrov in Bulgaria, Tito announced the formation of a customs union, to be followed by the establishment of a Balkan Federation. Stalin opposed this, and although Bulgaria backed down, Tito refused. Later, in March 1948, Stalin withdrew all Soviet economic and military advisers from Yugoslavia in order to topple Tito. However, Tito resisted; the Yugoslav Communist Party backed him, and he then arrested Stalin's Yugoslav supporters.

In June 1948, Yugoslavia was expelled from Cominform and, under pressure from the Soviet Union, the other Eastern European countries broke off diplomatic and trade links. This was followed by a purge of 'Titoists' in the Eastern European communist parties.

ACTIVITY
Draw up a chart, as follows:

Stalin's foreign policy 1945–48		
Stalin's aims	Stalin's actions	Results
Reparations from Germany		
Buffer zone		
Weakening Germany		

Then, using what you have studied in this chapter so far, and any other resources available to you, identify the aims (for example, seeking reparations, weakening Germany, establishing a buffer zone in Eastern Europe), and for each one complete the chart to show what Stalin did and what he actually achieved.

Finally, write a short paragraph to show whether you think that, overall, Stalin's foreign policy had succeeded or failed by 1948.

The continuing problem of Germany, 1948–49

While Eastern Europe was important to Soviet security concerns, Germany remained a serious potential threat – a buffer zone would provide little security from a revived and aggressive Germany. The failure to secure agreement over Germany led Stalin to insist on stronger control of Eastern Europe. The still-unresolved question of reparations continued to cause problems between the Soviet Union and the other Allies. But the major problem centred on the intention of Britain and the US, from September 1946, not only to merge their economic zones in Germany into one, but also to encourage a revival of German industry.

In January 1947, the British and US zones had been merged into what became known as Bizonia. Then, in February 1947, Britain stated that it might have to pull out of Bizonia if German heavy industry was not revived. After the Truman Doctrine and the Marshall Plan, announced in June 1947, the USSR began to see these steps as an attempt to build up the economy of a Western Germany which – as it contained 75% of the German population and the important industrial regions – might once again become a military threat: especially if it were allied to what the Soviet Union perceived to be an increasingly hostile US.

The US and Britain agreed to develop Bizonia and introduce currency reform, as preliminary steps to the establishment of a separate West German state. On 7 June 1948, France agreed to join its zone to Bizonia to form Trizonia. On 18 June, without consulting the Soviet Union, the West introduced a new currency, the Deutschmark, to replace the Reichsmark; on 23 June, this was extended to West Berlin.

QUESTION

Why did a crisis break out over Germany in 1948?

The Soviet Union, opposed to the idea of a separate West German state, tried to prevent this by putting pressure on West Berlin: on 24 June, the Soviet Union cut off all road, rail and freight traffic to West Berlin, in what became known as the Berlin Blockade. The Allied response was the massive Berlin Airlift, in which tons of food, fuel and other basic items were flown from Trizonia into West Berlin to supply its 2 million citizens. It lasted for almost a year, until May 1949, when Stalin called off the blockade.

The Berlin Blockade, designed to make the West drop its idea of a separate West German state, actually speeded up the very thing it was intended to stop. The West portrayed it as an attempt by the Soviet Union to drive the Allies out of West Berlin in preparation for taking over the Western zones of Germany. In May 1949, the new Federal Republic of Germany was set up. This confirmed Stalin's fears that the West wanted a revived Germany, closely allied to the US.

On 7 October, the USSR finally accepted the division of Germany and announced the transformation of its Eastern zone into a new state, called the German Democratic Republic (GDR).

Western military alliances

Stalin was further concerned by moves towards the creation of a Western military alliance. When Roosevelt had been US president, he had not seen the Soviet Union as a serious threat to US security – he was thus prepared to make some concessions in three key areas. These were: a Soviet sphere of influence in Eastern Europe (to include, if possible, those Middle Eastern and Asian states, which also had borders with the USSR); reparations from former Axis powers (especially Germany); and US financial support in reconstructing the USSR.

However, Roosevelt's death and Truman's accession meant concessions would only be forthcoming if the Soviet Union accepted that the US should be the strongest power, based on its nuclear monopoly. The Soviet Union then turned to the pursuit of security via tight control over Eastern Europe and the development of its own atomic weapons.

As well as looking to the US for economic assistance, the Western states also came to depend on its military strength. At first, though, the US believed that it could win the developing Cold War by stimulating massive economic growth in the West which could then 'win' the Eastern European states away from the Soviet Union.

In March 1948, the Western European countries formed the Brussels Treaty Organisation. After the Berlin Crisis was over, Britain worked hard to include the US in a European alliance. On 4 April 1949, the BTO became the North Atlantic Treaty Organisation (NATO), with the US and Canada as new members. The Treaty was signed in Washington – from the beginning, NATO was based on the USA's nuclear monopoly, which was seen as allowing the Western European economies to recover and become prosperous (thus also reducing the appeal of communism).

The Soviet response

In January 1949, Stalin announced the formation of the Council for Mutual Economic Assistance (CMEA) – known as Comecon – which bound the Eastern European states even more closely to the Soviet Union. It was the Soviet response to the Marshall Plan, and was intended to coordinate the industrial development and the trade of the Soviet Union and its Eastern European satellites, tying them more closely together and so preventing trade with the West. Initially, Stalin insisted on preferential terms for the Soviet Union, especially in relation to the supply of raw materials which he wanted for the reconstruction of Soviet industry.

The Soviet Union and Post-Soviet Russia (1924–2000)

The creation of NATO in April 1949 raised huge security concerns in the Soviet leadership as the USSR was, at most, only a regional power, whereas the USA was already clearly established as a global superpower. It was not until May 1955, when West Germany became a member of NATO and was allowed to re-arm, that the USSR formed a rival military alliance – the Warsaw Pact. However, in August 1949, the Soviet Union exploded its first atomic bomb – this significant development gave a new dimension to international relations between East and West. The US nuclear monopoly was ended, and a nuclear arms race began, as the US was determined to keep well ahead of Soviet military capabilities.

ACTIVITY

Imagine you are one of Stalin's foreign policy advisers. Write a short paper to advise him (a) about what you see as the main threats to Soviet security in 1949, and (b) what he should do in response. Give specific examples, dates, and so on in your paper.

The Sovietisation of Eastern Europe

At first (though some historians disagree on this), even after the formation of Cominform, it seemed as if Stalin aimed to create 'people's' democracies' in Eastern Europe – run by coalition governments, made up of various 'democratic' (meaning not hostile to the USSR) parties, though the local communist parties would have significant representation.

However, by the summer of 1948, as Cold War tensions increased, non-communists had been removed from these coalition governments via rigged elections, intimidation, arrests, show trials and political purges. Local communist party leaders were then replaced with those selected by Stalin, so strengthening Soviet control. As disagreements over Germany became more serious, Stalin's intentions moved towards establishing regimes in Eastern Europe which were to be organised along political and economic lines similar to those of the Soviet Union. This process in the Eastern European states was known as 'Sovietisation', and took place during 1948–49.

SOURCE 4.5

...Remarks by Stalin suggest that he wanted a 'democratic' (and even 'socialist') East-Central Europe that had to be friendly to the Soviet Union... Indeed, none of the major Soviet diplomats... foresaw or recommended a Sovietised East-Central Europe after the war...

It does not seem to be the case that either side had intended to partition Europe in 1945... even in May 1946, Stalin did not have outright Sovietisation in mind... Intensive archival work during the last decade or so after the formerly closed Soviet archives began to open up has not produced convincing evidence for a Soviet master plan to bolshevise the countries under Soviet occupation. The possibility cannot be excluded that the entire scheme of the 'people's democracy' was pure deception by Stalin to serve as cover for a cleverly hidden script of Sovietisation, but this appears unlikely.

Kuromiya, H., 2005, **Stalin**, *Pearson/Longman, Harlow, pp. 183–7.*

At the same time, the Stalinist model of state security, based on an extensive secret police system, and under close Soviet supervision, was introduced. Once Soviet control was established in Eastern Europe, Stalin was determined to maintain it.

DISCUSSION POINT

Do you think Stalin would have Sovietised the countries of Eastern Europe if the West had stuck to its earlier agreement to support the Soviet Union's demands for war reparations from Germany?

In many ways, this process of 'consolidation' brought little lasting benefit to the Soviet Union. Most Eastern European economies stayed relatively weak, and soon needed Soviet assistance, while the land buffer zone was made virtually obsolete as the US quickly built up a nuclear weapons arsenal based on bomber income and, later, on missiles.

Figure 4.7: Rudolph Slánsky, secretary-general of the Czech Communist Party, during his show trial in 1952.

Figure 4.8: The extent of the Soviet sphere of influence by the end of 1949.

Paper 3 exam practice

Question

Discuss the extent to which Stalin's foreign policy after 1945 was mainly conservative and defensive, with the sole aim of obtaining security for the Soviet Union. **[15 marks]**

Skill

Planning an essay

Examiner's tips

As discussed in Chapter 3, the first stage of planning an answer to a question is to think carefully about the wording of the question so that you know what is required and what you need to focus on. Once you have done this, you can move on to the other important considerations:

- Decide your **main argument/theme/approach** before you start to write. This will help you identify the key points you want to make. For example, this question clearly invites you to make a decision or judgement about the degree to which Stalin's foreign policy was essentially conservative and defensive. Deciding on an approach helps you produce an argument which is clear, coherent and logical.
- Plan **the structure of your argument**: the introduction, the main body of the essay (in which you present precise evidence to support your arguments), and your concluding paragraph.

For this question, whatever overall view you have about the aims of Stalin's foreign policy after 1945, you should try to make a **balanced argument**, by presenting points and evaluating evidence both in support of *and* against the view that his foreign policy was essentially defensive. If the question were about the extent to which Stalin's foreign policies were successful, you would need to decide whether you think that, overall, they were or were not successful.

As a rough guide for this type of question, you would need to deal with both the 'yes' and 'no' arguments – for example on the basis of 60% for your view and 40% for opposing views or interpretations.

4 The Soviet Union and Post-Soviet Russia (1924–2000)

Whatever the question, try to **link** the points you make in your paragraphs, so that there is a clear thread which follows through to your conclusion. This will help to ensure that your essay is not just a series of unconnected paragraphs.

You may well find that drawing up a spider diagram or mind map helps you with your essay planning. For this question, your spider diagram might look this:

When writing your essay, include **linking words or phrases** to ensure that each paragraph dealing with one of the smaller 'bubbles' is linked to the 'main bubble' (the question). For example:

__Although__ Stalin's foreign policy after 1945 can be seen as expansionist – especially as regards to the countries of Eastern Europe, it is possible to argue that this had more to do with valid concerns about the weaknesses of the Soviet Union resulting from the very destructive impacts of the Great Patriotic War. As well as suffering over 25 million deaths, many of the economic gains achieved during the period before 1941 had been destroyed. As the Soviet Union had twice been invaded by Germany in the period between 1914 and 1941, it *can be argued that Stalin's desire for a buffer zone of friendly countries on the USSR's western borders was essentially defensive…*

In addition, *his foreign policy after 1945 was, to an extent, shaped by the rapidly deteriorating relations between the US and the USSR. As Stalin was acutely aware of just how much destruction the Soviet Union had suffered between 1941 and 1945, he appears to have been worried by the abrupt change in US attitudes which resulted when Truman replaced Roosevelt as president of the US. The refusal of the US to share its nuclear weapons technology, its opposition to massive war reparations from Germany, and the conditions it insisted on if economic aid was to be forthcoming from the US, all combined to make Stalin feel insecure…*

Furthermore, *as recently as October 1944, Churchill and Stalin had met in Moscow, where they had made the 'Percentages Agreement', which seemed to accept that the Soviet Union had legitimate security interests in Eastern Europe. Although Roosevelt had not been present, he had not objected when informed of the details of the Agreement…*

However, *many historians have presented opposing arguments about Stalin's foreign policy. Some see his actions in Eastern Europe after 1945 as merely a continuation of the pre-1917 imperial expansionism of tsarist Russia – with Stalin being depicted as a 'Red Tsar'. Others have argued that Stalin's foreign policy after 1945 was an attempt to spread communism – first to Eastern Europe, and then to Western Europe…*

There are clearly many aspects to consider, which will be difficult under the time constraints of the exam. Producing a plan with brief details such as dates, main events/features under each heading will help you cover the main issues in the time available. It will also give you something to use if you run out of time and can only jot down the main points of your last paragraph(s). The examiner will be able to give you some credit for this.

Common mistakes

Once the exam time has started, one common mistake is for candidates to begin writing *straight away*, without being sure whether they know enough about the questions they have selected. Once they have written several paragraphs, they may run out of things to say – and then panic because of the time they have wasted.

Producing plans for *each of the three questions* you intend to answer in Paper 3 at the *start* of the exam, *before* you start to write your first essay, will help you see if you know enough about the questions to tackle them successfully. If you don't, then you need to choose different ones!

Activity

In this chapter, the focus is on planning answers. So, using the information from this chapter, and any other sources of information available to you, produce essay plans – using spider diagrams or mind maps – with all the necessary headings (and brief details) for well-focused and clearly structured responses to **at least two** of the following Practice Paper 3 questions. Remember to refer to the simplified Paper 3 mark scheme in Chapter 10.

Paper 3 practice questions

1   'The USSR was able to survive the Great Patriotic War of 1941–45 mainly because of Stalin's reconstruction of the Soviet economy in the 1930s.' To what extent do you agree with this statement?

2   Evaluate the reasons why, after 1945, Stalin continued to maintain strict political control within the Soviet Union.

3   Discuss the extent to which the US nuclear monopoly was the main reason why the Soviet Union extended its control over Eastern Europe in the period 1945-47.

4   Compare and contrast Soviet policies and actions in any two Eastern European states in the period 1946-49.

5   Discuss the consequences of Soviet foreign policy in relation to Germany in the period 1945–49.

Khrushchev and De-Stalinisation, 1953–64

5

5

Introduction

Following Stalin's death in March 1953, there soon began a power struggle between the top leaders but, from 1955, Nikita Khrushchev began to emerge as the most prominent. A limited form of 'de-Stalinisation' took place which became more marked after 1956, when Khrushchev made a 'secret speech' criticising Stalin at the 20th Congress of the CPSU. However, Khrushchev was often erratic in his policies, some of which angered the political and administrative bureaucracy. These, and some foreign policy reverses, led to his removal from power in 1964 by his opponents.

TIMELINE

1953 Mar: Death of Stalin; start of collective leadership

Jun: Beria overthrown; protests in East Germany

Sept: Khrushchev becomes First Secretary

1954 Jan: Khrushchev launches 'Virgin Lands' scheme

1955 Feb: Malenkov demoted; Khrushchev now the main power

1956 Feb: Khrushchev's 'secret speech'

Jun: Anti-Soviet unrest in Poland; Gomulka allowed to carry out some reforms

Oct/Nov: Hungarian Revolt; Soviet military intervention

1957 Jun: Anti-Party Group defeated

Oct: *Sputnik 1*

1958 Mar: Bulganin forced to resign; Khrushchev becomes premier

Nov: Khrushchev's 'Notes' on Germany

1960 Jun: Split between USSR and China becomes public

1961 Apr: Yuri Gargarin first person in space

Jun: Khrushchev presents Berlin ultimatum

Aug: Berlin Wall completed

1962 Oct: Cuban Missile Crisis

1963 Jun: Valentina Tereshkova first woman in space; Moscow-Washington hotline established

Aug: Nuclear Test-Ban Treaty

1964 Oct: Khrushchev forced to resign

KEY QUESTIONS

- What were Khrushchev's main political reforms?
- How did Khrushchev try to reform the Soviet economy?
- What were the main features of Khrushchev's foreign policy?

Overview

- When Stalin died in 1953, most communist leaders wanted to end the terror associated with Stalin's rule, and to bring in a more liberalised regime.
- At first, a collective leadership took over – with Malenkov, Beria and Molotov as the most important ones. However, Beria was arrested and executed shortly afterwards and, in 1955, Malenkov began to lose power to Khrushchev. By 1958, Khrushchev was both First Secretary of the CPSU and premier.
- Khrushchev favoured economic reforms – including some de-centralisation – in order to improve industrial productivity. In agriculture, he launched his 'virgin lands' scheme. However, his reforms had mixed results.
- In 1956, in a 'secret speech' to the 20th Congress of the CPSU, he attacked Stalin for his crimes. This began a limited period of de-Stalinisation – sometimes referred to as the 'thaw'.
- Khrushchev's 'secret speech' encouraged many in Eastern Europe to think they would be able to reduce Soviet control and reform their political and economic systems – resulting in the Hungarian Revolt.
- Other foreign policy setbacks in the early 1960s included a public split with China and the Cuban Missile Crisis with the US. Khrushchev also had to deal with a crisis over Berlin, which ended in the building of the Berlin Wall. These blows to his foreign policy undermined Khrushchev's position.
- In 1964, growing opposition to his leadership, including his changes to party organisation, resulted in his removal from power.

Figure 5.1: Khrushchev and Stalin in discussion during the Second World War.

QUESTION

What does the photograph in Figure 5.1 suggest about (a) Khrushchev's importance before 1953, and (b) his relationship with Stalin?

5.1 What were Khrushchev's main political reforms?

During the 1941–45 war, Khrushchev had acted as a political commissar in the Red Army, organising military and civilian resistance to the German occupation of Ukraine. He had also fought in the battle of Stalingrad. The experience of war, with its massive human costs, made him genuinely concerned to improve people's lives, and to modernise the Soviet Union in a humane way.

Khrushchev's rise

When Stalin died in 1953, there was initially a period of collective leadership, during which there was a struggle for power. All the leading Communists were agreed that they wanted no return to the purges and terror which had marked Stalin's rule for the past 20 years. However, no one wanted to radically reform the 'system' under which the Soviet Union had survived and won the Great Patriotic War – and which had enabled them to rise to top positions. Instead, they wanted modifications – though this implied that the system could be modified without weakening its hold on the USSR and Eastern Europe.

In March 1953, the collective leadership was as follows: Malenkov (Premier), Beria (Minister of Internal Affairs), Molotov (Foreign Secretary), Bulganin (Deputy Premier) and Khrushchev (First Party Secretary). The three most powerful leaders were Beria, Malenkov and Molotov. Khrushchev had been a loyal supporter of Stalin since the 1930s and, in 1949, Stalin had made him Secretary to the General Committee and gave him special responsibility for agriculture. However Khrushchev's apparently open and talkative manner led others in the Politburo to underestimate his desire for power.

The first to lose in the developing power struggle was Lavrenti Beria. Beria, who was still head of the Ministry of Internal Affairs and its secret police, was intelligent and had plans to modernise the Soviet Union. These included separating party and state functions, to allow for more efficient government, with the party concentrating on ideology and propaganda. He also wanted to release about 1 million of the 2.5 million prisoners in the Gulag labour camps. However, the other political leaders feared him, while the army resented him for the purge of the military in 1937 and 1938.

Khrushchev led the plot against Beria and was able to persuade Zhukov, the commander-in-chief, to provide troops to arrest Beria in June 1953: he was given a summary secret trial, and was subsequently shot. In future, however, the worst fate for those who lost out in power struggles would be demotion or dismissal. This made a significant break from the attitudes of Stalin's rule, marking the beginning of what became known as the 'thaw'.

The Soviet Union and Post-Soviet Russia (1924–2000)

QUESTION

Why do you think Beria was removed so quickly by the other Soviet leaders?

The relative easing of tensions and controls associated with the 'thaw' had much to do with Malenkov. He was keen to raise living standards and increase the number of consumer goods, and was prepared to cut back on investment in heavy industry in order to do so – this was all part of what he called his 'New Course'. As early as October 1953, he announced ambitious new targets for consumer industries for 1954 and 1955, over and above those set out in the current Five-Year Plan.

At first, as part of the power struggle against Malenkov, Khrushchev allied himself with the heavy industry and defence sectors. In agriculture, Malenkov – like Khrushchev – favoured reducing taxes on peasants' private plots, and raising the price the state paid for grain.

Malenkov also wished, like Beria, to separate party and state, and to allow the state – where he was strongest – to have greater autonomy from the ruling party bodies. In foreign affairs, he favoured establishing better relations with the West.

Malenkov's progressive ideas were not popular among the other leaders, and Khrushchev, as head of the party, gradually undermined Malenkov's position as head of the government. Moreover, Khrushchev, like Stalin, began to place his supporters in positions of power.

By 1955, Khrushchev was already the most influential of the leaders. Then, following a poor grain harvest, Malenkov publicly admitted his responsibility and resigned in February 1955. His place as premier was taken by Bulganin. At first, Bulganin and Khrushchev ruled as equals, but it soon became clear that Khrushchev was the dominant figure.

De-Stalinisation

From 1955, Khrushchev consolidated his position and, although Malenkov's more liberal policies had been one of the reasons for his fall, Khrushchev was soon to show that he, too, favoured more liberal directions and methods. However, he intended to maintain the CPSU's dominant position.

By 1956, Khrushchev was secure enough in his powers to launch a strong political attack on Stalin and his rule. At the 20th Congress of the CPSU, on 24–25 February 1956, Khrushchev delivered a lengthy 'secret report', which pointed out Stalin's many errors during the 1930s. In it, Khrushchev referred to Lenin's Testament, and listed Stalin's abuses of power – in particular, the purges of the 1930s.

ACTIVITY

Research the full text of Khrushchev's 'secret speech' of 25 February 1956. How does its content support what you have found out in Chapter 3 about Stalin's political actions in the 1930s? As you go through this chapter, try to list the number of actions taken by Khrushchev which actually changed the things he attacked in his speech.

Khrushchev did not just attack Stalin for the purges – he also criticised him for his leadership during the war; and for various foreign policy failures, especially his relations with the Eastern European countries. Although some aspects of Stalin's regime remained almost intact, R. Service has nonetheless described the speech as 'a turning point in the USSR's politics'.

Theory of Knowledge

History, ethics and individual responsibility

In his 'secret speech', Khrushchev seemed to lay the blame for the Great Terror on Stalin alone. Yet he – and many of the Soviet leaders listening to his speech in 1956 – had occupied important positions in the 1930s, and many had been close to Stalin. Khrushchev, for one, had helped carry through the purges in Ukraine. Yet humans have developed moral reasoning, and ideas about what we should and should not do. Does fear of the consequences for him – and possibly for his family – if he had opposed Stalin absolve Khrushchev of individual and moral responsibility for these events? Is it morally legitimate for a person to claim, as a defence, that they were 'only carrying out orders'?

The Soviet Union and Post-Soviet Russia (1924–2000)

Khrushchev only allowed an edited version of his report to be sent out to local party committees for discussion. Yet, although not officially published in the USSR, the contents of his 'secret speech' soon circulated – and even became known in the West and in Eastern Europe (see 5.3, Eastern Europe).

Figure 5.2: Khrushchev delivering his 'secret speech' at the 20th Congress of the CPSU, February 1956.

Khrushchev clearly wished to humanise the Soviet system, and wanted the party to be accepted as the legitimate authority without having to depend on terror and repression. However he did not want to introduce far-reaching liberalisation or democratisation of the system. His 'de-Stalinisation' was intended very much as a 'top-down' process, under the control of the party.

Culture and the arts

Censorship was eased, and there was a move away from the strict conformity established by Zhdanov. For instance, Soviet citizens had access to a wider range of foreign literature and films – though only those considered 'safe' by the Soviet authorities. In addition, artists and writers who had suffered or been banned under Stalin were rehabilitated. An early sign of the changes to come appeared in 1954, when Ilya Ehrenburg's novel *The Thaw* was published. The classical composer Shostakovich was allowed to perform and publish his works; while Khrushchev personally intervened in 1962 to ensure that Solzhenitsyn's novel *One Day in the Life of Ivan Denisovich* (an account of conditions in Stalin's Gulag camps) was published. Another writer who had suffered bans under Stalin was the poet Anna Akhmatova. Nearly all her work was published after Stalin's death and the start of the 'thaw', and she was readmitted to the Writers' Union.

ACTIVITY

See what else you can find out about conditions in the Gulag labour camps. You could watch the 1970 film made of Solzhenitsyn's novel *One Day in the Life of Ivan Denisovich* – clips can be found on YouTube. Why do you think Khrushchev allowed the book to be published in the Soviet Union?

There were limits to this 'thaw' in cultural matters – for example, Boris Pasternak's novel, *Doctor Zhivago*, which dealt with the early days of the Revolution, was banned. Other writers, classified by the authorities as 'dissidents' because of their outspoken criticisms of the regime, were harassed by the secret police, and sometimes imprisoned.

In practice, most Soviet citizens did not give much support to dissident artists, writers and intellectuals. Khrushchev's aims of modifying the worst aspects of Stalinism, and improving living standards meant that most Russians tended to see dissidents as unpatriotic rather than defenders of freedom, and as undermining a regime which was giving them significantly improved benefits.

Legal reforms

One important change after 1956 was the end of arbitrary terror – citizens who conformed could feel reasonably safe. Large numbers of political prisoners were also released from the Gulag labour camps. Although serious opposition or dissent was still suppressed by the regime, a new criminal code in December 1958 stated that citizens could no longer be tried by emergency or military courts; while certain 'crimes' (such as being an 'enemy of the people') were abolished. Also, confessions alone were no longer enough to secure a conviction, and the death penalty was given only for the crime of treason.

The Soviet Union and Post-Soviet Russia (1924–2000)

Political reforms

Khrushchev's attacks on Stalin and Stalinism were made partly to prepare the way for a series of economic reforms which he wanted to introduce. Although he fully intended that the party should continue to be the main force in the Soviet system, to carry through the economic reforms he felt that some changes to party structure and administration were needed.

Although no one was dropped from the Politburo immediately after the 'secret speech', Khrushchev did ensure that some of his supporters were added to it – one of those was **Leonid Brezhnev**.

Leonid Brezhnev (1906–1982):

During the late 1920s, he was involved in the collectivisation of agriculture and, in 1931, became a full party member. He was promoted by Khrushchev and was a political commissar during the Second World War – and maintained close links with the military. In 1952, he was appointed to the Politburo, but lost his new positions after Stalin's death. Though reinstated by Khrushchev in 1956, he was a 'man of the centre'; he began to distance himself from Khrushchev and eventually helped overthrow him.

In October 1961, Khrushchev launched a new Party Programme, claiming that by 1970, the USSR would have laid the basis for true communism and would have surpassed the productivity, scientific and technological levels, and the living standards, of the USA. He asserted that by 1980, the foundations for achieving communism would be complete.

SOURCE 5.1

Khrushchev was a reformer, not a state-builder; an impatient, impetuous leader with a propensity for large-scale – and sometimes risky – panaceas. On occasion, he could be truly bold. The 'secret speech' against Stalin at the Twentieth Congress was his own initiative; he stuck with it and imposed it on recalcitrant colleagues without regard for the rules or niceties. And thus the Congress suddenly learnt that [Stalin]... was a bloody mass murderer. For the anti-Stalinists, it was a shocking revelation. As for the Stalinists of various hues, they were more than embarrassed and claimed that the picture was exaggerated, when in fact it was very incomplete. For inveterate Stalinists, the most embarrassing thing was to see so many high-ranking leaders evince their astonishment: how could they pretend that they knew nothing about the scale of the atrocities? In fact, only a few insiders were aware of the true scale of things... The shock therapy applied by Khrushchev cost him dearly politically... the denunciation of Stalin was not restricted to words, but was preceded and succeeded by deeds: a large-scale process of 'rehabilitation' and a dismantling of the MVD's industrial complex...

Some of his ideas were very dangerous for the apparatchiks... Some say that the Brezhnevites ousted him on account of this. For others, the 'conservatives' never forgave him for 'de-Stalinisation'...

Lewin, M., 2005, The Soviet Century, *London, Verso, pp. 239–43.*

5.2 How did Khrushchev try to reform the Soviet economy?

Khrushchev began a process which soon became known as 'reform communism' – an attempt to reform certain aspects of the system, while still maintaining the essential features of it, such as one-party rule, and a state-owned, planned economy.

Agriculture

Shortly after Stalin's death, Soviet leaders began to acknowledge that collectivisation of agriculture had not really solved the problems of inefficiency and insufficient food production. To deal with these, Khrushchev made it clear that major reforms were needed.

His main approach was to encourage local initiatives and decision-making; he also got the state to pay higher prices for grain and to reduce some quotas, while taxes on farming profits from private plots were reduced. Khrushchev merged many of the collectives into larger state farms, over which the government had greater control. At the same time, experts were sent from Moscow to advise on more modern methods, while the Machine-Tractor Stations were disbanded in February 1958, and instead became repair shops, with the tractors being sold to the state farms and to peasant farmers.

The net effect of these reforms and new incentives was to increase production modestly, while living standards of those working in the countryside, both on state farms and on the collectives, more than doubled between 1952 and 1958.

Khrushchev also launched the ambitious 'Virgin Lands' policy in January 1954. The idea was to farm land previously not used for agriculture. A large state investment – including 120 000 motorised tractors – was provided, along with incentives. In the first year, more than 6 million acres were ploughed. However, despite Khrushchev's efforts, there had been inaccurate appreciation of local conditions, and there was often insufficient fertiliser to rejuvenate the quickly exhausted soil.

Although there was an increase in overall grain production, this was more to do with the usual grain-producing areas rather than the result of success in the virgin lands. A record harvest was announced in 1962, but the reality was that many areas had failed to meet their production targets. To make matters worse, the harvest of 1963 was disastrous – grain production dropped by nearly 30%, creating a serious shortage in animal fodder. Large quantities of North American and Australian grain had to be bought – this clear dependency on the West was a security worry, and angered many of Khrushchev's opponents.

QUESTION
Why were Khrushchev's agricultural reforms largely unsuccessful?
Is it fair to lay the main blame on the way in which he tried to
implement these reforms?

Industry

In the main, Khrushchev's industrial policies were an extension of those originally put forward by Malenkov. However, Khrushchev pursued these policies with much more enthusiasm and energy. In particular, he wanted to reduce investments in heavy industry, and instead bring about diversification by concentrating on light engineering and chemicals. He also wanted to reorganise the structure and management of industry, in order to encourage initiatives which would lead to greater efficiency and production.

Although he needed great efforts from workers to achieve his plans, unlike Stalin he did not rely on coercion. Instead, Khrushchev's approach was based on incentives. Although central planning continued, Khrushchev wanted to reduce central bureaucracy from the levels it had reached under Stalin. He tried to streamline the administrative system, and push aspects of economic planning from the centre to local areas.

His first measures included, in May 1956, establishing 105 regional ministries based on the existing administrative structures. During February and March 1957, he abolished most of the all-union economic ministries in Moscow, and carried out reform of Gosplan. Such reforms clearly upset central bureaucrats, and began to create growing opposition to him within the party.

When Stalin had died in 1953, the Fifth Five-Year Plan was about halfway through. Following Malenkov's policies, Khrushchev tried to steer the plan into consumer goods, but met opposition from the planning administrators. In 1955, a Sixth Five-Year Plan was drawn up and introduced in January 1956, but this was soon seen to have set unrealistic targets. In 1957, it was revised; then, in January 1959, it was scrapped, and replaced by a Seven-Year Plan. Khrushchev pushed for this to concentrate on consumer production, light industry, chemicals and plastics, and on newly discovered mineral resources.

Khrushchev also tried to focus on regional development, in an attempt to create a more balanced Soviet economy. Thus 40% of investment was directed to the relatively neglected eastern regions of the Soviet Union. However, despite some successes, not all the plan's targets were met; and old problems remained. In October 1961, the Seven-Year Plan was replaced by the Seventh Five-Year Plan.

SOURCE 5.2

Khrushchev at last felt well placed to rectify the inadequacies in consumer-goods production in Soviet factories. Malenkov's priority became his own. This adjustment of policy, however, unsettled the institutional support that had facilitated his rise to power since Stalin's death: the traditional lobbies in the army and the heavy-industrial civilian administrations were appalled by what they saw as his treachery. Conflict was avoided mainly because Khrushchev did not push his wishes too hard. In any case he adhered to his original contention that agricultural improvements remained more urgent than changes in industrial investment policy... Thus his basic economic preferences were much more conventional than appeared from his declarations about the need to satisfy all the aspirations of Soviet consumers... [However] Shortages of meat, butter and milk... [led] the Presidium... on 31 May 1962, to increase the prices charged to the urban consumers. It was officially pointed out that these prices had been held at the same level since the First Five-Year Plan, but the economic explanation did not interest most people... Popular opinion was outraged... There had been urban disturbances before, notably in Karaganda in 1958... In 1962, popular disturbances broke out in Riga, Kiev, and Chelyabinsk... on 1 June 1962 an uprising took place in Novocherkassk.

Service, R., 1997, A History of Twentieth-Century Russia, *London, Allen Lane/The Penguin Press, pp. 347 and 364.*

The space programme

In January 1960 Khrushchev announced that the Soviet armed forces were to be reduced by half. He hoped the money saved could be diverted into light industry, newer chemical and electrical production, and also the space programme, in order to catch up with the West. In fact, the USSR was ahead of the USA in the space race: in October 1957, *Sputnik 1*, the world's first artificial satellite, was successfully launched, followed by *Sputnik 2* in November. In September 1959, the USSR landed a rocket on the Moon and, in April 1961, the USSR scored another first when Yuri Gargarin became the first person to travel in space. In June 1963, Valentina Tereshkova became the first woman to do so.

Figure 5.3: Valentina Tereshkova, the first woman in space, 1963.

Other space firsts came in 1964 and 1965. However, this level of spending and use of sophisticated engineering was not matched in other areas of the Soviet economy.

Success and failure

Production and efficiency

In industry, the results of Khrushchev's Seven-Year Plan in 1965 (one year after his overthrow) show, according to official statistics, that by 1965, gross national income had grown by 58%, industrial output by 84% and consumer goods by 60%. There was also a significant increase in foreign trade.

The Soviet Union and Post-Soviet Russia (1924–2000)

SOURCE 5.3

	1958	1965 (plan)	1965 (actual)
National income	100	162–165	158
Gross industrial output (index)	100	180	184
Producers' goods	100	185–188	196
Consumers' goods	100	162–165	160
Iron ore (million tons)	88.8	150–160	153–4
Pig iron (million tons)	39.6	65–70	66.2
Steel (million tons)	54.9	86–91	91.0
Coal (million tons)	493	600–612	578
Oil (million tons)	113	230–240	242.9
Gas (billion cubic metres)	29.9	150	129.3
Electricity (billion Kwhs)	235	500–520	507
Mineral fertiliser (million tons)	12	35	31.5
Synthetic fibres (thousand tons)	166	666	407
Machine tools (thousands)	138	190–200	185
Tractors (thousands)	220	–	355
Commercial timber (million cubic metres)	251	275–280	273
Cement (million tons)	33.3	75–81	72.4
Cotton fabrics (million cubic metres)	5.76	7.7–8.0	7.08
Wool fabrics (million cubic metres)	303	485	365
Leather footwear (million pairs)	356.4	515	486
Grain harvest (million tons)	134.7	164–180	121.1
Meat (total) (million tons)	3.37	6.13	5.25
Workers and employees (millions)	56.0	66.5	76.9
Housing (million square metres)	71.2	650–660*	79.2

* Total for seven years, 1959–65

Nar. Khoz., 1960, pp. 210–12; Nar. Khoz., 1965, pp. 136–9, 262, 557, 609; seven year plan, 1959–65.

Table 5.1: *Results of Khrushchev's Seven-Year Plan.*

> QUESTION
>
> What can you learn from Table 5.1 about (a) the overall success
> of Khrushchev's reforms, and (b) the biggest problems still facing
> Soviet leaders by the time Khrushchev was overthrown in 1964?
> What are the values and limitations of such sources for historians
> trying to study the Soviet economy during this period?

So, despite the inefficiencies and administrative irrationalities, and the
bureaucratic obstruction which continued to be a problem for any
seriously reformist leader, Khrushchev had managed to achieve some
impressive industrial growth. Certainly, until Gorbachev came to power
in 1985, no other leader had tried harder to reform things.

However, Khrushchev's boast that the Soviet Union would overtake the
West economically and so show the superiority of Soviet 'socialism' was
not met. Despite some successes, Khrushchev often acted to impose new
priorities which then created shortages elsewhere. This increasing lack
of a coordinated and coherent investment programme resulted, in 1963
and 1964, in the lowest economic growth rates in peacetime since 1933.
In addition, many of the problems which had emerged under Stalin
continued – historians such as J. Keep and P. Kenez have pointed out
that, despite some sound attempts to improve agriculture, the underlying
problems remained.

Consumers and living standards

Khrushchev had promised that a more productive and efficient Soviet
economy would also meet the needs of consumers for more and
better products. Reforms improving people's quality of life included
the introduction, in September 1956, of minimum wages for urban
and rural areas, in an attempt to reduce wage differentials between
jobs and professions. Working conditions were also improved, with the
introduction of a shorter working day, more holidays, longer maternity
leave, better pensions and other social benefits. Also in 1956, education
provision was improved in the poorer republics, and it was decided to
extend secondary education for all. Scientific and technical education
was prioritised, and this paid dividends in the series of space 'firsts' (see
above). Medical care was improved, with a significant decline in infant
mortality between 1950 and 1965.

However, Soviet living standards still remained low compared with those in the West, although it is important to consider the subsidised food, energy and transport prices. According to M. McCauley, real personal disposable income increased by just over 4% a year under Khrushchev. Although the number of consumer goods also increased, the quality of many items was still poor, and shortages in some areas continued. By the time Khrushchev was overthrown in 1964, only 5 in 1000 citizens owned a car, only 82 in 1000 owned a television, and only 40 in 1000 owned a refrigerator.

Khrushchev never lost sight of the need to significantly improve living standards. His relative failure in this respect – and his failure to seriously improve the efficiency and productivity of Soviet industry – ended by increasing the amount of opposition to his rule.

5.3 What were the main features of Khrushchev's foreign policy?

Eastern Europe

Many people in Eastern Europe – and some in the West – took Khrushchev's attacks on Stalin as indicating that the Soviet Union would be going to go far down the road to freedom and tolerance. For instance, after his 'secret speech' Khrushchev had issued a declaration promising more equal relationships between the USSR and the satellites.

However, Khrushchev was very mindful of the needs of Soviet security in the Cold War, and had no intention of losing control of the security belt of satellite states in Eastern Europe which Stalin had established after the war. If the governments which ruled these states were seriously challenged from below, then the Soviet Union would move to shore them up – with military force if necessary. This had happened in June 1953, just after Stalin's death, when Soviet insistence on taking massive post-war reparations from their zone of East Germany had led to protests and riots.

ACTIVITY
Try to find out more about the protests in East Germany after
Stalin's death. Do you think they were mainly anti-communist or
anti-Soviet?

Still, the first signs of de-Stalinisation in Eastern Europe did seem to
reflect a change in direction. Firstly, as early as 1953, the USSR began
to slacken the pace of 'Sovietisation' in Eastern Europe – especially
as regards collectivisation of agriculture. Secondly, Khrushchev
moved to heal the disagreement with Yugoslavia and, in May 1955,
visited President Tito in Belgrade. Although Yugoslavia remained an
independent Communist country, it seemed the USSR now accepted
that countries could develop their own style of Communism – this was
a clear move away from the monolithic model imposed by Stalin.

Some Eastern European leaders saw Khrushchev's approach to
Yugoslavia as indicating that they could attempt to renegotiate their
relations with the Soviet Union, and gain greater national independence
for their own countries. At first, Khrushchev seemed willing to accept
this. As a result, there were significant stirrings in some countries to
reduce Soviet control. In Poland, for example, there were protests by
industrial workers in June 1956. Although these were put down with
the help of Soviet forces, some reforms were allowed.

The Hungarian Revolt, 1956

These developments encouraged Communist reformers in Hungary. At
first, Khrushchev followed the policy he had adopted in Poland: **Imre
Nagy**, a Communist who had been ousted two years before by the
hardliner Matyas Rakosi, was allowed to become the new leader of the
government.

The Soviet Union and Post-Soviet Russia (1924–2000)

Imre Nagy (1896–1958):

He fought with the Bolsheviks during the Russian Revolution, and was part of Bela Kun's short-lived Soviet Republic of Hungary which collapsed in November 1919. In July 1953, with support from Soviet premier Malenkov, he became Prime Minister but, shortly after Malenkov was ousted in 1955, he was forced to resign. In October 1956, following the 20th Party Congress in Moscow, demonstrators called for his return to power, and Nagy was allowed to form a coalition government that included three non-communists.

However, the situation in Hungary proved to be quite different from that in Poland, where workers had demanded radical and left-wing reforms. In Hungary, the protests soon went beyond demands for de-Stalinisation to a campaign for the ending of communism – increasingly backed by conservative peasants and the churches. When Nagy's government began to tolerate anti-Soviet demonstrations, Khrushchev and the Soviet government began to conclude that the 'thaw' in Hungary had gone too far.

At this stage, Khrushchev seemed to think it would be possible to find a solution similar to the one reached in Poland. However, Soviet fears were revived when the West decided to make Hungarian independence an issue at the UN while, at the same time, Nagy began to tolerate non-Communist political groups. Also worrying was the increasing emergence of right-wing nationalist groups. Then, on 1 November, Nagy announced his wish to leave the Warsaw Pact – which had only been formed in May 1955 – and for Hungary to become neutral.

ACTIVITY

Carry out some additional research on developments in Hungary and the Soviet response. How do you think comments made by Western politicians contributed to the unfolding of events? You could start by watching the documentary videos on YouTube called 'Hungarian Uprising 1' and 'Hungarian Uprising 2'.

SOURCE 5.4

We should re-examine our assessment and should not withdraw our troops from Hungary and Budapest. We should take the initiative in restoring order in Hungary. If we depart from Hungary, it will give a great boost to the Americans, English and French – the imperialists. They will perceive it as a weakness on our part and will go on the offensive. We would then be exposing the weakness of our positions. Our party will not accept it if we do this. To Egypt they [the imperialists] will then add Hungary. We have no other choice...

An extract from Khrushchev's address to the Central Committee on 5 November, about what the USSR should do in relation to the growing unrest in Hungary, taking account of Britain and France's attack on Egypt in what became known as the Suez Crisis.

In Williamson, D., 2008, **Europe and the Cold War 1945–91**, *London, Hodder Education, p. 112.*

After several threats had no impact on Nagy, Khrushchev ordered in the Red Army. Nagy's government was overthrown. He was arrested, flown back to Moscow and, along with several others, tried in secret. They were found guilty of treason and were executed in June 1958.

The suppression of the Hungarian Revolt showed that, if Soviet security was threatened, Khrushchev would not hesitate to take strong action to maintain the Eastern European security belt. Nonetheless, Janos Kadar, who became the head of a new pro-Soviet government, was allowed to implement several of the reforms favoured by Nagy; this indicates that Khrushchev's main concerns were security ones. Once the crisis in Hungary was over, Soviet armed forces were withdrawn from several Eastern European states.

In the short term, though, the problems which arose in 1956 meant that pressures within the Soviet leadership to halt de-Stalinisation grew. Khrushchev's actions were seen as having weakened Soviet security and undermined the position of the governments in Eastern Europe. There was also the growing fear that if reforms were allowed in these states, there would be increasing demands for similar reforms within the USSR itself.

Figure 5.4: Soviet tanks suppress the Hungarian Revolt, in Budapest, November 1956.

Relations with the West – peaceful co-existence

Khrushchev followed a policy known as 'peaceful co-existence', first stated in his 'secret speech' of 1956. This was based on the argument that it was possible for different social systems to live in peace with each other. He stated that violent conflict between the Soviet Union and the West was not inevitable – thus allowing the Soviet Union to divert money towards the civilian economy. This was important, as the Soviet economy, being so much weaker than the USA's, found the burden of defence spending had a much more negative impact.

In 1955, Khruschchev and Bulganin went on a tour of various Western countries, and also visited Yugoslavia and China – something that would have been unthinkable under Stalin. Meetings with President Eisenhower in September 1959, at Camp David, led to improved East-West relations, and to what was known as the 'spirit of Camp David'. However, in May 1960, this positive spirit ended during the Paris Summit because of the controversy surrounding a US U-2 reconnaissance spy plane, which had been shot down over the Soviet Union. Eisenhower (who had previously denied that the US were using spy planes over the USSR) refused to apologise for sending the plane, and the summit broke up. Eisenhower's replacement by Kennedy in 1961 only partially repaired relations.

ACTIVITY

How different was Khrushchev's foreign policy from that followed by Stalin in the period 1930–45? Write a couple of paragraphs which compare and contrast the foreign policies of these two Soviet leaders.

The German problem

One important reason why relations did not improve was the question of Germany which, despite the Yalta agreement that the occupying powers should eventually leave, had become divided into two separate states by 1949 (see Chapter 4).

Russia's aims regarding Germany have been the subject of some historical debate. It appears that even under Stalin (at least for a time) the USSR wanted a united, independent – but neutral – Germany. For instance, this seems to be what was offered in March 1952, in the 'Stalin Notes' which were presented to the West. Although these proposals were rejected by the West, Stalin continued to make such offers until his death – even though the East German communists were unhappy at the prospect of losing their newly formed state. This has been how revisionist historians such as W. Loth and R. Steininger have interpreted

Stalin's policy – they argue that it was only the riots in East Germany in June 1953 which prevented a deal. However, post-revisionists such as John Gaddis have seen Stalin's stance as merely temporary propaganda ploys, which he calculated would please France, and which he knew would be rejected by the West; instead, they argue that, at bottom, he was determined to keep control of a 'socialist' East Germany.

Khrushchev's early policies in this area were designed to force the West – which recognised the legitimacy of the new West German state – into also recognising East Germany. In 1955, a USSR-GDR treaty was drawn up, giving East Germany full powers to conduct its own foreign policy. In November 1958, Khrushchev's 'Notes' accused the West of using West Berlin 'as a springboard for espionage and anti-Soviet acts', and said the West had six months to recognise East Germany – if it did not, then the USSR would conclude a separate peace treaty with the GDR. When the West refused to comply with his ultimatum, Khrushchev withdrew it and, at a summit meeting in March 1959, accepted the rights of the West in West Berlin. Further summits, with Eisenhower and then Kennedy, saw Khrushchev modify his demands – but he remained insistent that the 'German problem' needed to be resolved.

KEY CONCEPTS ACTIVITY

Causation: Carry out some further research about the main reasons which led to the various developments in Berlin during the period 1945–59. How valid were Khrushchev's accusations about Western use of Berlin for espionage and sabotage against Soviet interests? To what extent did the USSR use Berlin for the same purposes?

The Berlin Crisis

Much of this 'German problem' concerned the issue of Berlin. As a result of Marshall Aid, West Berlin – like West Germany – had prospered economically. This made a stark contrast with East Germany which, in the early years of the Cold War, suffered from a lack of resources and investment – partly because the USSR was taking reparations for the war damage suffered during 1941–45. As a result, between 1949 and 1957, over 2 million people had fled into West Germany via West Berlin. As many of these were skilled and professional people, this had a serious impact on plans to improve the economy of East Germany.

At a meeting with Kennedy in June 1961, Khrushchev renewed the earlier ultimatum – that the West had six months to settle the question of Germany, or they would be required to leave West Berlin. One result of this was that the number of refugees fleeing to West Berlin increased dramatically, to about 1000 a day. This presented real problems for the East German economy so its leader, Walter Ulbricht, ordered the construction of the Berlin Wall; in July, Khrushchev gave his approval. In August, construction began on a barbed wire fence; later that month it became a concrete wall.

Although some feared that the building of the wall might lead to conflict between the US and the Soviet Union, in some ways it actually formalised things. It also saved the East German economy from collapse – which meant that the East German government was unlikely to take any desperate measures which the USSR would have to support. However, Khrushchev's failure to solve the 'German problem' by ultimatums was a setback for him, and was to provide ammunition for his opponents back in the USSR.

SOURCE 5.5

In November 1958 Khrushchev demanded that the USSR and the western powers negotiate and conclude a peace treaty with Germany (there... was no final peace settlement). Khrushchev also demanded that the treaty include an agreement to transform West Berlin into an international, demilitarised city... Khrushchev's immediate purpose was to bolster the East German communist regime... by involving the GDR in control of the city as a whole – a city which, after all, was located deep inside East German territory. Khrushchev may also have entertained broader objectives: forcing the west to negotiate over the future of Germany; disrupting NATO's planned nuclearisation of West Germany; generally strengthening the Soviet position in central and eastern Europe following the events of 1956... [However] more recent research... has shown that an important player in the crisis was Walter Ulbricht, the East German communist leader. Ulbricht pressurised Khrushchev into taking action over West Berlin... Ulbricht, it seems, played a particularly important role in the decisions leading to the building of the Berlin Wall.

Roberts, G., 1999, **The Soviet Union in World Politics: Coexistence, Revolution and Cold War 1945–1991**, *London, Routledge, pp. 49–50.*

The Soviet Union and Post-Soviet Russia (1924–2000)

QUESTION

What were the different reasons for the building of the Berlin Wall? Which reason do you think was the most important one?

The Cuban Missile Crisis, 1962

In 1959, the right-wing dictator of Cuba – an ally of the US – had been overthrown by a revolution led by Fidel Castro. As Castro tried to end US domination of Cuba's economy, and the US tried to undermine his government, Khrushchev moved quickly to give Cuba economic and political support – for instance, by buying Cuban sugar on which the US had placed an embargo.

After a failed US-backed attempt to invade Cuba in April 1961, Castro openly spoke of the 'socialist' nature of his revolution, and appealed to the USSR for protection. This offered Khrushchev a chance to balance the threat posed by US missiles based in Turkey and Italy, by placing Soviet nuclear missiles in Cuba.

However, when the US discovered the sites in October 1962, it led to the 13-day Cuban Missile Crisis in which it seemed to the world that a nuclear war was imminent. Kennedy, the US president, placed a blockade (illegal under international law) on Cuba, threatening to stop and search any ships bound for the island. The US also placed its nuclear forces on war alert.

After an exchange of letters, it was agreed that the Soviet Union would remove its missiles from Cuba, in return for a US promise not to invade Cuba. In a secret deal, Kennedy agreed to withdraw US missiles from Turkey (in fact these had already been made redundant by the deployment of nuclear missiles placed on submarines, which were much more difficult to detect than land-based missile sites). However, as this part was kept secret – the US government did not admit to Americans that it had had missiles in Turkey until 1969 – it seemed as though Khrushchev had backed down and gained very little.

Dispute with China

The Soviet Union had eventually welcomed the Communist victory in China October 1949, as it gave it an ally in the rather one-sided Cold War which had just broken out. However, apart from the fact that China

152

was hardly a powerful ally in 1949, there had been considerable tension between Stalin and China's leader, Mao Zedong. Initially, Stalin had been against the Communists taking power in China, as he had wanted to avoid upsetting the US in its 'sphere of influence'. In addition, the Soviet leaders were dismissive of the chances of socialism in such an overwhelmingly underdeveloped and agricultural country. However, while Stalin was alive, these tensions remained concealed and, in 1950, the two countries had signed a Treaty of Friendship, Alliance and Mutual Assistance.

After 1953, Mao became more openly critical of the USSR, stating that Khrushchev's policy of peaceful co-existence was a 'revisionist' betrayal of international revolutionary Marxism. These tensions sparked off a struggle for the political leadership of world communism. China openly attacked Soviet foreign policy in June 1960. The following month Khrushchev ordered the withdrawal of all Soviet technicians and economic assistance from China. As a result, the international Communist movement became split into pro-Moscow and pro-Beijing parties.

Figure 5.5: Tensions were hidden in October 1959, when a Soviet delegation attended the tenth anniversary of the People's Republic of China; Khrushchev (left) and Chinese communist leaders Mao Zedong (front, centre) and Liu Shaoqi (right) are shown surveying the Chinese troops.

5

Khrushchev's fall, 1964

Khrushchev's foreign policy failures in Germany and Cuba and the
breach with communist China, along with the effects of de-Stalinisation
in Eastern Europe, increased the opposition to his policies that he
had faced since 1957. These factors combined with the impact of his
various political and economic reforms in the USSR to bring about his
downfall in 1964.

Since 1957, Khrushchev's opponents in the Politburo – led by
Malenkov, Molotov and Kaganovitch – had argued that de-Stalinisation
had gone too far, and that Khrushchev was to blame for the anti-Soviet
protests and revolts in Eastern Europe. In June 1957, they voted 7:4 to
dismiss him as Party Secretary. However, Khrushchev insisted that the
full Central Committee would have to agree before he would resign. He
then worked with Zhukov and the army to ensure that his supporters
were flown in for the meeting, enabling him to survive this first attempt
to unseat him. He then accused his opponents of forming an 'Anti-Party
Group', and they all resigned their government posts.

In 1958, Khrushchev accused Bulganin of being involved. In March,
Bulganin confessed to his connections: he resigned as premier, and was
removed from the Central Committee. Shortly afterwards, Khrushchev
combined his role as Party Secretary with that of premier – once again,
one man was holding both posts. However, unlike Stalin, Khrushchev
remained answerable to both the Politburo and the Central Committee.

Many of the older party members – at both national and regional levels
– had been worried by, and even opposed to, Khrushchev's attacks on
Stalin. His attempts to modernise administration, and to reduce perks
and privileges, had led to growing opposition from the bureaucratic
elites, while party leaders worried that the greater freedom given
to some writers and artists to criticise aspects of Soviet history and
society was dangerous. When his policies of decentralisation and greater
efficiency led to many party officials losing their posts, opposition to
Khrushchev began to organise once more.

Essentially Khrushchev was attempting to undo some aspects of 30 years
of Stalinist practice – but came up against the power of entrenched
interest-groups who benefited from the system, and tried to protect
their positions, powers and privileges. Gorbachev was to face the same
problems in the 1980s.

By 1964, Khrushchev's failures had begun to outweigh his successes, and he had lost the support of the military – partly because he had diverted money away from it to consumer and light industries, and partly because of his foreign policy failures.

In October 1964, while Khrushchev was on holiday at the Black Sea, the Politburo finally decided he had to go. A special meeting of the Central Committee was held, and Khrushchev was informed that he had 'retired' because of ill-health and age, and that his positions had been filled by Leonid Brezhnev and Alexei Kosygin. Realising he had no allies, Khrushchev went into obscure retirement.

ACTIVITY

The reasons for Khrushchev's downfall form a popular examination question. So, make a chart of all the factors that you think may have contributed to Khrushchev's overthrow in 1964. Against each one, give brief details (such dates, Khrushchev's aims, what happened). Then try to rank them in order of importance – placing a number against each one.

Khrushchev left the Soviet Union with almost as many problems as he had inherited and tried to solve. In particular, the crucial question which had faced the Soviet Union in 1924 – how to guarantee its security when surrounded by more powerful potential enemies – remained. In addition, 40 years on from 1924, the USSR still suffered from a relatively underdeveloped economy – with agriculture remaining a particular problem.

Paper 3 exam practice

Question

Discuss the main effects of Khrushchev's economic policies in the period 1955–64? **[15 marks]**

Skill

Writing an introductory paragraph

Examiner's tips

Once you have planned your answer to a question (as covered by Chapters 3 and 4), you should be able to begin writing a clear introductory paragraph. This needs to set out your main line of argument and to **outline briefly** the key points you intend to make (and support with relevant and precise own knowledge) in the main body of your essay. Remember: '*Discuss…*', '*Evaluate….*' or '*Examine…*' questions (just like '*To what extent…?*' questions) clearly require **analysis** of opposing arguments, interpretations or explanations – not simply description. If, after making your plan, you think you will be able to make a clear overall or final judgement, you might find it a good idea to flag up in your introductory paragraph what overall line of argument or judgement you intend to make.

Depending on the wording of the question, you may also find it useful to define in your introductory paragraph what you understand any 'key terms' to mean – such as 'reform communism', 'virgin lands scheme', 'collectives', 'Seven-Year Plan'. For example, 'reform communism' could cover various political and legal changes, as well as how economic policies were implemented.

For this question, you should:

1   establish Khrushchev's economic policy aims

2   consider his various policies and their successes and failures

3   write a concluding paragraph which sets out your judgement about their overall effects.

You will need to:

- cover the various aspects and details of Khrushchev's agricultural and industrial policies during the relevant period (that is, the whole period of Khrushchev's rule)
- outline the actual results of those various policies
- provide a judgement about whether these reforms were, overall, successful or unsuccessful, or whether the picture was more mixed.

Setting out this approach in your introductory paragraph will help you keep the demands of the question in mind. Remember to refer back to your introduction after every couple of paragraphs in your main answer.

Common mistakes

A common mistake – one that might suggest to an examiner a candidate who hasn't thought deeply about what's required – is to fail to write an introductory paragraph at all. This is often done by candidates who rush into writing *before* analysing the question and doing a plan. The result may well be that they focus entirely on the words 'economic policies' and on the dates, an approach that may simply result in a narrative of Khrushchev's economic policy. Even if the answer is full of detailed and accurate own knowledge, this will *not* answer the question, and so will not score highly.

Sample student introductory paragraph

After Stalin's death in 1953, Khrushchev began to consider how best to improve the Soviet economy. In particular, he – and other Soviet leaders – recognised that Stalin's collectivisation of agriculture had not really solved underlying problems of inefficiency and under-production. One of his main agricultural policy aims was to increase grain production – the 'Virgin Lands' scheme was an important part of this. He also wanted to extend and modernise the Soviet Union's industrial sector. However, unlike Stalin, he did not want to do this by coercion and setting unrealistic production targets. Instead, he tried to modernise the Soviet economy via methods which have been called 'reform communism'. As well as liberalising some aspects of the political and legal systems (especially as part of the 'de-Stalinisation' process which followed on from his 'secret speech' against Stalin's rule), he also wanted to increase production of consumer goods, and to raise living standards. This was particularly shown by his Seven-Year Plan which was introduced in early 1959. One of the objects of his industrial policy was also to show the superiority of Soviet 'socialism' in relation to Western capitalism. However, as with agriculture, the results of his industrial powers were mixed. One reason for this was that some of his reforms were opposed by some leading members of the Soviet government, and by Communist Party officials in the regions. Despite some successes, it is probably fair to conclude – as have several historians – that, overall, the positive effects of his economic policies were mainly short-term, and that by the time he was deposed in 1964, they were largely unsuccessful.

EXAMINER'S COMMENT

This is a good, if rather long, introduction, as it shows a good grasp of the topic, and sets out a clear and logical plan, clearly focused on the demands of the question. It shows a sound appreciation of the fact that to discuss and assess the effects of Khrushchev's economic policies, it is necessary to identify aims, and it explicitly demonstrates to the examiner what aspects the candidate intends to address. This indicates that the answer – if it remains analytical, and is well-supported – is likely to be a high-scoring one.

Activity

In this chapter, the focus is on writing a useful introductory paragraph. So, using the information from this chapter, and any other sources of information available to you, write introductory paragraphs for **at least two** of the following Practice Paper 3 questions. Remember to refer to the simplified Paper 3 mark scheme in Chapter 10.

Paper 3 practice questions

1 Examine the reasons for Khrushchev's victory in the power struggle which followed the death of Stalin in 1953.

2 Discuss the degree to which Khrushchev's policy of 'de-Stalinisation' brought about real change in the Soviet Union.

3 Evaluate the achievements of Khrushchev's economic policies in the years 1955–64.

4 Discuss the impact of Khrushchev's 'secret speech' of 1956 on relations between the USSR and the countries of Eastern Europe between 1956 and 1964.

5 'Khrushchev's pursuit of his policy of "peaceful co-existence" in the period 1955–64 was inconsistent.' To what extent do you agree with this statement?

6 | The Brezhnev Era: Stagnation and Drift, 1964–85

Introduction

This chapter deals with the main political, economic and foreign policy developments from 1964 to 1985. This period saw the emergence of significant problems. To a large extent, the response (or lack of response) to these issues by Brezhnev and his successors played a significant role in the eventual collapse of the USSR. The reluctance of most of the Soviet leadership to openly acknowledge these growing political and economic problems brought the party and its rule into increasing disrepute.

TIMELINE

1964 Oct: Brezhnev replaces Khrushchev as First Secretary of the CPSU; Kosygin becomes prime minister

1965 Sept: Start of Kosygin's reforms

1968 Aug: Warsaw Pact invasion of Czechoslovakia

Nov: 'Brezhnev Doctrine' announced

1971 Ninth Five-Year Plan

1973 Oct: Start of world oil crisis

1975 Aug: Helsinki Final Act

1976 Tenth Five-Year Plan

May: First Helsinki monitoring group established in USSR

1977 Jun: Brezhnev replaces Podgorny as head of state

Oct: New ('Brezhnev') constitution

1979 Dec: Soviet Union intervenes in Afghanistan; start of Second Cold War

1980 Dec: Kosygin dies

1981 Jan: 26th Congress, CPSU; Eleventh Five-Year Plan

1982 Sept: Helsinki groups in USSR disbanded

Nov: Brezhnev dies, replaced by Yuri Andropov

1984 Feb: Andropov dies, Konstantin Chernenko takes over

1985 Mar: Chernenko dies, Gorbachev takes over

6

The Soviet Union and Post-Soviet Russia (1924–2000)

KEY QUESTIONS

- What were the main political developments in the USSR, 1964–85?
- What were the main features of the Soviet economy, 1964–85?
- How did Soviet foreign policy develop during this period?

Overview

- During the period 1964–85, the Soviet Union – despite seeming to be at its most powerful – began to experience some serious political and economic problems.
- Despite the collective leadership established when Khrushchev had been overthrown in 1964, Brezhnev became increasingly dominant, with party and state bodies dominated by ageing conservatives reluctant to make radical changes to the system.
- Khrushchev's economic reforms were at first put on hold but, in September, prime minister Kosygin received approval to introduce some similar economic reforms.
- However, many Soviet leaders – including Brezhnev – were not supportive and, by 1970, many of Kosygin's reforms had been blocked. Economic problems were made worse as defence expenditure continued to increase because of the Cold War.
- There were also political problems related to both Eastern Europe and the continuing Cold War. Reform in Czechoslovakia was stopped in 1968, but from 1980 unrest in Poland created growing concerns.
- Relations with the West at first improved under détente, but this eventually gave way to a Second Cold War – especially after the Soviet Union sent troops into Afghanistan in 1979.
- When Brezhnev died in 1982, some limited political and economic reforms were introduced by Andropov, but when Andropov then died in 1984, there was a period of 'drift' before Gorbachev took over the leadershp in 1985.

Figure 6.1: From left to right: Nikolai Podgorny, Leonid Brezhnev, and Alexei Kosygin.

6.1 What were the main political developments in the USSR, 1964–85?

After Khrushchev's overthrow in 1964, a collective leadership was established – it moved quickly to reassure military leaders, government administrators and economic managers that the instability and unpredictability which had characterised much of Khrushchev's time in office would end.

The Brezhnev era, 1964–82

At first, it seemed as though the members of this new leadership were co-equals. Brezhnev was given the post of First Secretary of the CPSU, **Kosygin** became prime minister, and Podgorny became chair of the Presidium of the Supreme Soviet and thus head of state.

> **Aleksei Kosygin (1904–1980):**
>
> During the Second World War, he was a member of the State Defence Committee; once Khrushchev had become leader, he was appointed in 1959 as chairman of *Gosplan*, before becoming first-deputy of the Council of Ministers. He was one of the more reform-minded of the top Soviet leadership, and had favoured a more liberal solution to the events in Czechoslovakia in 1968 known as the 'Prague Spring'. He also opposed the sending of troops into Afghanistan.

However, Brezhnev soon began to assert his dominance. At the 1966 Party Congress, his title was changed to General-Secretary – the post that had been used by Stalin. In contrast to Khrushchev, though, Brezhnev's watchwords were stability, continuity and conservatism. He quietly removed possible rivals them from their posts, or moved them to less important positions. In June 1977, Podgorny was removed from the Politburo – this meant he lost his position as president of the Supreme Soviet. Brezhnev then took over this position as head of state, while retaining his post as General-Secretary. By then, he had even been able to sideline or block many of Kosygin's attempts at economic reform (see 6.2, The economy under Brezhnev, 1964–82).

The *Nomenklatura* system and corruption

By 1971, the Politburo was dominated by Brezhnev's supporters, and by 1981, eight of the 14 full Politburo members were his protégés: four of these were part of the 'Brezhnev Mafia' (the men who had worked with him since the 1940s). These appointees opposed significant or radical changes, and increasingly undermined efforts by would-be reformers such as Kosygin, in both political and economic areas.

To maintain stability, Brezhnev continued to use the established *nomenklatura* system – this was essentially a long list of 'reliable' party members who could be appointed to state and administrative positions. The most senior enjoyed special privileges – such as special shops, special rooms in hospitals, and privileged access to elite schools for their children.

Brezhnev gave his son and his son-in-law high positions, and other family members and friends were also promoted. This nepotism (showing favouritism to close relatives in appointments to offices and official positions) increasingly led to corruption. Younger party members, such as Gorbachev, were appalled by this corruption and complacency, and awareness of it among the general public did much to undermine respect for the party and the system.

DISCUSSION POINT

The incidence of corruption under Brezhnev is seen as a significant factor in the political and economic problems building up in the Soviet Union. Was corruption inevitable under such a centralised political and economic system? Does it exist in all types of social and economic systems?

ACTIVITY

Carry out some additional research on the extent of the corruption which began to flourish under Brezhnev – including the involvement of members of his own family. Why did it later become significant that the KGB were aware of much of this?

Neo-Stalinism and political dissidents

Brezhnev and other conservatives were determined to maintain party control. Though Brezhnev made it clear that there would be no return to Stalin's methods, it was obvious that dissent would not be tolerated. However, as the Soviet system produced more and more well-educated people, these people became increasingly frustrated, and some turned to protest and dissent.

Under Brezhnev, some decided to push their rights as citizens to the limits, by protesting against political and cultural restrictions: these were the dissidents, who became confident that Soviet leaders had no wish to go back to the harshness and brutality of the Stalin era. As early as December 1965, a group of artists and scientists demonstrated in Red Square in Moscow, calling for the individual freedoms in the 1936 constitution to be honoured. Though detained and questioned, the dissidents – who included Andrei Sakharov – were then released.

As a result of these protests, Brezhnev strengthened some aspects of state control in 1966: it became illegal to circulate 'false information';

and police powers were increased. Increasingly, the Soviet Union under Brezhnev began to treat all serious critics of the regime as traitors in the pay of the West, who undermined the Soviet system. Some dissidents were classified as psychologically disturbed, and placed in psychiatric hospitals or wards – thus allowing the authorities to avoid any trial.

For a brief time, there was a softening of attitudes in the arts. However, this was then followed by another crackdown – some of the more famous of the dissidents affected included Andrei Sinyavsky in 1973 and **Alexander Solzhenitsyn** in 1974, after his book *The Gulag Archipelago*, about his experiences in the labour-camps system, had been published abroad.

Alexander Solzhenitsyn (1918–2008):

The author of *One Day in the Life of Ivan Denisovich* – which had been published under Khrushchev – and other books (such as *Cancer Ward*), Solzhenitsyn was later felt by many in the West to have 'lost the plot' when, after being expelled from the USSR in 1974, he called for the US to launch a nuclear war against the Soviet Union. One headline in a British newspaper was: 'Solzhenitsyn: Saint or Fool?' His reactionary form of Russian patriotism, and his adherence to the Russian Orthodox religion, also increasingly lost him supporters both within and without the USSR.

Theory of Knowledge

History, sources and 'truth'

During the Brezhnev period, many underground pamphlets were distributed by dissidents. The Soviet media clearly gave only a partial view of life and events in the USSR; but are these dissident publications any more reliable than official statements for historians trying to study life in Brezhnev's Soviet Union? As this underground literature was produced by dissident groups with very divergent views, how can historians make choices about which ones to rely on?

Dissidents were encouraged by the period of détente (meaning an easing of tensions and improved relations) between the West and the USSR, when human rights became one of the issues. In August 1975, the Soviet Union endorsed the Helsinki Accord (part of the Conference on Security and Cooperation in Europe (CSCE)). This committed the USSR to upholding the basic principles of human rights, such as free speech and freedom of assembly and conscience. Several 'Helsinki groups' were established in the USSR in 1976 and, in theory, Brezhnev allowed them to monitor the Soviet record on human rights. However, in practice, their leading members – including Dr Andrei Sakharov, Elena Bonner and Yuri Orlov – were often hounded by the authorities.

Figure 6.2: The Russian dissident brothers: Zhores (left) and Roy (right) Medvedev.

After 1977, Brezhnev's regime cracked down harder. In January 1980, Sakharov was placed under house arrest in Gorky, and in September 1982, the Helsinki monitoring groups were disbanded.

SOURCE 6.1

In 1970 the biologist and dissenter Zhores Medvedev was locked up in a lunatic asylum. Only the timely intervention of his twin brother Roy and others, ... secured his release... Solzhenitsyn, too, was subjected to involuntary emigration in 1974. Vladimir Bukovski suffered the same fate a year later ... In 1980 Sakharov was subjected to an order confining him to residence in Gorki, a city which it was illegal for foreigners to visit.... Within a year of the signature of the Helsinki Final Act in 1975, informal 'Helsinki groups' in the USSR were drawing the world's attention to the Soviet government's infringements of its undertakings... Three figures stood out amongst the dissenters in Russia: Sakharov, Solzhenitsyn and Roy Medvedev... What Sakharov, Medvedev and Solzhenitsyn had in common was that they detested Stalin's legacy and knew that Brezhnev's Politburo had not entirely abandoned it. But on other matters their ideas diverged... This [anti-Soviet] attitude [of Sakharov and Solzhenitsyn] was uncongenial to Medvedev, a radical communist reformer who argued that there was nothing inherently wrong with the Leninism enunciated by Lenin himself.

Service, R., 1997, **A History of Twentieth-Century Russia**, *Allen Lane/ Penguin, pp. 412–14.*

Yet there were few signs of really determined and overt political opposition to the Soviet regime under Brezhnev. For many people, standards of living were higher than they had been in 1964, there was a shorter working week, and education had improved. Most Soviet citizens seemed reasonably content.

Nationalism

However, during this period, nationalist unrest began to emerge in some non-Russian republics. At first, during the early 1970s, this exhibited itself in the Baltic republics, increasingly influenced by events in Poland in the late 1970s and early 1980s. There were also signs of growing unrest in the USSR's Central Asian republics which bordered on Afghanistan, and which had mainly Muslim populations. In fact, there is evidence to suggest that this (often fundamentalist religious) unrest was being fostered by the CIA – *before* the Soviet Union sent troops into Afghanistan in December 1979 (see 6.3, Afghanistan).

Such nationalist protests were a sign of a significant political crisis emerging in the Soviet Union. Under Brezhnev, though, all forms of dissent were essentially controlled, and did not appear to pose much of a threat to the continuation of Soviet rule.

ACTIVITY

Carry out some additional research on dissent in the Soviet Union under Brezhnev. Then draw up a KGB report for Brezhnev about some of the main dissidents, their criticisms and their activities. In particular, try to show that these groups often differed greatly from each other.

Political developments under Andropov, 1982–84

In the late 1970s, Brezhnev's increasingly serious health problems triggered a power struggle, in which Brezhnev seemed to favour Konstantin Chernenko. Chernenko's main rival was **Yuri Andropov**.

Yuri Andropov (1914–1984):

He was Soviet ambassador to Hungary when Soviet troops suppressed the Hungarian Rising of 1956. By 1957, he had been promoted to the Central Committee and, in May 1967, he became head of the KGB. However, he did not favour total repression of dissent, and he emphasised the need to establish and follow proper legal procedures. Later, when he took charge of ideology, he used his contacts in the KGB to undermine the position of Chernenko – a rival for the post of General-Secretary.

In November 1982, Brezhnev suffered a fatal stroke, and Andropov was immediately appointed as General-Secretary. Although prime minister Tikhanov had nominated Chernenko, Andropov was backed by the military and the KGB.

On becoming General-Secretary, Andropov made a number of personnel changes at intermediate and lower levels in the economic and party apparatuses. He also decided to take a much tougher line on corruption – several of Brezhnev's associates were executed for this. However, Andropov had no plans for any fundamental political changes, and the main focus was on economic reform. Although he put his own team in place as far as possible, the number of Brezhnevites in post – at both senior and intermediate levels – meant that he had to go cautiously. Andropov's main aim was to reform the administration to help push through his economic reforms.

Andropov was not a liberal, and had been in charge of the KGB before 1982. He had been responsible for Sakharov's exile to Gorky in 1980 and, after Andropov came to power, Sakharov and his wife were continually harassed, while **Roy Medvedev** was warned to stop his 'anti-Soviet activities'. Other dissidents were firmly repressed.

> **Roy Medvedev (b. 1925):**
>
> He was a dissident Marxist historian who was expelled from the CPSU in 1969 for his book, *Let History Judge*, which was highly critical of Stalin. He called for a return to Leninism, and a reformed, democratic socialism. In 1970, along with Sakharov and other dissidents, he signed an open letter to the Soviet leadership. He was a supporter of Gorbachev's reforms, rejoining the CPSU in 1989.

Nevertheless, Andropov also encouraged ordinary citizens to voice complaints to officials, and he took a more sympathetic attitude to nationalist unrest. He even made attempts to try to persuade certain dissidents that their criticisms were harming the country. According to M. Lewin, fear of the secret police, which had been lessening since the 1960s, had mostly faded by the1980s. This made dissidence and other forms of political activity more possible – but, ironically, by relaxing controls and repression, it helped undermine the Soviet regime.

By mid-1983, it was clear that Andropov's health was fast declining, and those opposed to reform began planning their moves. In December, Andropov removed a few more Brezhnevites from top positions but, on 11 February 1984, he died. Andropov had not had sufficient time to push ahead with his reforms, or to overcome the obstructionism which tried to neutralise their impact. Yet his attempts had encouraged others to think in similar ways about reform – and had led to the emergence of reform-minded politicians such as **Mikhail Gorbachev**.

> **Mikhail Gorbachev (b. 1931):**
>
> He had studied law at Moscow University, graduating in 1955 and beginning work in the public prosecutor's office in Stavropol. He was horrified by the corruption he saw and, in 1970, became First Party Secretary there. It was here that Andropov met him, and decided to support his rise. By 1980, aged only 49, he was a full member of the Politburo – the average age of Politburo members then was over 70. Though not a liberal, he was, like Khrushchev, Kosygin and Andropov, a communist reformer who wanted to make the Soviet system more efficient and democratic.

Gorbachev was the youngest member of the Politburo, and was Andropov's main protégé and supporter, and it appears that Andropov hoped Gorbachev would replace him. Gorbachev typified those who were frustrated by the conservatism and stagnation represented by the leaders who had come to power under Brezhnev.

Political developments under Chernenko, 1984–85

However, the Brezhnevites were still strong enough to ensure that their preferred candidate, Chernenko, succeeded Andropov as the next General-Secretary rather than Gorbachev. At 72, Chernenko was the oldest man ever to become Soviet leader – more importantly, he was the candidate favoured by the conservative anti-reform faction. Chernenko's approach was designed to maintain 'stability', and his main political 'initiatives' were to carry on with Andropov's campaign against corruption, and to concentrate on education. He also tightened censorship, and took a hard line on dissent; though he did try to address some of the issues of the non-Russian nationalities. Significantly, though, he dropped plans to reduce the bureaucracy.

In August 1984, Chernenko became seriously ill. By this time, Gorbachev had become chairman of the Foreign Affairs Committee of the Soviet Union – he then took charge of ideology, which made him apparently Chernenko's unofficial deputy. In early 1985, Chernenko's health deteriorated further and there began a jockeying for position between those supporting Gorbachev and a younger set of enthusiastic reformers, and those favouring stability and more experienced personnel. Gorbachev made it known that he was strongly in favour of reducing military expenditure and securing arms reductions by negotiations with the West.

On 10 March 1985, Chernenko died. Supported by those in favour of reform, Gorbachev became the next General-Secretary – at 54, he was the youngest member of the Politburo.

6.2 What were the main features of the Soviet economy, 1964–85?

In the period 1964–85, there were increasingly serious signs of economic slowdown – and arguably of actual decline.

The economy under Brezhnev, 1964–82

Evidence of the growing economic problems facing the Soviet Union at that time is mixed. By the late 1970s, just as signs of a serious slowdown in economic growth were emerging, many Soviet citizens enjoyed a higher standard of living than they had done before Brezhnev – and much higher than they would experience after the Soviet Union collapsed in 1991.

The centrally planned Soviet economy was largely under the control of the Communist Party – though the Soviet government was responsible for the day-to-day direction of the economy, through planning departments which decided the rate of growth to be carried out by the industries and state farms, and also the prices and amounts of materials, energy, labour and goods. Many assumed that this Soviet economy – which had achieved several 'firsts' in space technology – would carry on more or less as it had done.

However, though not apparent to most people until the 1980s, the Soviet model of state planning was showing signs of an impending economic crisis as early as the mid-1970s. Aspects of this are examined in the following sections.

Industry and the Kosygin reforms

At the beginning of Brezhnev's rule, there were some attempts at industrial reform. The main person responsible for these was Aleksei Kosygin who, as prime minister, pushed hardest for increased investment and real economic reforms. He tried to make the economy more efficient and dynamic – especially in increased production of consumer goods. In September 1965, he resurrected Khrushchev's 1962 plans to give greater autonomy to factory managers over certain decisions.

However, the desire to give extra powers to managers – and so reduce the influence of Gosplan – had political repercussions. In particular, it decreased the authority of the various economic ministries and of the CPSU itself. Many of Kosygin's colleagues therefore opposed his plans. Although Kosygin was given formal approval by the Central Committee to press ahead with his plans, Brezhnev decided not to support Kosygin against his party critics – and did what he could behind the scenes to impede Kosygin's reforms.

There were some successes and improvements during the Eighth Five-Year Plan, 1965–70 – by 1970, the output of factories and mines had risen 138% compared with 1960. However, these increases in production were not maintained, and plan targets were increasingly not met.

KEY CONCEPTS ACTIVITY

Change and continuity: Find out what you can about Kosygin's industrial reforms – and why they were opposed. Then draw up a chart, with headings for: Khrushchev, Kosygin and Gorbachev. Complete it for the first two, showing aspects of change and continuity between them. Once you have studied Chapters 7 and 8, complete the chart by filling in the section on Gorbachev.

SOURCE 6.2

[Kosygin's] remarkable administrative skills made him indispensable. It was known in top circles that the economy rested on his shoulders – and that nobody else possessed such broad ones... he knew better than anyone else how to make the administrative machinery work... Kosygin was also known for the interesting economic reform he launched, which was scuttled by the conservatives, who continued to hold it against him... Dedicated to the system, he was also well aware of the need to reform it; and around 1964 everything still seemed possible. He believed in semi-public companies and cooperatives. He was conscious of the West's superiority and the need to learn from it. He believed in initiating gradual changes, setting in train a transition from a 'state-administered economy' to a system in which 'the state restricts itself to guiding enterprises'... when Kosygin tried to convince Brezhnev to elaborate a genuine economic strategy and discuss it at a Politburo meeting... Brezhnev used delaying tactics, which amounted to burying the idea. Kosygin emerged from such conversations completely demoralised.

Lewin, M., 2005, **The Soviet Century***, London, Verso, pp. 248–9.*

By the beginning of the 1970s, the majority of Politburo members believed they could stabilise the Soviet order. Indeed, in the early 1970s, the Soviet Union seemed to be stable and strong – its military strength almost equalled that of the US and it was the world's second largest industrial economy. There were even those in the West (not supporters of the USSR) who thought that the centrally planned economy might succeed in out-producing advanced capitalist states in many economic areas.

Figure 6.3: A satirical cartoon from the Soviet Union, which mocks the state of industry under Leonid Brezhnev in the 1970s. Despite modern technology, Soviet industry was still largely labour-extensive compared to the West.

The USSR thus continued with Five-Year Plans – the Ninth was to run from 1971 to 1975. This projected a slight increase in the production of consumer goods, such as furniture and radios. However, as before, the bulk of government funding went to medium and heavy industry. As a consequence, by 1975, consumer goods had expanded at a rate 9% *lower* than the increase in industrial goods.

In addition, the USSR – a major oil and natural gas producer – failed to take advantage of the 1973–74 world oil crisis (during which oil prices rose extremely high) to develop more modern fuel-efficient technology. By increasing oil prices to the Soviet-bloc counties, Brezhnev contributed to their economic problems, forcing those regimes to take measures – such as increasing prices to consumers, and borrowing from Western financial institutions – which contributed, ultimately, to the eventual collapse of the security belt of satellite states in Eastern Europe.

The Tenth Five-Year Plan

It was during the Tenth Five-Year Plan (1976–80) that signs of a real slowdown in growth became apparent. The planned increase in industrial production for 1979 was 5.7%, but the *actual* increase was

3.4%. The *official* statistics insisted that industrial output rose by 4.4% a year in the period 1976–80. Yet, even according to official statistics, this actually showed a steady *decrease* in the rate of expansion: as, in 1966–70, official statistics had claimed that the annual rise was 8.5%. Yet the situation under Brezhnev seemed likely to continue in this way, and great things were expected from the planned Baikal-Amur Magistral (BAM) railway line, which would link Siberia (rich in coking coal, iron, copper, timber and especially oil and natural gas) to the Pacific.

There was little fresh thinking in the Politburo about the economy or other related aspects – the members' increasingly unfounded belief was that the USSR could make steady economic advances without any major reforms. Nonetheless, Brezhnev did allow the creation of 'associations' (*ob'edineniya*), where factories with complementary activities could join to help each other. Such associations were expected to operate on a self-financing basis. However, this reform was undermined by the fact that central authorities still retained much control over investment, prices, and wages. Additionally, old problems continued. For example, because the Soviet Union's planned economy meant there was no unemployment, a labour shortage emerged. As a result, many workers held more than one job, and split their time between them.

Agriculture

As early as March 1965, Brezhnev insisted on a bigger allocation of resources for agriculture – for more chemical fertilisers and advanced mechanical equipment – in order to overcome grain shortages. This took resources away from Kosygin's industrial plans, but did increase state investment – as well as having the knock-on effect of industrial reforms initiated by Khrushchev and Kosygin which led to an improvement in agricultural production. From 1960 to 1970, Soviet agricultural output increased at an annual average of 3%.

Output quotas were still established from the centre, along with instructions on what crops to plant or sow. Brezhnev shared Khrushchev's idea that amalgamating farms to form bigger *kolkhozes* would raise productivity, and in 1976, the Politburo issued a resolution calling for this. However, despite the massive state subsidy for food and agriculture, many *kolkhozes* operated at a loss. This was partly because charges for fuel and machinery went up, thus wiping out any advantage from increases in state prices for farming produce.

In 1977, and again in 1981, Brezhnev authorised a decree which increased the size of private plots that peasants could have to half a hectare. Peasants preferred to work on these rather than the collective's land – by the 1970s, over 30% of agricultural produce was from these private plots, although they comprised only 4% of arable land.

To keep *kolkhoz* workers happy, Brezhnev decided to increase the prices paid to them – while subsidised food prices for consumers were kept low, thus satisfying industrial workers. For example, the state subsidy for meat meant it was sold to consumers at half cost-price. This was fine while the Soviet Union was benefiting from increased oil and commodity prices, but it was not a long-term solution. Although there had been a record harvest in 1978 (235 million tonnes of grain), the following year produced only 179 million tonnes – about 47 million tonnes short of the target. This resulted in the embarrassing situation of the Soviet Union having to depend on buying 20 million tonnes from Canada and the US.

Brezhnev's response was simply to increase state investment and subsidies – though he did also support plans for land reclamation and improved irrigation. Those who favoured significant reform tended to remain silent; however, some reform-minded party officials at the local level (such as Mikhail Gorbachev) did introduce some changes.

Consumer goods and the social wage

Khrushchev had aimed to increase the supply of consumer goods, and this policy was continued by Brezhnev and Kosygin. One reason for this was to avoid any dissatisfaction and protest which might arise if workers did not see improvements in their living standards. Hence the temptation was to make concessions *before* trouble appeared – even if this actually hindered fundamental economic reform. So Brezhnev tried to reduce wage differentials and, in particular, ensured that industrial and other blue-collar workers were paid better than various professional groups.

Under Brezhnev's rule, the numbers of families owning electrical goods such as refrigerators and televisions increased significantly – from 32% to 86%, and 51% to 86%, respectively, in the period 1970–80. Even though investment in the industrial consumer-goods sector fell behind plan projections, the situation did improve. There was, however, a slowdown in the production of some consumer goods after 1976.

For ordinary Soviet citizens, many aspects of life improved under Brezhnev. In addition to state-subsidised prices for the main foodstuffs (such as bread, potatoes and meat), there were other elements of the Soviet people's social wage (a term that refers to measures of economic and social well-being other than wages, such as job security). These benefits included cheap prices for clothing, electricity, gas and coal, and subsidised rents and public transport.

It is estimated that the prices paid by people in the USSR for such items were not much higher than those paid during Stalin's First Five-Year Plan of 1928–32. In addition, trade unions opened more holiday centres for their members on the Baltic and Black Sea coasts. Yet people took all these advantages – along with sanitation, health care and education – for granted.

ACTIVITY

Draw a spider diagram to identify and illustrate the economic problems and policies in both industry and agriculture during the period 1964–82. Then carry out some brief research to see what economic problems were experienced by the US and other Western capitalist countries during this period. How were these problems similar, and how were they different?

The Soviet economy, 1982–85

When Brezhnev died in November 1982, he had been in power for 18 years – the longest tenure of office of a Soviet leader after Stalin's. His rule had seen considerable stability and continuity, and consequently the reality of economic stagnation had been hidden from many observers. However, even Brezhnev had been prepared to admit the existence of economic problems. At the 28th Party Congress in 1981, while he had spoken of the impact of a difficult world economic situation, he had also drawn attention to domestic economic weaknesses, such as shortages of food and consumer goods. These problems remained for his successors.

Andropov's time in Hungary meant he had seen at first hand Hungarian attempts to introduce more liberal economic reforms and policies by reducing the influence of central planning agencies. His attitude to reform was also influenced by his career in the KGB, as he had received accurate reports about economic situations both in the USSR and abroad. This meant he knew before he became leader of the USSR what the main problems were.

Though he was not a political 'liberal', Andropov did want to reform and modernise the Soviet economy to make it more efficient and productive. In many ways, his attitudes and policies were similar to Khrushchev's. However, in the end, he was only in power for 15 months – much less than the 10 years he believed were needed to carry through a meaningful reform programme.

Andropov's first campaign was against absenteeism from work – a report in 1982 showed that, at any one time, 30% of people of working age were absent from work for 'personal reasons'. His speeches warned that improvements in wages, and in working and living conditions, would only come from hard work and greater productivity. One of the main reasons for absenteeism was drunkenness and even alcoholism – so Andropov also launched a campaign against alcohol abuse.

To help carry through his reforms, Andropov quickly appointed those who supported him and his aims, and moved to demote some who favoured continuing with Brezhnev's 'drift'. After becoming General-Secretary, Andropov's reforms included setting up smaller enterprises, and increasing productivity in different sectors of the economy. In January 1984, steps were taken to give more powers to factory managers – in what was called a 'limited industrial experiment' – in branches covered by five industrial ministries. In particular, managers were to have more powers relating to production and use of profits. Wages and bonuses were to be more closely linked to production and sales. However, central planning bodies and structures would remain.

These early reforms were limited, but seemed to point in a clear direction. However, Andropov's health was poor, and this affected his ability to push his reforms through against the opposition and inertia he encountered.

QUESTION

What was involved in the 'limited industrial experiment' introduced by Andropov in 1984?

When Chernenko took over, he did not press ahead with economic reforms. Indeed, although Gorbachev was now speaking for a reduction in defence spending so that more could be done on consumer-goods production, the conservative military/anti-reform group managed to get a 12% increase in the defence budget. Thus, during Chernenko's limited time in power, little was done to address the ever-increasing signs of an approaching economic crisis.

> ACTIVITY
>
> Carry out some further research on Andropov and Chernenko. Then write obituaries for them, which assess their attempts at economic reform during the period 1982–85.

The Soviet economy and the Cold War

To understand the increasing problems of the Soviet economy – and the reasons for them – it is important to assess the growing impact of the Cold War and the costs of the arms race associated with it.

By 1976, many leaders accepted that the Soviet economy had fallen behind the advanced capitalist countries of the West in civilian technology, and that more needed to be done about increasing productivity, and the availability of consumer goods. The Cold War was a significant factor behind this – and indeed behind the crisis and ultimate collapse of the Soviet economy. For, in addition to the cost of massive food-subsidies, a huge part of the annual budget was taken up by the nuclear arms race.

Concerned with both defence and deterrence after the Second World War, all Soviet leaders had been determined to develop and maintain a strong military capability, both conventional and nuclear. Brezhnev's foreign policy (see 6.3, below) was based on the assumption that Soviet military strength, combined with an approach of reasonableness, would result in détente, with the West agreeing to weapons reductions and loans; this in turn would then enable the Soviet economy to be better funded and so improve.

However, the massive defence spending this incurred placed an increasingly heavy burden on the economy. The huge sums diverted from civilian to military expenditure as a result of the Cold War restricted the ability of the USSR to respond to increasing demands from civilians for continued improvements in living standards and the availability of newer consumer goods. Brezhnev's approach came seriously unstuck in the late 1970s, as the West began to abandon détente and instead embarked on a Second Cold War, with the development and deployment of newer and more expensive nuclear weapons. In fact, according to F. Halliday in *The Making of the Second Cold War*, 1986, one of the main reasons for the US launching this Second Cold War was so that it would destabilise the Soviet economy. CIA experts reported that the economy was extremely weak, and that increased defence spending could cause serious problems for the Soviet Union and its control of Eastern Europe. After 1977, this US policy was stepped up – arguably as a form of economic warfare.

By 1980, Brezhnev's determination to catch up with, and then maintain parity with, US rearmament was coinciding with increasing signs that the Soviet economy was slowing down. As a result, the production of more and better consumer goods began to decline and economic stagnation continued. The crisis threatening the Soviet economy was now clear.

One obvious way to fund a rapid growth of the economy would be to greatly reduce the defence budget and so fund increased investment in the civilian economy. The two other main options were to cut the real living standards of the Soviet people, thus releasing funds; or to borrow heavily abroad from capitalist states. All three options were seen as unacceptable by many Soviet leaders.

ACTIVITY

'During 1964–85, external pressures, not internal weaknesses, were the main reason for the growing problems of the Soviet economy.' With a partner, produce two short discussion papers (or speeches) – one of you to support the statement, and the other to oppose it. Then swap your work, and assess each other as regards:
a   clear argument
b   precise supporting evidence
c   reaching a judgement.

6.3 How did Soviet foreign policy develop during this period?

The main foreign policy issues for the Soviet Union in this period remained those concerned with Soviet security. As before 1964, these were the maintenance of the 'buffer zone' in Eastern Europe and the ongoing attempt to maintain satisfactory relations with the West. Additional complications – also connected to the ideas of 'spheres of influence' and security belts – were firstly Afghanistan, and secondly the additional threat of the Second Cold War. These factors all adversely affected the Soviet Union's ability to address its domestic political and economic problems.

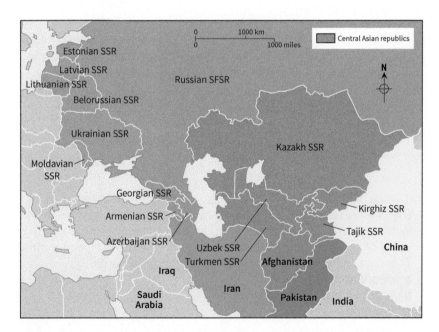

Figure 6.4: A map showing Afghanistan and the Soviet Central Asian republics; three of these Soviet republics had common borders with Afghanistan.

Brezhnev's foreign policy, 1964–82

From the start, Brezhnev had been keen to improve relations with the West – mainly for economic reasons. In addition to the cost of maintaining parity with the US in the nuclear arms race, the USSR was suffering from the impact of the worsening rift with China; this entailed greater military expense, in having to defend the long border with China.

Détente

These problems made détente with the West an attractive proposition. The invasion of Czechoslovakia in 1968 initially prevented better East–West relations, but from around 1969 Brezhnev's attitude was an important factor in the development of a period of détente. Kosygin, in particular, worked hard to improve relations with the West, as he hoped the Soviet economy could gain from increased access to Western technology.

> QUESTION
> **Why was Kosygin keen to develop closer relations with Western states?**

Brezhnev reasoned that, from a position of strength, he could negotiate a reduction in nuclear weapons and import Western technology. This policy of negotiating with the West for weapons reductions really got underway in 1969 and 1970, with the beginnings of the SALT (Strategic Arms Limitations Treaty) talks. In 1972, further agreements were made which attempted to slow down the nuclear arms race; while in August 1973, the Conference on Security and Cooperation in Europe (CSCE) eventually led to agreements which recognised existing borders in Europe. At the same time, several trade deals were signed with the US and its Western allies, including West Germany. So until the mid-1970s, Brezhnev's foreign policies brought some benefits as a result of reasonably stable East–West relations.

> **SOURCE 6.3**
>
> The conference [CSCE] concluded with the signature in August 1975 of a wide-ranging agreement... Not everything in the CSCE agreement was to Soviet liking..., Moscow saw [the protection of human rights] as a device for western interference in its internal affairs. But the Warsaw Pact had been campaigning for such a conference since the 1950s and Helsinki was viewed by Moscow as a significant success for Soviet diplomacy and as one of the high points of détente. Particularly pleasing for the Soviets were the CSCE agreements' underwriting of the territorial and political status quo in Europe – a final rubberstamping of the de facto post-Second World War peace settlement which had emerged during the early years of the Cold War. Whatever it might mean to Moscow in other contexts, détente in Europe was about freezing the outcome of the Cold War and the maintenance on a stable, predictable and orderly basis of Soviet control of eastern Europe. Moscow's determination that détente should underwrite its position in eastern Europe had, in fact, only very recently been reinforced by events in Czechoslovakia in 1968 which had revealed once again the fragility of Moscow's communist bloc in eastern Europe.
>
> *Roberts, G., 1999,* **The Soviet Union in World Politics: Coexistence, Revolution and Cold War 1945–1991,** *London, Routledge, p. 68.*

However, in December 1978, there was a big increase in US defence spending, which began a new arms race. This marked the unofficial start of the Second Cold War. As a result of this, a second SALT agreement was never ratified by the US.

Eastern Europe

Developments in Eastern Europe continued to be of crucial importance to the Soviet Union. Brezhnev's main aim in Eastern Europe was to maintain the USSR's buffer zone of satellite states established by Stalin after the end of the Second World War. The first serious issue arose in Czechoslovakia, where problems came to a head in January 1968, when **Alexander Dubcek** became the country's First Secretary, with Brezhnev's approval. Dubcek had been an admirer of Khrushchev's reforms, and called for significant reforms in Czechoslovakia. He also travelled to Moscow, in an attempt to reassure Brezhnev that the reforms would not threaten the Warsaw Pact and Soviet security. At first, the Soviet leadership appeared prepared to accept his plans. Dubcek's reforms, known as the 'Prague Spring', were intended to create 'socialism with a human face'. Though the Czechoslovak Communist Party retained its leading role, non-communist organisations began to appear. Soon, an opposition party of sorts was formed.

Alexander Dubcek (1921–1992):

He was a Slovak politician and a reform Communist. In his brief time as leader of Czechoslovakia in 1968, he attempted to build 'socialism with a human face' in what became known as the 'Prague Spring'. After the fall of communism in 1989, he was briefly the Chairman of the federal Czech-Slovak parliament, before Czechoslovakia split into two states in 1993.

When these political developments were combined with Dubcek beginning negotiations with the IMF and other Western financial organisations to arrange loans, the USSR became increasingly concerned. In July, Eastern European leaders sent the Warsaw Letter to Dubcek, warning him to stop his reforms – but he refused. Brezhnev then authorised an invasion of Czechoslovakia by Warsaw Pact forces in August 1968 to end the 'Prague Spring'. Dubcek was removed from power, and replaced by Gustav Husak.

Shortly after the invasion of Czechoslovakia, in November 1968, Brezhnev made a declaration known as the Brezhnev Doctrine which claimed the right to interfere in the internal affairs of its Comecon and Warsaw Pact allies if Soviet security, or the gains of the people's republics, were under threat. In effect, this was a statement of intent – the Soviet Union would intervene if necessary to prop up the existing regimes in Eastern Europe.

QUESTION

What were the main points of the Brezhnev Doctrine?

6

Figure 6.5: Czech students protest against the 1968 invasion of Czechoslovakia.

Towards the end of his rule, Brezhnev had to deal with growing unrest in Poland, where the unofficial trade union Solidarity organised growing protests and strikes against the government's economic policies. Moreover, during Brezhnev's time in office, some Eastern European countries, such as Hungary and Romania, were increasingly taking actions independently from Moscow. To an extent, this was because, as part of détente, many had made trade and finance deals with Western states and banks. These independent actions were continued after Brezhnev's death, and contributed to the crisis which unfolded in the late 1980s.

By the early 1980s, Brezhnev's concerns about security in Eastern Europe were intensified as détente had given way to the Second Cold War.

Afghanistan

Of all aspects of Brezhnev's foreign policy, perhaps the one that had the greatest impact on Soviet security was the decision to send troops into Afghanistan in December 1979. Although it was not the main cause of the end of détente, it was the final act which officially brought détente to a close. Intended as a step to maintain Soviet security, it actually ended up undermining it because of the economic and political problems the intervention caused.

As Afghanistan had common borders with the USSR's Central Asian republics, it had been generally accepted by the West that it lay within the USSR's 'sphere of influence'. Hence, when the People's Democratic Party of Afghanistan (PDPA) carried out a military coup in April 1978, the West accepted the new communist government.

However, this pro-Soviet PDPA government soon came under attack from conservative feudal landowners and religious fundamentalists who opposed its reforms. Brezhnev's government became increasingly worried by the threat of Islamist fundamentalism spilling across the borders into the Central Asian republics – especially when evidence mounted that Pakistan (with US support) and Iran were already supporting such groups. Brezhnev was also concerned that failure to intervene in this Soviet 'sphere of influence' might lead the communist states in Eastern Europe to think that the USSR was no longer willing to act on the Brezhnev Doctrine to maintain Soviet control there, or to resist US power.

Consequently, following a new coup in December 1979, when the new communist government in Kabul requested military assistance, the Soviet Union sent in troops. By April 1980, there were over 100000 Soviet troops in Afghanistan.

DISCUSSION POINT

Why do you think the US began supporting Islamist fundamentalist military groups in Afghanistan in 1978? To what extent has this possibly contributed to problems with such terrorist groups in the 21st century?

SOURCE 6.4

The end of détente came suddenly in December 1979... when the USSR sent its forces over the Soviet-Afghan border. Communists in Afghanistan had for months begged Moscow to help them militarily against their many religious and political enemies. The Politburo gave permission for KGB special forces and paratroops to give them secret assistance, but, under Kosygin's influence, stood out against all-out intervention by the Soviet army. But the pleas from Kabul grew more insistent. Brezhnev [and] his leading confidants ... resolved to dispatch a military contingent...The rest of the Politburo gave subsequent approval. The decision was motivated by the wish to prevent power being seized in Kabul by anti-communists supported by the USA, and the USSR put its troops over the border with reluctance... The Americans were eager to supply all the material aid requested by the insurgents. The fact that the revolt was led by Moslem fanatics – the mujehaddin – did not bother the Americans at the time... Brezhnev had thought he was throwing a lasso around the neck of an adjacent country, Afghanistan. Instead he had tied a cord round the neck of the Soviet order and pulled it tight.

Service, R., 2007, **Comrades: Communism – A World History,** *London, Macmillan, pp. 329–330.*

The Soviet leaders expected no serious consequences, and were greatly surprised by the strength of the US response. As well as ending détente and launching the Second Cold War, the US imposed a boycott on exports of grain and technology to the USSR, and other countries followed suit. These actions led to some shortages in the USSR. The Soviet invasion of Afghanistan soon became a massive drain on both manpower and the already-struggling Soviet economy. By the time Brezhnev died, it was clear that this had become the USSR's 'Vietnam' – a war it could not win; and it was one of the most important factors behind Gorbachev's push after 1985 for the need for 'new thinking'.

In fact, events in Afghanistan illustrate the wider impact of Brezhnev's aim to maintain Soviet defences at levels comparable with the USA's. Although he had achieved parity with the US in many areas, the domestic effect was an increasing shortage of certain consumer goods. This not surprisingly contributed to growing dissatisfaction and thus a developing domestic and foreign political crisis with which Brezhnev's successors had to try to deal.

ACTIVITY

Using the information in this chapter, and any other sources available to you, prepare a brief for a court case arguing that the Soviet intervention in Afghanistan was essentially defensive – and, in part, a reaction to earlier actions by the US. Then develop a counter-argument.

Foreign policy, 1982–85

Both Andropov and Chernenko followed an essentially conservative approach to foreign policy. In particular, Andropov – one of the leaders who had strongly advised Brezhnev to send in the troops in the first place – never seriously considered withdrawing troops from Afghanistan, even though this had become a major source of discontent within the USSR.

However, he did suggest further arms controls in November 1982 and, in 1983, he reduced the Soviet space programme in an attempt to save money. In 1983, he called again for arms controls, and even offered a 'freeze' on anti-ballistic missiles and the reduction of Soviet missiles in Europe. But the US and its allies refused to make similar concessions, so the offer fell. Although there was another attempt at Geneva at the end of November 1983, no agreements were reached – and by then Andropov was seriously ill.

Under Chernenko, there were attempts to resume good relations with the US and the West – despite the opposition of some Soviet military leaders. However, the continued Soviet presence in Afghanistan, along with the US determination to continue with the Second Cold War, made this almost impossible, so little was achieved.

Paper 3 exam practice

Question

'Brezhnev's economic policies in the period 1964–82 resulted in falling living standards and industrial and agricultural stagnation.' To what extent do you agree with this statement? **[15 marks]**

Skill

Avoiding irrelevance

Examiner's tips

Do not waste valuable writing time on irrelevant material – by definition, if it is irrelevant, it won't gain you *any* marks. Writing irrelevant information can happen because:

- the candidate does not look carefully enough at the wording of the question (see the skill section at the end of Chapter 3)
- the candidate ignores the fact that the questions require selection of facts, an analytical approach, and a final judgement; instead the candidate just writes down all that she or he knows about a topic (relevant or not), and hopes that the examiner will do the analysis and make the judgement
- the candidate has unwisely restricted his or her revision. So, for example, if a question crops up on Brezhnev's economic policy, rather than the expected one on Stalin's or Khrushchev's economic policy – the candidate tries to turn it into the question he or she wanted! Whatever the reason, such responses rarely address any of the demands of the question asked.

For this question, you will need to:

- cover the various aspects and details Brezhnev's industrial and agricultural policies during the relevant period (that is, the whole period of his rule)
- outline the actual results of those various policies as regards both living standards and stagnation
- provide a judgement about the extent to which you agree with the statement – for instance, whether the results were mixed.

Common mistakes

One common error with questions like this is for candidates to write about material they know well, rather than material directly related to the question.

Another mistake is to present too much general information, instead of material specific to the person, period and command terms.

Finally, candidates often elaborate too much on events outside the dates given in the question (see the skill section in Chapter 3).

Sample paragraphs of irrelevant focus or material

Before trying to decide whether Brezhnev's economic policies resulted in falling living standards and economic stagnation, it will be necessary to explain the state of the Soviet economy in the period before 1964. In particular, the situation Brezhnev inherited from Khrushchev is relevant to answering this question.

After Stalin's death in 1953, Soviet leaders realised they would need to address the problems of agriculture which had not really been solved by Stalin's collectivisation policies. Once Khrushchev gained control, he tried various new policies – these included reducing quotas for the collectives, and cutting the taxes placed on profits from private plots. He also raised the prices paid by the state for grain, and merged many of the collectives into larger state farms which he believed would be more productive. In addition, agricultural experts were sent out to the state farms, to encourage more modern methods. As a result, living standards for those employed in agriculture increased significantly. However, the increases in production were much more limited – even taking into consideration his 'virgin lands' scheme...

[There then follow several more-detailed paragraphs about Khrushchev's agricultural policies – especially about the 'virgin lands' scheme]...

As a result of all this, just before Brezhnev took over, the 1963 harvest was very poor – so poor, that the Soviet Union had to import large quantities of grain from North America and Australia. It was this situation that Brezhnev inherited in 1964.

As regards industry, Khrushchev's policies had been more successful. He tried to increase production by giving greater incentives to workers, and also tried to decrease central control in order to allow for more local initiative. In particular, he shifted resources from heavy industry into light industry and consumer goods production…

[There then follow several detailed paragraphs about Khrushchev's industrial policies and administrative plans during the period 1955-58]…

These aims were then pushed forward by his Seven-Year Plan which began in January 1959. However, there had been opposition from the central planning bureaucrats to his attempts to increase regional planning; as a result, his Seven-Year Plan had been ended in 1961, and replaced by a Five-Year Plan. This was because…

[There then follow more paragraphs about Khrushchev's industrial policies from 1961-64]…

Nonetheless, his industrial policies were generally successful – and Brezhnev inherited these gains. For instance, the figures for 1965 showed his policies had led to an 80% increase in overall industrial production, while foreign trade had also significantly increased. However, , in 1963 and 1964 – in part because of his rather uncoordinated investment programme – the Soviet Union experienced its lowest peacetime economic growth rates since 1933. This was the situation Brezhnev faced when he took over in 1964.

EXAMINER'S COMMENT

This is an example of a weak answer. Although a brief comment on the state of the Soviet Union before 1964 would be relevant and helpful, there is certainly no need to go into detail about the period 1955–64. Thus virtually all of the material is irrelevant (marked in blue), and will not score any marks. In addition, the candidate is using up valuable writing time, which should have been spent on providing relevant points and supporting knowledge.

Activity

In this chapter, the focus is on avoiding writing answers which contain irrelevant material. So, using the information from this chapter, and any other sources of information available to you, write an answer to **one** of the following Practice Paper 3 questions, keeping your answer fully focused on the question asked. Remember – making a plan *first* can help you maintain this focus. Remember to refer to the simplified Paper 3 mark scheme in Chapter 10.

Paper 3 practice questions

1   Examine Brezhnev's attempts to control the emerging dissident movement in the Soviet Union in the period 1964–82.

2   Discuss Brezhnev's success in reforming the Soviet economy in the period 1964–82.

3   'If Andropov had been in power long enough, his reforms would have solved the USSR's political and economic problems.' To what extent do you agree with this statement?

4   Compare and contrast the impact of the Soviet Union's policies and actions in two Eastern European states in the period 1964–82.

5   Evaluate the success of Brezhnev's military intervention in Afghanistan.

7

Gorbachev and the Years of Reform, 1985–89

Introduction

When Gorbachev came to power in March 1985, his main aims were to establish and maintain a reformed socialist system – and to revitalise the CPSU – by economic reforms combined with greater freedoms and political democracy. On several occasions, he said he wanted to return to the early ideals of the Bolshevik Revolution, when Lenin was in charge. He wanted to avoid the excesses of both Russia's Stalinist past and Western capitalism, in order to create a 'self-managing socialism', in which there would be less state domination of the economy.

In fact, many of Gorbachev's ideas were close to those advocated by Leon Trotsky in the late 1920s and the 1930s, before and after his expulsion from the Soviet Union. For example, Gorbachev established a new form of Lenin's New Economic Policy (NEP), returned parts of farming to family production, and set up genuine cooperatives in the service sectors of the economy. All these strategies had also been proposed by Trotsky in the 1920s and 1930s. He, like Gorbachev, argued for a reformed, efficient and properly planned state sector to oversee such changes.

In 1986, Gorbachev announced that these aims were to be achieved via three main policies: *perestroika*, *glasnost* and *demokratizatsiya*. These mean, respectively: restructuring, openness and democratisation. *Perestroika* is normally associated with Gorbachev's economic reforms, which were meant to make the Soviet economic system more modern and so increase productivity. However, the term also soon came to be applied to aspects of political reform, all of which were intended to modernise the USSR. In fact, Gorbachev often spoke of *perestroika* in this wider sense, applying it to the entire Soviet system.

Gorbachev also adopted a very different foreign policy from that of his predecessors. This was characterised by what he called 'New Thinking'. As well as wanting to improve international relations in general, and to end the Soviet presence in Afghanistan, he aimed to loosen the Soviet Union's control over, and economic support of, the states of Eastern Europe. In part, this changed foreign policy was in order to cut costs and use the money saved to modernise the Soviet economy.

TIMELINE

1985 Mar: Gorbachev becomes General-Secretary of the CPSU; Ryzhkov becomes prime minister; Gorbachev abandons the Brezhnev Doctrine

Jun: Gorbachev informs Central Committee of economic problems

Jul: Romanov sacked

Dec: Grishin replaced by Yeltsin as party boss of Moscow

1986 Feb/Mar: 27th Congress of CPSU; official launch of *perestroika*; 12th Five-Year Plan

Apr: Chernobyl disaster

Nov: Law on Individual Labour Activity

Dec: Law on Joint Enterprises

1987 Jan: Central Committee agrees on limited competitive elections

May: Law on State Enterprises

Jun: First competitive elections in some areas

Oct: Solidarity re-forms in Poland

1988 Jan: Central Committee extends competitive elections to all soviets; Law on State Enterprises comes into effect

Feb: Gorbachev announces withdrawal of Soviet troops from Afghanistan

Apr: Geneva Conference

May: Law on Cooperatives; Grosz replaces Kadar in Hungary; Moscow summit

Jun: 19th Party Conference

Jul: Strikes by miners in Kuzbass region

Dec: Congress of People's Deputies votes for Abalkin Programme of economic refoms; Electoral Law

1989 Mar/Apr: Elections for new Congress of People's Deputies

Apr: Nationalist unrest in Georgia

May: First meeting of new CPD and Supreme Soviet

Nov: GDR opens Berlin Wall

KEY QUESTIONS

- What were Gorbachev's main economic policies, 1985–89?
- How did Gorbachev try to democratise the Soviet political system?
- What were the main consequences of Gorbachev's foreign policy during the 1980s?

Overview

- In 1986, Gorbachev launched his new economic reform policy. This was *perestroika*, or restructuring. However, economic decline, along with political opposition to his reforms, continued. So he also began to implement two political programmes: *glasnost* and *demokratizatsiya*.
- Gorbachev tried to separate party and state bodies, and introduced more democracy into the CPSU. However, his conservative opponents in the party became increasingly concerned that these reforms would lead to the break-up of the Soviet Union.
- Nationalist unrest began to emerge in many of the Soviet republics; by 1989, these developments had become very significant.
- From 1985, Gorbachev applied 'New Thinking' to Soviet foreign policy. He announced the abandonment the Brezhnev Doctrine in Eastern Europe, and on a series of visits to the Eastern European states, encouraged Communist leaders to adopt economic and political reforms.
- The first significant moves in Eastern Europe began in 1987. By 1989, many Eastern European leaders had been replaced by reform Communists.
- The pace of change then rapidly took off. However, in many countries, it soon became clear that revolution rather than reform was what the people wanted. By the end of 1989, all these governments had stepped down (or, in Romania's case, been overthrown) in the face of mass protests.

7.1 What were Gorbachev's main economic policies, 1985–89?

By the mid-1980s, the centralised economy had managed to deliver – for most people – full employment; cheap housing, fuel and transport; and subsidised food prices. Given that only 70 years (many of which had seen political turmoil and wartime destruction) had passed since the Bolshevik Revolution of 1917, this was perhaps no mean achievement.

Yet these successes hid some fundamental underlying problems in the economy. By 1985, according to some estimates, the average annual growth rate of the Soviet gross national product (GNP) was down to 2% a year – not enough to do all that was necessary or expected by consumers. This figure masked a continuous decline in the average annual growth rate: from 5% by 1965, to 3.75% in 1975, and 2.5% in 1980. Yet consumer demands and expectations were rising just when it became increasingly clear that the Soviet economy was showing serious signs of stagnation. These signs included labour shortages and low productivity, along with poor-quality goods in certain areas.

It was estimated that a rate of growth of 4% or 4.5% (or 3% according to some) was the *minimum* needed to ensure the Soviet economy could fulfil its three main objectives: investment to improve industrialisation and modernisation; military spending to maintain 'parity' with the West; and improving living standards for the general population. Any drop below these figures would mean that the USSR would no longer be able to meet these three objectives, which had been more or less achieved following the death of Stalin in 1953.

However, several historians – such as Jacques Sapir – have argued that even these worrying figures understated the real economic decline in the Soviet economy. According to him, the true average percentage of annual growth rates was much lower than the official figures showed. This view was shared by **Abel Aganbegyan**, who became Gorbachev's main economic adviser.

Abel Aganbegyan (b. 1932):

He was a member of the Soviet Academy of Sciences, and had been one of the principal economic advisers at the time of the Kosygin reforms. He played a key role among the young technocrats who favoured radical reform of the Soviet economy. However, because of the failure of the Khrushchev and Kosygin reforms of the 1960s and early 1970s, Aganbegyan and others tended to be cautious about making practical proposals.

In Aganbegyan's view, during the course of the Eleventh Five-Year Plan (1980–85), the annual growth rate of the Soviet economy was zero.

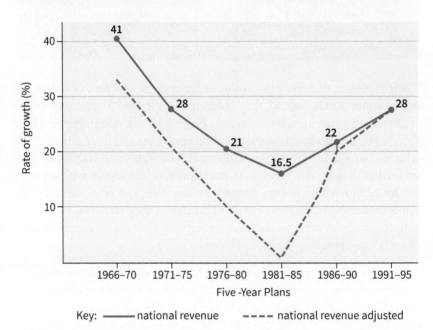

Key: ——— national revenue   – – – – national revenue adjusted

Figure 7.1: Abel Aganbegyan's statistics on the growth of the Soviet Union's national revenue, 1966–85; the adjusted figure takes account of price rises.

Gorbachev's ideas and first steps

Gorbachev and the reformist wing of the Soviet bureaucracy wished to overcome the growing problems of economic stagnation and technological decline by modernising the system. This reformist section of the party enjoyed a certain amount of support. Since the final days of Brezhnev, Aganbegyan and **Tatiana Zaslavskaya** (whose ideas also influenced Gorbachev's reforms) had both been arguing that there was a fundamental problem in the Soviet economy.

> **Tatiana Zaslavskaya (1927–2013):**
>
> She was an economic sociologist working at the Novosibirsk Institute, specialising in agriculture. In 1968, she was elected to the Soviet Academy of Sciences. In 1983, a report she had written on the structural problems of the Soviet economy – especially in agriculture – was leaked. This report became known as the Novosibirsk Report – it emphasised the need to strengthen central planning and the powers of the directors of enterprises, and to reduce the intermediate layers of bureaucracy. However, like earlier suggestions put forward under Khrushchev and Kosygin, most of her reform proposals were limited and vague.

Their view was that this problem went beyond the problem of shortages of consumer goods. Instead, they claimed that the Soviet economy was approaching a state in which it would begin to break down. However, there were also many scientists, technical specialists and intellectuals who also supported Gorbachev's attempts – though some wanted to go further than he did. They were not dissidents but people who were interested in having greater contact with the West, and who wanted opportunities to make more money. This meant they were not so concerned about keeping the basic underlying philosophy and ideology of socialism operating.

Yet, despite all this support, Gorbachev faced enormous resistance to his reforms. The conservative layers of the bureaucracy, especially the *nomenklatura*, did not grasp the depth of the economic and political crisis facing the USSR by the mid-1980s, and so were reluctant to support radical changes which undermined their power and privileges. So, Gorbachev moved some of his supporters into the Politburo in April 1985, including Yegor Ligachev and Nikolai Ryzhkov. Ligachev started to oppose Gorbachev and was sacked in 1987, replaced by Alexander Yakovlev. In July 1985, Gorbachev's rival Grigori Romanov was sacked and, at the end of the year, Viktor Grishin was replaced as head of the Moscow party by **Boris Yeltsin**.

Boris Yeltsin (1931–2007):

Appointed by Gorbachev as the new head of the Moscow party, to replace the corrupt Viktor Grishin (who had links with an 'economic mafia'), Yeltsin was at first a supporter of Gorbachev, but it soon became clear he wished to go further and more quickly than Gorbachev. When Yeltsin launched a strong attack on Ligachev, he was forced to resign from the Central Committee, and was later removed as party boss of Moscow.

ACTIVITY

Carry out some additional research on the following reformers who supported Gorbachev's initiatives after 1985: Abel Aganbegyan, Tatiana Zaslavskaya, Yegor Ligachev, Nikolai Ryzhkov, Alexander Yakovlev and Eduard Shevardnadze. Then place them in order, from 1 (most) to 6 (least), as regards how far each of these reformers wished to go towards:
a democratising the political system
b introducing market mechanisms in the economy.

Gorbachev's emphasis was on modernisation to ensure more rational use of investments – in particular, modernising existing factories and machinery. From 1985 to 1986, he followed an approach known as *uskorenie* ('acceleration' or 'accelerated growth') to achieve increased production by making the existing unreformed system work more efficiently. To achieve a rapid increase in the quantity and quality of consumer goods, he called for greater administrative efficiency from managers responsible for delivering the targets set for the Twelfth Five-Year Plan for 1986–90.

QUESTION

What was meant by *uskorenie*?

Perestroika, 1986–89

In 1986, Gorbachev officially launched his *perestroika* programme of economic reforms. It called for a great reduction in detailed centralised planning, with more self-management at local enterprise levels; and announced the end of subsidised prices.

In February 1986, at the 27th Congress of the CPSU, precise details of Gorbachev's *perestroika* plans were lacking. Nevertheless, he made it clear that administrators who adopted a 'wait and see' approach to implementing the new changes would not keep their jobs. Following this Congress, factory and farm managers were given a greater say in what they produced and whom they employed. Eventually, from 1987 to 1989, self-financing was phased in, with enterprises paying for their operating costs out of their profits.

Figure 7.2: Gorbachev explaining his reforms to factory workers near Moscow in 1987.

In April 1987, Ryzhkov, the new prime minister, reported a *decline* in economic growth, while a drop in world oil and gas prices had led to *increased* foreign debt with the West. The result was a large and increasing budget deficit. In 1985, it had been 3% of national income, but by 1989, it had grown to 14%.

Gorbachev began to make some far-reaching reforms in agriculture and in the service industries. In these areas, *perestroika* became in effect a partial re-privatisation. Gorbachev wanted to stimulate private production by agricultural workers on both *kolkhozy* (cooperative) and *sovkhozy* (state-run) farms. As a result of encouraging greater use of private plots and cooperatives, these sectors soon accounted for 25% of all agricultural production in the Soviet Union. In November 1986, the Law on Individual Labour Activity allowed individuals in the service sector to start private enterprise concerns – such as private taxi services. Further legislation came in May 1987.

In terms of heavy industry and the planning system, Gorbachev's often vague proposals aimed to create a modern and efficient socialist economy – not to restore capitalism. Conservative hardliners and bureaucrats often managed to stop or blunt these attempts. However, despite such opposition, Gorbachev began to implement changes in the central industrial organisation, by attempting to reduce the 60 or more industrial ministries and state committees to six or seven 'super-ministries'.

In December 1986, Gorbachev pushed through the Law on Joint Enterprises. This was meant to get foreign companies to invest in joint schemes in the USSR. But there were significant problems, including both confusion and corruption.

Reducing state control

In 1988, on a visit to Britain, Aganbegyan argued that there needed to be a fundamental shift in Soviet priorities, in relation to three areas: social provision (housing, food supplies, health and education); improved industrial technology and efficiency; and reforms in the way large enterprises were managed. Though state ownership of the main parts of the economy was to be retained, any moves away from strict central control would have political implications, because of how closely the state and the Communist Party were connected. Moreover, it was evident that the removal of price controls would hit Soviet citizens hard.

A small number of contemporary Soviet political commentators began to fear that many of Gorbachev's reforms could lead to the re-emergence of capitalism. In particular, they began to echo the warnings made by Trotsky in the 1930s. They believed the Soviet Union in the 1980s was still a transitional society (halfway between capitalism and socialism); and argued that it could not remain in that situation forever, but would have to either return to private enterprise or forge a stronger drive to socialism (based on a more efficient economy), and then move on to communism.

SOURCE 7.1

It would be truer, therefore, to name the present Soviet regime [1937] in all its contradictoriness, not as a socialist regime, but a preparatory regime transitional from capitalism to socialism... To define the Soviet regime as transitional, or intermediate, means to abandon such finished categories as capitalism (and therewith 'state capitalism') and also socialism. But besides being totally inadequate, in itself, such a definition is capable of producing the mistaken idea that from the present Soviet regime only a transition to socialism is possible. In reality a backslide to capitalism is wholly possible... Without a planned economy the Soviet Union would be thrown back for decades. In that sense, the [Soviet] bureaucracy continues to fulfil a necessary function. But it fulfils it in such a way as to prepare an explosion of the whole system which may completely sweep out the results of the [1917] revolution.

Trotsky, I., 1972, **The Revolution Betrayed: What is the Soviet Union and Where is it Going?***, New York, Pathfinder Press, pp. 47, 254 and 285–6.*

QUESTION

What are the values and limitations of Source 7.1 for historians studying the problems associated with Gorbachev's planned reforms?

ACTIVITY

Several political commentators – starting with Trotsky – and historians have referred to the Soviet Union as a transitional society: halfway between capitalism and socialism. Carry out some additional research on this issue.

Even the reformers were uncertain about what to do, so initially Gorbachev decided that what was needed was more political reform. This meant further reducing the power of the CPSU and the Soviet state industrial ministries in Moscow over the economy.

In January 1988, the Law on State Enterprises came into effect. In total, 60% of state enterprises were shifted from tight central control to control by their managements. This meant, among other things, that they could set their own prices, and negotiate and trade with other firms for the products they needed. In 1989, the remaining 40% of state enterprises were similarly released from central control.

In May 1988, there was a new law on cooperatives. This built on the 1986 Law on Individual Activity, by allowing small and medium-sized private cooperative enterprises to operate not only (as before) in the service sector, but also now in manufacturing and even foreign trade. In addition, workers' cooperatives and even small private businesses could be set up. But, as with the 1986 law, there was both bureaucratic obstruction and lack of funds, as these businesses were not entitled to state subsidies. They also faced tight employment restrictions (in order to avoid exploitation of workers) and heavy taxes, though the latter were later reduced.

QUESTION

Were the two 1988 laws – on state enterprises and on cooperatives – evidence that Gorbachev wanted to transform the Soviet planned economy into a market economy?

In agriculture, from 1988, Gorbachev continued with moves to carry out some kind of privatisation, along the lines of extending the private plots that peasants already had. Peasants and farmers were now allowed to take out long-term leases on land belonging to the collectives – the ownership of land would thus still remain with the state. It was hoped this would lead to increased productivity. Farmers would pay for the leases, and be taxed on the profits. But many collective farm managers were reluctant to lease land out.

SOURCE 7.2

We have got to be self-critical; we must see clearly that despite all the positive effects, the state of affairs in the economy is changing too slowly. Some advances are on hand. But they cannot satisfy us... And those who are holding up the process, who are creating hindrances, have got to be put out of the way. Difficulties arose largely due to the tenacity of managerial stereotypes, to a striving to conserve familiar command methods of economic management, to a resistance of a part of the managerial cadre. Indeed, we are running into undisguised attempts at perverting the essence of the reform, at filling the new managerial forms with the old content...To put it plainly, the reform will not work, will not yield the results we expect...

Extracts from Gorbachev's address to the 19th Party Conference, Moscow, June 1988.

By the end of 1988, in some areas rationing had to be brought in for certain foods. In July 1989, miners in the Kuzbass region went on strike in protest against shortages. Soon, over 500 000 were on strike, along with over 150 000 other workers. They soon moved on to demanding better working conditions – and even a 'free' trade union like Solidarity in Poland. Further significant signs of labour unrest occurred in the next two years.

Although some things did actually improve – for example, advances in medical care reduced infant mortality by 10% in the late 1980s – these successes received little publicity. Instead, most workers just felt that their living conditions had got worse – it seemed that the system that had worked for them before 1985 was now being destroyed by *perestroika*. The unrest and instability led to an economic slowdown and then even decline.

Figure 7.3: Striking miners, Kuzbass, July 1989.

Why were strikes such as the one shown in Figure 7.3 a worrying sign for Gorbachev and those supporting his attempted reforms?

7.2 How did Gorbachev try to democratise the Soviet political system?

Once elected as general-secretary of the CPSU, Gorbachev immediately announced that the posts of president and head of the party would not be combined, as they had been under Brezhnev. Gorbachev used his position as general-secretary of the CPSU to concentrate on party and economic reform. Gorbachev saw his main political policies as necessary pre-conditions for the successful implementation of his economic reforms – in part, by stimulating some public pressure from below to help him overcome his conservative opponents in the bureaucracy. These opponents included Grigori Romanov (a leading Politiburo member) and Viktor Grishin (the party boss of Moscow). However, foreign minister Andrei Gromyko, who was an important member of the Politiburo, backed him. Gorbachev – mindful of how the reforms of Khrushchev and Kosygin had been blocked and 'absorbed' by their opponents in the bureaucratic apparatus – initially focused on strengthening his position, by promoting those who supported him.

Theory of Knowledge

History, language and meaning

When historians write about political change, terms such as 'conservative', 'liberal', 'radical', 'reformer' and 'reactionary' are often used. However, do these words always mean the same, or do their meanings depend to an extent on the historical context: such as the particular time or nature of the society being studied? Are such problems of meaning greater in one-party states such as the USSR?

At first, Gorbachev's reforms were limited and gradual so as not to upset the party apparatus. Then, from 1986 – when it became increasingly clear that *perestroika* would not benefit the mass of Soviet workers in the short term – he began to push for more far-reaching political reforms which he hoped would 'sweeten' the economic 'medicine', which was likely to lead to higher prices and temporary unemployment. This particular approach became more marked with the 19th Party Conference, held in June 1988.

His political reforms were built on the twin policies of *glasnost* and *demokratizatsiya*. Initially, *glasnost* was about greater openness in government policy, but Gorbachev also wanted people to be able to voice criticisms of the CPSU leadership and government policies. In part, this was to allow him and his team of reformers to carry out a political purging and modernisation of all branches of the bureaucracy.

Demokratizatsiya was intended to make the Soviet system more democratic, by reforming election procedures and allowing political clubs to exist outside party control, and to make the state more independent of party control. To a large extent, Gorbachev's political reform programme was linked to his aim of pushing through the economic reforms he believed were essential. He also soon came to realise that the nationalist tensions emerging in some of the Soviet republics would also have to be addressed politically.

At first, several commentators saw Gorbachev as representing a progressive, reformist current within the Soviet elite who, in his attempts to preserve the Soviet Union, would initiate a far-reaching political revolution. However, to do this, he needed to reform the Communist Party so that it became a popular and progressive force. Eventually, Gorbachev and his supporters concluded that economic reform would not succeed without significant democratisation. However, they also realised that shaking up the upper levels of Soviet society by encouraging a partial re-politicisation and mobilisation of the lower levels would be very risky. In particular, they feared events might escape their control – possibly resulting in a Soviet version of the 'Prague Spring' in Czechoslovakia in 1968. In fact, just six years after Gorbachev began his reforms, the Soviet Union collapsed. Thus many historians have ascribed the fall of the Soviet Union to political rather than economic factors.

Gorbachev's early aims

When Gorbachev came to power in March 1985, there was no obvious sign of any political crisis. There was no internal opposition of any significance; the dissident movement had been isolated and defeated by 1980, and many of its leaders were in exile. Nor was there serious discontent within the working class. Despite increasing signs of stagnation, the Soviet economy was still growing (unlike many major Western economies in the early 1980s), although at much slower and smaller rates than in previous decades. However, though not very visible at first, there was a crisis within the political leadership of the CPSU itself: this was the result of fundamental differences over how things should continue. Gorbachev was just one of several younger, reform-minded, modern and sophisticated leaders who had emerged during the Brezhnev era, and who had been helped into positions of power by Andropov.

Because the USSR was a planned economy, politics was of central importance in the planning mechanisms. In particular, because the Soviet Union – unlike Western economies – had virtually full employment, the Soviet system had to devise positive incentives to encourage workers to achieve higher productivity. This involved more than just financial incentives – it also involved respect for the party leadership, and faith in the leaders' ability to keep the economy growing. Unlike in capitalist economies, there was no 'market' or profit motive in the socialised Soviet economy; and the absence of economic and political democracy impeded the development of the full potential of total planning. Realising that *perestroika* would have some negative short-term economic effects, Gorbachev felt he needed to improve the political position for Soviet citizens by giving them more influence over how the country was governed.

By 1985, several sections of the leadership – including the one headed by Gorbachev – were convinced that the old framework was bankrupt, and that therefore change was necessary if a catastrophe were to be averted. Gorbachev and his team of reformers therefore drew up a political strategy involving three elements:

- liberalisation of the media and citizens' right to criticise
- a purging and modernisation of all branches of the political apparatus
- greater freedoms and flexibility for the political institutions which exercised power.

However, if the economy did not improve sufficiently, the political process would be seriously threatened, as workers would lose interest, preferring better living standards to greater democracy. This would leave Gorbachev with no socio-political base outside the ranks of his supporters in the bureaucracy – this was something that many of the hardliners were hoping for.

The determination of Gorbachev and his supporters to challenge the ideological basis of the party and the state ultimately split the superstructure of the Soviet state. As early as February 1986, at the 27th Congress of the CPSU, Gorbachev made his intentions clear, in a speech which included references to Lenin's own struggles, at times, against the leadership of the Russian Bolsheviks. Yet only a few Western observers noted at the time the potential seriousness of the changes Gorbachev was attempting to make.

SOURCE 7.3

These facts [about the conflict over the April Theses] were not written about in the Soviet Union, in the decades that followed Lenin's death in 1924, but they were talked about a great deal. So Gorbachev's listeners in February 1986 would have understood (and many did, especially his opponents) that this particular reference to Lenin implied that what was at stake was nothing less than an assault on the entire tradition of the present CPSU (a tradition, it should be pointed out, that dates back to the Thirties). Gorbachev was calling into question the entire programmatic orientation of the Party... So we note that everything – the entire future of the Soviet state and of the Communist Party – is at stake in the current turn. If it fails, everything could fail... What is being stated is that a crucial section of the Soviet leadership considers that the state and the Party are facing one of the most serious crises in its history. Gorbachev is arguing that the Party is not politically prepared for confronting and overcoming this crisis.

Ali, T., 1988, Revolution from Above: Where is the Soviet Union Going?, *London, Hutchinson, pp. 5–6.*

Glasnost and *demokratizatsiya*

Glasnost

Glasnost was the first of Gorbachev's political reforms, and signified 'openness', and 'publicity' – the latter meaning that the government should explain its policies to the public. Gorbachev's initial aim was not for full freedom of information and expression. What he wanted was a greater willingness to admit problems and failings, and to allow ordinary people to voice concerns and criticisms. For example, if there was more openness about corruption and incompetence, it would make it easier for him to identify and remove corrupt and incompetent individuals from their positions of power. He believed all this would make it easier to achieve reform, and increase popular support for the system.

At first, *glasnost* did not get off to a good start. On 26 April 1986, a nuclear reactor exploded at the Chernobyl nuclear plant in Ukraine. This spread high levels of radiation – but it was not reported at first by the plant to the government; nor then by the media or the Soviet government. Even after it was admitted, the extent of the accident was not fully revealed. There is some evidence that, on 28 April, Gorbachev called for full reporting, but was blocked by the Politburo. This was a clear sign of the unaccountability the Soviet system in 1986.

Figure 7.4: The Chernobyl nuclear power plant three days after the explosion in April 1986.

Despite this setback, *glasnost* continued. Yakovlev, as minister responsible for the media, gave the media greater freedom to publish critical commentaries. Television often showed discussions in which people made criticisms to ministers who answered them. Even Western politicians were interviewed on television. There was not complete freedom, as publishers – rather than the party as previously – were still meant to 'vet' new works. Nonetheless, previously forbidden books (for example, by Pasternak and Nabokov, and by foreign writers) were legalised, while the press and films dealt with contemporary social problems such as alcohol and drug abuse, abortion, suicide and crime. This more open atmosphere led some émigrés to return to the Soviet Union.

Another aspect of *glasnost* was the decision to open the state archives: this gave historians – and, later, the public – access to information in order to re-examine aspects of Soviet history, including the Stalin era. This soon led to an increasingly open debate on past policies, such as forced collectivisation and central planning. Some of this fed into debates about the economic reforms of *perestroika*. Many former 'enemies of the state' were politically rehabilitated. There was also a more liberal attitude to contemporary internal critics and dissidents: for instance, Sakharov was released from internal exile and allowed to travel abroad – even though he made speeches about repression and the Soviet gulags. Though he was widely known and admired in the West, his support within the USSR was more limited.

While intellectuals were pleased by the more relaxed policy, there was a mixed response within the top levels of the party. Hardline conservatives, in particular, objected to the printing of attacks on Stalin – and even on Brezhnev. In part, this was because they feared that such openness and freedom would lead to social and political instability, and so undermine the Soviet system.

Demokratizatsiya

As part of *demokratizatsiya*, his programme to increase democracy in the USSR – and to sideline opponents of his economic reform – Gorbachev made various changes, as described below. Despite opposition from many of the bureaucratic caste (the *nomenklatura*) – who worried that many of their special privileges would be lost – Gorbachev had a reasonable chance of successfully implementing these changes. Though the bureaucracy was powerful, it was also divided, with Gorbachev and his supporters making up one wing of it. In addition, the bureaucracy did not have popular support in the country, so that any mass mobilisations (especially if encouraged from the top) would soon expose its weaknesses.

SOURCE 7.4

[The bureaucracy's] power is exceptional because it is economic, political and cultural at the same time. Yet, paradoxically, each of these elements of power has had its origins in an act of liberation [the November 1917 Revolution]... Because of the workers' inability to maintain the supremacy they held in 1917, each of these acts of liberation turned into its opposite.... But the conflict between the origins of the power and its character, between the liberating uses for which it was intended and the uses to which it has been put, has perpetually generated high political tensions... which have again and again demonstrated the lack of social cohesion in the bureaucracy... They have not eradicated from the popular mind the acts of liberation from which they derive their power; nor have they been able to convince the masses – or even themselves – that they have used the power in a manner compatible with those acts. In other words, [the bureaucracy] has not obtained for itself the sanction of social legitimacy.

Deutscher, I., 1969, **The Unfinished Revolution: Russia 1917–1967,** *Oxford, Oxford University Press , pp. 57–8.*

Historians and the bureaucracy

This diversity of opinion within the Soviet leadership after 1985 came as a surprise to those who had described the USSR as a totalitarian state, but was less unexpected for those who had seen it as a bureaucratic pluralist regime. The orthodox Cold War theories of totalitarianism, as applied to the USSR, came under attack from revisionist historians as early as the beginning of the 1970s. Such historians included R. Daniels, S. Cohen, and J. F. Hough, who challenged the idea of the Soviet Union as a passive, inert society dominated by a united and all-powerful elite. Hough believed that pluralism in the USSR and the USA had a number of common features. Daniels did not go this far, but he described the USSR as having tried – since Khrushchev's time – to form a 'participatory bureaucracy'.

SOURCE 7.5

Gorbachev also granted much power to the regions. This had an effect he had not foreseen as several Soviet republics followed their own national agendas in opposition to the wishes of the 'centre'. Likewise many members of the Russian intelligentsia, freed from fear of retribution, advocated ideas for the future different from his own... Gorbachev... genuinely wanted a more democratic USSR... His political attitudes were formed in the Khrushchev years and he truly believed that the country suffered from a deficit of democratic procedures. He detested the Stalinist legacy and felt disgust at what his country had done to Hungary in 1956 and Czechoslovakia in 1968... His conversations with Western leaders encouraged him to go on thinking that his strategy had credible chances of success.

Service, R., 2007, **Comrades: Communism – A World History,** *London, Macmillan, pp. 451–2.*

ACTIVITY

Carry out some research on the various groupings in the CPSU during the period after 1985. How could it be argued that Gorbachev's chances of success seemed quite good?

Gorbachev's main political reforms, 1986–89

Gorbachev's intention was to reform the Soviet political system in all its main aspects – the role of the party, the electoral and legislative system, and the executive and administrative bodies. His first attempt to change things took place at the 27th Congress of the CPSU, which met during February and March 1986.

27th Congress of the CPSU

At this Congress, Gorbachev announced his intention to push ahead with party reform. To begin with, this Congress gave a larger role to the Central Committee Secretariat; while Alexandra Biryukova was put in charge of light industry, food and consumer services – this was the first time a woman had held such a high-level job since Khrushchev's administration. The Congress also approved a new Party Programme which, for the first time, modified the one drawn up under Khrushchev in 1961. This new programme publicly stated that progress to communism would be difficult, and criticised the years of 'inertness'.

However, although this Congress confirmed Gorbachev as general-secretary, the bureaucracy tried to keep some control over him and his reforms. Yegor Ligachev – a senior member of the Politiburo, who supported economic reform but opposed democracy – was put in charge of party ideology; while it was made clear that Ryzhkov, the prime minister, would be in charge of implementing policy. In addition, the majority of the old Central Committee initially stayed in place.

Despite this, Gorbachev was determined to push ahead with party reform: after making some changes to the leadership bodies, he insisted on the calling of a Party Conference in order to gain approval for a new set of guidelines, which would supersede those made at this Congress. Among other things, he was determined to avoid the fate of Khrushchev who had been overthrown in 1964 to prevent him implementing plans to totally reorganise the leading bodies of the CPSU.

In January 1987, at a Central Committee meeting, Gorbachev announced that the Soviet economy and society were in crisis – and that to solve these problems, the party and state political systems needed to be democratised. To start with, there were to be competitive elections, with a choice of candidates, for members of some local soviets, which would in future be directly elected by the people. There were also to be direct elections to other important soviet posts. In this way, he hoped to weaken party control over the state and to increase the number of supporters of reform.

Gorbachev reiterated his determination to press ahead with his democratisation policies – by then, under heavy criticism from sections of the bureaucracy – at the 18th Congress of Soviet Trade Unions in April 1987. As well as arguing for workplace democracy to ensure *perestroika* was a success, he advised union officials to stop 'dancing cheek to cheek' with economic managers and, instead, urged them to protect the interests of their members.

SOURCE 7.6

We possess [the] necessary political experience and theoretical potential to resolve the tasks facing society. One thing is clear: we should advance without fail along the path of reorganisation. If the reorganisation peters out the consequences will be far more serious for society as a whole and for every Soviet citizen in particular...

I will put it bluntly: those who have doubts about the expediency of further democratisation apparently suffer from one serious drawback which is of great political significance and meaning – they do not believe in our people. They claim that democracy will be used by our people to disorganise society and undermine discipline, to undermine the strength of the system... Democracy is not the opposite of order. It is the order of a greater degree, based not on implicit obedience, mindless execution of instructions, but on fully-fledged, active participation by all the community in all society's affairs... Democracy means self-control by society, confidence in civic maturity and awareness of social duty in Soviet people. Democracy is unity of rights and duties.

Extracts from Gorbachev's speech to the 18th Congress of Soviet Trade Unions, April 1987.

In June 1987, some multi-candidate elections were held in some constituencies. Then, at a meeting of the Central Committee on 27–28 January 1988, further reforms were proposed. These included a choice of candidates for elections to all local and regional soviets, and this was eventually established by a new electoral law in December 1988. There was also agreement on secret ballots for the election of party officials, and on a choice of candidates for the election of trade union delegates within enterprises.

SOURCE 7.7

We are obviously not going to change the system of Soviet power or its fundamental principles... [but] we attach priority to political measures, broad and genuine democratization, the resolute struggle against red tape and violations of the law, and the active involvement of the masses in managing the country's affairs. All of this is directly linked to the main question of any revolution, the question of power... The perestroika drive started on the Communist Party's initiative, and the Party leads it... Hence we must – if we want perestroika to succeed – gear all our work to the political tasks and the methods of the exercise of power...

When the command-economy system of management was propelled into existence, the soviets were somehow pushed back... This lessened the prestige of the soviets. From that moment the development of socialist democracy began to slow down. Signs appeared that the working people were being alienated from their constitutional right to have a direct involvement in the affairs of state.

Gorbachev, M., 1987, **Perestroika***, London, HarperCollins, pp. 54–5 and 111.*

19th Party Conference

On 28 June 1988, the CPSU's 19th Party Conference was held in Moscow – this took place at Gorbachev's insistence, and was the first time since 1941 that a party conference had been held. At this conference, Gorbachev launched radical reforms meant to further reduce party control of the government apparatus. He successfully proposed a new executive in the form of a presidential system, as well as a new all-union legislative body, to be called the Congress of People's Deputies. This would have 2250 seats to be directly elected by the people. Two-thirds of this Congress was to be elected by universal suffrage, and one-third (750 seats) from 'people's organisations' – of which the CPSU (which had 100 seats allocated) was to be only one. Only Congress would be allowed to amend the constitution.

Figure 7.5: Gorbachev at the 19th Party Conference, Moscow, June 1988.

Congress would then elect from among its members deputies to sit in a new permanent 400-member all-union Supreme Soviet – the Congress would have the power to ratify or amend any laws coming from the Supreme Soviet. This new Supreme Soviet would sit twice a year for sessions lasting several months, and would have the power to make laws and to ratify (or not) ministerial appointments – including the president's choice of prime minister. It could also question ministers, and set up commissions and committees. This two-tier structure was also to be set up in the various republics, where elections would take place in March 1990. However, at first, Gorbachev intended to keep the one-party system.

Gorbachev also proposed making all party officials accountable to the law. This was to be achieved by making judges and the legal system independent of the CPSU. There would also be a new constitution that would guarantee civil rights, and separate party and state organisations. This new constitution was finally drafted in June 1989.

SOURCE 7.8

The main direction of the democratisation of our society and state is the restoration in full of the role and authority of Soviets of People's Deputies as sovereign bodies of popular representation. V. I. Lenin discovered in the Soviets, born of the experience of revolutions in Russia, a political form in accordance with the nature of socialism. At once representative bodies of power and mass organisations of the population, the Soviets organically combine the principles of statehood and self-government...

At the same time, we see serious shortcomings in the activity of the Soviets and dissatisfaction with their work among the working people. As a result of well-known deformations, the rights and powers of the representative bodies have been curtailed, and Party committees continue to exercise unwarranted tutelage over them. In many instances, ministries and departments resolve questions of economic and social development behind their backs... It is necessary to change this situation fundamentally and to return real governing powers to the Soviets...

Extracts from the Central Committee Theses, passed by the 19th Party Conference of the CPSU, Moscow, June 1988.

QUESTION

What were the main decisions made in 1988 concerning the electoral and legislative procedures of the Soviet political system? Did these mean Gorbachev was trying to introduce a multi-party system?

The 1989 elections

Elections to the Congress of People's Deputies were held throughout the Soviet Union in March and April 1989. This was the first semi-free election in the Soviet Union since 1921, with some non-CPSU candidates allowed to stand for election – including dissidents such as Andrei Sakharov. Almost 90% of registered voters turned out to vote. About 50 senior regional party secretaries who did not have reserved seats were defeated, as were many local government officials and military candidates. These elections marked a weakening of party control – this was noted in many of the Eastern European states.

The Congress met on 25 May 1989, to elect representatives from its members to sit on the Supreme Soviet of the Soviet Union. Gorbachev was elected chairman – or head of state – of this Supreme Soviet. Nonetheless, the Congress posed problems for Gorbachev: its sessions were televised, airing more criticism and encouraging people to expect ever more rapid reform. In the elections, many Communist Party candidates were defeated. Furthermore, Yeltsin – who, in November 1987, had been sacked as Moscow party leader and had not been nominated for one of the CPSU's reserved seats – was elected in Moscow for one of its territorial seats. He then returned to political prominence and became an increasingly vocal critic of Gorbachev.

Figure 7.6: Sakharov at the podium, addressing the first session of the Congress of People's Deputies, 25 May 1989. He was one of several dissidents elected.

Other deputies also proved to be critics of the government, the Supreme Soviet and the CPSU. In July 1989, Yeltsin and some of these other opponents of Gorbachev, created the Inter-Regional Deputies' Group. Yeltsin then managed to get into the new Supreme Soviet, when one of the elected members stood down to let him have the seat.

These developments encouraged the formation of political clubs outside the Congress – the first of which had emerged as early as 1987. For the first time since the 1921 ban, there were in effect organised factions, if not opposition political parties. While most of these political groupings were either centrist or right-wing, there were also left-wing socialist, green and anarchist groups. These included the Popular Front for Perestroika, the Soviet Communist Party of Bolsheviks; and the Moscow People's Front, whose co-ordinator was **Boris Kargarlitsky**.

> ### Boris Kargarlitsky (b. 1958):
>
> He was a left-wing Marxist dissident in the 1970s and 1980s, editing and contributing to various *samizdat* (underground) journals. In 1982, he was imprisoned for 'anti-Soviet' activities. After his release, he published his first book, *The Thinking Reed: Intellectuals and the Soviet State from 1917 to the Present*. In 1987, he played a leading role in the establishment of the Federation of Socialist Clubs in Moscow. In 1990, he was elected to the Moscow City Soviet, and to the executive of the Socialist Party of Russia. After the collapse of the USSR in 1991, he co-founded the Party of Labour in October 1992, which opposed Yeltsin's neo-liberal programme of market privatisation of state property.

Reforming the CPSU

Gorbachev wanted the party to retain its leading political role; however, he realised it would have to reform itself. He wanted it to be more open, more tolerant of differing viewpoints, and less interfering and autocratic. As early as January 1987, when Gorbachev had first proposed holding a party conference, he had said that he envisaged this as coming up with ways 'to further democratise the life of the Party and society as a whole'; and that he saw it as 'a serious step toward making our Party life more democratic in practice and developing the activity of communists'. Yet he made it clear that there would not be multi-party elections. His reforms within the party, though, included genuine elections, with competing candidates, for party officials and conference delegates.

The 19th Party Conference, in June 1988, decided that the party was to lose its control of economic policy, with the Politburo now dealing only with internal party affairs. However, it retained its leading position in the military and the KGB. The conference also decided that party positions could not be held for more than two consecutive terms of five years. To help separate party and state, it was agreed that nobody could hold both a party and a state position at the top levels – though Gorbachev did not at first apply this restriction to himself.

The problem was that, though his reforms did indeed weaken the party's economic control, the separation of party and state also weakened Gorbachev's position, as being General-Secretary of a weakened CPSU was no longer so important, while the new state structures had yet to establish their authority. In addition, contrary to Gorbachev's expectations, the introduction of greater democracy led many to leave the party. Though those leaving in 1988 and 1989 only numbered just over 150000 – out of a total membership of 20 million – it was a worrying sign that many were confused about the significance of the party after these reforms. In 1990, over 3 million left the CPSU.

Nationalism and the Union

At the same time that Gorbachev was reforming party and state structures, the unrest which had been building in many of the Soviet republics led to calls for greater autonomy and even full independence from 1987 onwards.

This was especially marked in Transcaucasian republics such as Georgia, and Central Asian republics such as Kazakhstan. As in Brezhnev's time, nationalism was also particularly strong in the Baltic republics, where many people disliked the number of Russians who migrated there because of the relatively higher standards of living – and the closeness to Western Europe.

A 'union of equals'?

In fact, much of the unrest in the republics was long-standing in that under Stalin, the Soviet Union had been set up as a much tighter system than the original federation which had existed under Lenin. It had been growing awareness of the nature of the new Soviet constitution, and Stalin's treatment of non-Russian nationalities, which had led Lenin (shortly before he died in 1924) to recommend that Stalin be deprived of his offices, including that of Minister for Nationalities. Lenin and Trotsky feared that Stalin was resurrecting the old Tsarist policy of Russification – trying to make all the states the same, with Russia dominant. Lenin, in fact, had said that 'Great Russian' chauvinism was wrong and that the former parts of Tsarist Russia should be free to secede – Finland had actually been allowed to do so.

However since 1924, the right to secede had only really existed on paper – and the USSR was not a true union of equals. Brezhnev had tried to create a 'Soviet' identity, to replace the various national identities

– for instance, the Russian language was prioritised, and was needed for promotion anywhere in the USSR. Yet, in 1971, only 54% of the 240 million population was Russian. The CPSU in Moscow was dominant, but each republic had its own party structure: provided they were loyal to the centre, they were allowed considerable leeway – which often resulted in corruption.

Growing unrest

Gorbachev had hoped that freer elections would see more reformers come to power – instead, nationalists were elected in many Soviet republics. Many of these were extremely right-wing, and often prejudiced against ethnic minorities – several were also anti-Semitic. Previously, the CPSU had managed to keep such attitudes under control. But in 1988 and 1989, ethnic tensions led to clashes between Azeris and Armenians in the Nagorno-Karabakh region. A speaker in the new Supreme Soviet referred to this crisis as a 'landmine under *perestroika*', while Gorbachev stated that if a solution was not found, it could have 'far-reaching consequences for all of *perestroika*'.

In addition, a popular movement calling for independence also began to emerge in Georgia in 1988. In April 1989, demonstrations turned to violence in which Interior Ministry special troops killed 23 people. In elections in October, the Georgian communists did badly, while a coalition of pro-independence groups won 54% of the vote. Later, in November 1989, the new Supreme Soviet of Georgia declared itself sovereign. However, given the amount of subsidies the republics received from the centre – even if some did not benefit as much as others – this was not likely elsewhere. Many of these republics, in fact, suffered real economic hardship once the Soviet Union had collapsed. Meanwhile, in the Baltic states, nationalist Popular Front movements – such as the Sajudis in Lithuania – were established during 1988, and began to demand greater sovereignty.

Consequently, from September 1989, the CPSU began to consider changes to its nationalities policies – including a looser federation, with more respect for the rights and cultures of the different republics.

SOURCE 7.9

The CPSU had been quite successful in getting people to identify themselves as 'Soviet' as well as identifying themselves with their ethnic group... on the whole, the federation's various republics and national territories seemed to be obedient to Moscow in all essential matters. In fact, the CPSU's management of inter-ethnic relations looked to be so successful, even by the mid-1980s, that there was enormous complacency both among the party's leaders who mostly insisted that the 'nationality question' ... had been largely 'solved'; and among outside observers of the Soviet scene, very few of whom considered that [this]... would ever become an unmanageable problem. This complacency was fatal as it turned out. We can now see that the Soviet federal system generated the potential for enormous conflict, first of all, because its internal structure was extremely complex. And, secondly, because it was in the federal system that the old contradictions and tensions of the Soviet system were most precariously balanced...

As long as the central party-state authorities retained their coercive control over society it proved possible to prevent these contradictions and tensions from becoming unmanageable. However, once the reform process began to undermine the power and authority of central institutions federal relations required much more careful and imaginative management than they actually received.

Walker, R., 1993, **Six Years that Shook the World: Perestroika – The Impossible Project**, *Manchester, Manchester University Press, pp. 166–67.*

7.3 What were the main consequences of Gorbachev's foreign policy during the 1980s?

When Gorbachev came to power in 1985, he adopted a very different foreign policy from that of his predecessors. To a large extent, his foreign policy aims were closely linked to his attempts to solve the Soviet Union's economic problems. His hope was that money and resources could be shifted from aid and armaments and, instead, used to overcome the stagnation of the Soviet economy and modernise Soviet industry. Gorbachev also wanted to obtain large-scale credits from the West in order to finance the rapid modernisation of the Soviet economy. This was something that Stalin had not managed to achieve at the end of the Second World War – hence Gorbachev's desire to end the Second Cold War and bring about a new period of détente.

These changes affected Soviet foreign policy with regards to East–West Cold War relations, Afghanistan and, in particular, to Eastern Europe. However, Gorbachev's foreign policy also impacted both on the Soviet Union, and on Gorbachev himself. Although his foreign policy made him very popular abroad – in both Western and Eastern Europe – the changes which resulted eventually undermined his political position at home.

The Cold War and Afghanistan

Gorbachev and his supporters were keenly aware that the Cold War – with its accompanying arms race – was crippling the Soviet economy, and was thus no longer financially bearable. In addition, in the context of the Second Cold War – which had begun in 1979, following the USSR's military intervention in Afghanistan – some of Gorbachev's advisers believed it vital for Soviet security to reach a reconciliation with the US. Alexander Yakovlev, for instance, was deeply concerned about the possible implications of the close connections (which Eisenhower had called the 'Military-Industrial Complex') between the government, the military and the largest corporations in the US.

Yakovlev saw these links as particularly close in US President Reagan's Republican administration, and feared US armaments companies might even push the US government into military interventions against the Soviet Union.

Afghanistan

Gorbachev was thus keen to end the Second Cold War and to end the trade and technological blockade the US had imposed since the Soviet intervention in Afghanistan. Consequently, he soon made it clear that the Soviet Union would end its costly intervention in Afghanistan. From mid-1986, the Soviet Union gradually withdrew troops and in April 1988, at the Geneva Conference, Gorbachev and Reagan agreed to end all foreign involvement in the Afghan civil war. By February 1989, after ten years of fighting, all Soviet troops had been withdrawn.

The arms race

Gorbachev also offered deep armaments cuts to the US. These were largely intended to ease the burden of military attempts to keep up with the much wealthier US. These offers led to a series of summit meetings with US president Reagan in November 1985, and in October 1986. Though the latter meeting resulted in no firm agreements, it laid the groundwork for the future. Gorbachev's visit to Washington in December 1987 led to the Intermediate Nuclear Forces (INF) Treaty which eliminated intermediate-range nuclear weapons from Europe. A further summit in Moscow in May 1988 saw the start of a new Strategic Arms Limitation Treaty (START). Although this was not finalised until 1991, both sides agreed to reduce their respective nuclear stockpiles: the USSR by 25%, the US by 15%. Overall, though, this was less successful than Gorbachev had hoped, as the US refused to abandon its 'Star Wars' (Strategic Defensive Initiative – SDI) project.

'New Thinking' and Eastern Europe

Ever since the start of the Cold War, the communist-ruled states of Eastern Europe had been politically, economically and militarily bound to the USSR, through the military alliance of the Warsaw Pact. This Soviet-led military alliance – initially created to counter the West's NATO military alliance which had been set up in 1949 – had dominated Eastern Europe since its formation in 1955. When Gorbachev came to power in 1985, he was aware that developments within the countries of Eastern Europe, as in the USSR itself, required some changes in policy.

In 1985, six Eastern European countries were allied with the USSR in the Warsaw Pact: the GDR, Hungary, Poland, Czechoslovakia, Bulgaria and Romania. However, the maintenance of this post-Second World War 'buffer zone' of satellite states involved an ever-growing cost for the Soviet Union in terms of aid and subsidies. Gorbachev believed that a reformed and more prosperous Eastern Europe, with links to Western Europe, would benefit the Soviet Union economically. He also hoped that money and resources shifted from aid to these satellite states could be invested in the Soviet Union's civilian economy. Moreover, like the USSR, these communist regimes were now facing economic and political crises. Gorbachev was aware that some reforms in these countries were vital if the communist regimes were to hold on to power. In addition, it would have been difficult to push through his political reforms in the Soviet Union, yet not allow the satellite states to do the same.

Gorbachev also seemed to have been motivated by a genuine commitment to end Soviet interference and to make Europe a safer place for all, both east and west. This 'Common European Home' policy was first mentioned by him in February 1986, and was repeated in April 1987. It seemed to be about to end the Second Cold War, and won him many supporters in Western Europe among those increasingly anxious about the number of US nuclear weapons deployed in their countries. In fact, this led to a period of worldwide 'Gorby mania' – though usually expressed by the citizens of various countries, rather than by some Western leaders. The British prime minister, Thatcher, for instance, initially retained her Cold War mentality, accusing Gorbachev of trying to extend communism worldwide.

ACTIVITY

Carry out some additional research on why Gorbachev was so popular in many Western European states. Do you think he deserved this popularity?

Although he negotiated an extension of the Warsaw Pact Treaty in 1985, it was soon clear that Gorbachev was genuinely committed to giving the countries of Eastern Europe the freedom to carry out reforms without fear of any Soviet or Warsaw Pact intervention. In March 1985 Gorbachev announced the abandonment of the Brezhnev Doctrine of November 1968. He made it clear that Soviet troops would no longer be sent into any Eastern European state, either to defend an existing regime or to crush reform communists or mass popular movements. He also made it clear that each member state of the Warsaw Pact had the right to make changes within its own country 'without outside interference'.

QUESTION

Why was the abandonment of the Brezhnev Doctrine seen as a really radical change in Soviet foreign policy? Why might some Soviet and Eastern European leaders have opposed this?

From 1985 Gorbachev gradually reduced Soviet control and economic assistance, and began encouraging the Eastern European states to follow their own 'paths to socialism' by beginning liberalisation reforms. In private discussions, he increasingly made it clear that Eastern European governments could no longer rely on Soviet economic or military help to get them out of any crisis. He also made public speeches which effectively appealed directly to the citizens of the Eastern European states.

In 1987, Gorbachev launched a serious discussion within the Warsaw Pact alliance on how to reduce Soviet troop levels in the countries of Eastern Europe. Significant withdrawals of Soviet troops from Eastern Europe began in 1989 (these were accelerated in 1990 and 1991). By giving up Soviet influence in Eastern Europe, Gorbachev was effectively marking the end of any Soviet aspirations towards being a global superpower like the US, as the USSR had no significant allies outside Eastern Europe.

QUESTION

How did Gorbachev's 'New Thinking' on Soviet foreign policy differ from Brezhnev's approach?

Significance: Draw up a table listing the main reasons for Gorbachev's new approach to relations with Eastern Europe, and giving the main facts in brief. Then try to place them in order of importance. Finally, write a short paragraph to justify the reasons for your decisions.

The 'velvet revolutions'

In many ways, Gorbachev's actions after 1985 undermined the authority and position of Eastern Europe's hardline rulers, and prepared the way for the events of 1988–89, which soon resulted in the downfall of the communist regimes in all the Eastern European states. These Eastern European regimes might have sometimes resented Soviet interference, but they had also relied on the moral and military support of the USSR to ensure their survival in the face of any serious internal oppositions. Hence, many of these leaders were unsettled by Gorbachev's reformist policies of *perestroika*, *glasnost* and *demokratizatsiya*.

Although the ruling communists in Hungary and Poland had welcomed the new opportunities for reform, those of the GDR, Bulgaria, Romania and Czechoslovakia had tried hard at first to limit news of Gorbachev's reforms in the Soviet Union. Nonetheless, dissidents in those states began to speak out and become organised. The more Gorbachev spoke of *glasnost* and democracy, the more these dissidents were encouraged to act.

As the protests and opposition movements grew and spread in these Eastern European countries from 1988, the rulers of these states (with the exception of the ruler of Romania) decided against using the force of the state to stop them. Instead, they stood down in the face of these mass popular revolts. By the end of 1989, the communist regimes in all the Eastern European states had been overturned in peaceful and bloodless political revolutions, which the Soviet Union did nothing to prevent. In addition, in November 1989, the Berlin Wall – a visible symbol of the Cold War since its construction in 1961 – was opened up, and talks for German reunification began almost immediately.

Because of the peaceful nature of these revolutions, they were known as the 'velvet revolutions', which was the description initially given to the changes in Czechoslovakia. However, these political revolutions –

much to the dismay of many of the dissidents – soon turned into social revolutions, which made more fundamental changes, including the restoration of an unregulated neo-liberal form of capitalism.

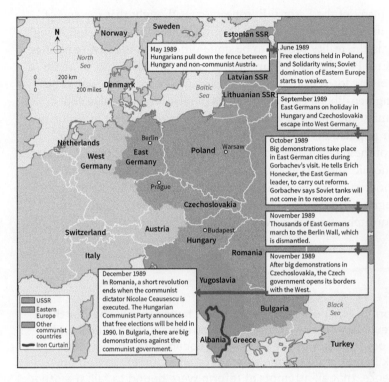

Figure 7.7: Changes and protests that took place in Eastern Europe in 1989.

Although the events in Eastern Europe of 1988 and 1989 took many people by surprise, changes had been taking place in many of the East European states since the start of the 1980s. These countries faced similar problems to those of the USSR: economic stagnation, indebtedness and the lack of consumer goods, as well as dissidence from those who resented Soviet interference in their country's affairs and challenged the bureaucratic rule of their governments. Nonetheless, when Gorbachev had come to power in 1985, most regimes in the Soviet bloc had seemed reasonably secure and stable. Many of Gorbachev's critics blamed the collapse of these countries' governments, in only four years, on his policies.

Some historians, such as M. McGwire, argue that Gorbachev and his supporters deliberately began policies which they knew would end in the collapse of communist rule in Eastern Europe. However, this is contested by others – R. Service, for example, argues that it was not his intention to bring about the collapse of these communist regimes.

While many of the Eastern European states thought that the end of communist rule would usher in a period of freedom and better living standards, the reality proved to be quite different in the first years after 1989. Eric Hobsbawm, a Marxist historian, warned that, as a condition for receiving loans from the West, such new governments would be applying neo-liberal capitalist policies in relatively underdeveloped economies, and that this would cause great hardship for the majority of their populations as both jobs and social services would be cut. Many of these newly liberated states would experience the full effects of economic 'shock therapy'. He also pointed out that, while moves to democracy were welcome, it was by no means certain that the new regimes would prove to be tolerant or even very democratic. Unfortunately, some of his warnings have proved to be quite well placed.

DISCUSSION POINT

Historians and political commentators have argued whether there was ever any chance of successfully reforming the political and economic systems of the Eastern European states in the 1980s. Work in two groups – one to produce an argument, based on evidence, that all attempts at reform were bound to fail; the other to argue that, with different approaches, it would have been possible to transform the states into thriving democracies.

Though Gorbachev hoped that the new governments would be reform communists or socialists, who would establish democratic socialism in Eastern Europe, the only certainty by late 1989 was that the old-style communist governments had gone. More significantly, the Soviet Union had allowed the disappearance of a security belt which had been the foundation and main aim of its foreign policy since 1945, and which had played a large part in the start of the Cold War. This loss of a security belt – along with the reductions in nuclear weaponry, which left the US advantages intact – did much to strengthen the resolve of those Soviet leaders opposed to Gorbachev's economic and political reforms within the Soviet Union.

Figure 7.8: In this cartoon, by American artist Jeff Koterba, the Soviet Union is portrayed as a dinosaur, with the Berlin Wall as its tail.

The cartoon in Figure 7.8 – like most good cartoons – has multiple meanings. What is its message concerning (a) the Soviet Union itself, and (b) the implications for the countries of Eastern Europe? How are these messages put across?

In particular, Gorbachev's foreign policy played an important part in an unsuccessful coup against him in August 1991. This was because to many leaders and people in the Soviet Union, his ending of the Soviet Union's security belt weakened the USSR, and seemed as big a threat as the growing movements for independence in the Soviet republics. Thus the crises and events in the 'communist' satellite states of Eastern Europe in 1988 and 1989 proved to be significant factors in the eventual collapse of the Soviet Union itself at the end of 1991.

Consequences: What were the main effects of Gorbachev's Eastern European policies on events in the USSR?

Paper 3 exam practice

Question

Evaluate the reasons for Gorbachev's abandonment of the 'Brezhnev Doctrine' in relation to the satellite states of Eastern Europe in the period 1985–89. **[15 marks]**

Skill

Avoiding a narrative-based answer

Examiner's tips

Even once you have read the question carefully (and so avoided the temptation of giving irrelevant material), produced your plan and written your introductory paragraph, it is still possible to go wrong.

By 'writing a narrative answer', history examiners mean providing supporting knowledge which is relevant (and may well be very precise and accurate) *but* which is not clearly linked to the question. Instead of answering the question, it merely *describes* what happened.

The main body of your essay and argument needs to be **analytical**. It must not simply be an 'answer' in which you just 'tell the story'. Your essay must **address the demands/key words of the question** – ideally, this should be done consistently throughout your essay, by linking each paragraph to the previous one, in order to produce a clear 'joined up' answer.

You are especially likely to lapse into narrative when answering your final question – and even more so if you are getting short of time. The 'error' here is that, despite all your good work at the start of the exam, you will lose sight of the question, and just produce an account, as opposed to an analysis. So, even if you are short of time, try to write several analytical paragraphs.

Note that such a question, which asks you to evaluate the different reasons why something was done, expects you to come to judgements about the relative significance of those various reasons. Very often, such a question gives you the opportunity to refer to different historians' views (see the skill section in Chapter 8).

A good way of avoiding a narrative approach is to continually refer back to the question and even to mention it now and again in your answer. That should help you to produce an answer which is focused on the specific aspects of the question – rather than just giving information about the broad topic or period.

For this question, you will need to:

- give brief explanations/definitions of the 'Brezhnev Doctrine' and the 'satellite states'
- supply a brief explanation of the historical context (the reasons for Stalin's decision to establish a 'buffer zone' after 1945; problems with some of the Eastern European states in the 1950s and 1960s)
- outline the problems faced by Gorbachev in 1985, especially in relation to Eastern Europe
- provide a consistently analytical examination of the reasons for the changes in Soviet foreign policy relating to Eastern Europe brought about by Gorbachev in the period 1985–89.

Common mistakes

Every year, even candidates who have clearly revised well, and therefore have a good knowledge of the topic and of any historical debate surrounding it, still end up producing a mainly narrative-based or descriptive answer. Very often, this is the result of not having drawn up a proper plan.

The extracts of the student's answer below show an approach which essentially just describes Gorbachev's foreign policy towards Eastern Europe, without any analysis or evaluation of the different reasons for his decisions.

Sample paragraphs of narrative-based approach

Note: This example shows what examiners mean by a narrative answer – it is something you should *not* copy!

The Brezhnev Doctrine had been announced by Brezhnev in November 1968, following the Warsaw Pact invasion of Czechoslovakia in August of that year. This Doctrine stated that the USSR and members of the Warsaw Pact had the right to intervene in the affairs of any member state of the Warsaw Pact if developments there threatened the security of the Soviet Union or other member states. Essentially, it meant the Soviet Union would intervene militarily, if it judged it necessary, to prop up the existing communist governments in Eastern Europe.

In 1985, Gorbachev became General-Secretary of the CPSU. As well as trying to reform the Soviet economic and political system, he also tried to reduce the USSR's foreign policy commitments which were costing the Soviet Union large sums of money which could have been spent on modernising Soviet industry and technology. For instance, the economic assistance and subsidies given to allies were reduced.

In March 1985, Gorbachev first publicly renounced the Brezhnev Doctrine – making it clear that the USSR would no longer interfere in the affairs of the satellite countries of Eastern Europe. In particular, he made it clear, in several statements, that the Soviet Union would no longer intervene militarily to prop up unpopular regimes or to quash reforming governments, as had happened in Hungary in 1956 and in Czechoslovakia in 1968. He also publicly encouraged the leaders of the East European satellites to introduce reforms similar to those he was trying to implement in the USSR; and said that the peoples of the Warsaw Pact countries should be able to choose their political and economic systems for themselves.

In February 1986, Gorbachev made the first mention of his plans for 'our common European home'. There had already been considerable political unrest in Poland since 1980. Then, from March 1986, there were signs of growing protest and unrest in Hungary.....

[There then follows several more paragraphs with precise and accurate own knowledge about events in Eastern Europe between 1986 and 1989, and Gorbachev's foreign policy reactions to them. However, these just describe his policies and his reactions to developments – without *any* evaluation or analysis of the various reasons for them.]

Activity

In this chapter, the focus is on *avoiding* writing narrative-based answers. So, using the information from this chapter, and any other sources of information available to you, try to answer **one** of the following Practice Paper 3 questions in a way which avoids simply describing what happened. Remember to refer to the simplified Paper 3 mark scheme in Chapter 10.

Paper 3 practice questions

1 Examine the success of Gorbachev's attempts to reform the Soviet economy in the period 1985-89.

2 Discuss the effects of Gorbachev's attempts to democratise the Soviet Union's political system between 1985 and 1989.

3 Evaluate the reasons for the growing significance of nationalism in the Soviet Union in the period 1985–89.

4 Compare and contrast the reactions to Gorbachev's foreign policy in the period 1985-89 in any two Eastern European states.

5 'By 1985, the collapse of communism in Eastern Europe was inevitable.' To what extent do you agree with this statement?

8

The Collapse of the Soviet Union, 1990–91

Introduction

As we have seen in the previous chapter, Gorbachev began as a communist reformer – not someone who wanted to replace socialism and instead create a capitalist state. Yet by 1991, after only six years in power, Gorbachev seemed to have acted as the 'grave digger' of the system he was trying to reform.

TIMELINE

1990 Feb: Article 6 of the constitution amended

Mar: Contested elections in all republics; Gorbachev becomes executive President; Lithuania votes to secede; free elections in Hungary see Communists outvoted; Warsaw Pact dissolved (the West does not dissolve NATO)

May: Russian Supreme Soviet votes for sovereignty

Jun: Free elections in Czechoslovakia

Jun–Jul: 28th Congress of CPSU

Aug: Shatalin Plan presented

Sept: Shatalin Plan rejected

Oct: German reunification

Nov: Draft of new Union Treaty

1991 Jan: Russian Supreme Soviet legalises ownership of private property

Mar: Referendum on new Union Treaty

Jun: Yeltsin elected president of Russia

Aug: Attempted coup; Gorbachev resigns as General-Secretary

Dec: Formation of CIS; Gorbachev resigns as Soviet president; collapse of USSR

KEY QUESTIONS

- What happened with Gorbachev's economic policies, 1990–91?
- What happened with Gorbachev's attempts to democratise the Soviet political system?
- Why did the Soviet Union collapse in 1991?

Overview

- After 1989, nationalist unrest in many of the Soviet republics became increasingly significant. In 1990, following freely contested elections in all Soviet republics, Lithuania became the first republic to vote to secede.
- Attempts to draw up a new Union Treaty for a looser federation of republics met with little success.
- However, a referendum in nine republics in March 1991 saw almost 75% vote in favour of keeping some federation.
- In June 1991, Yeltsin became president of Russia and began negotiations with the leaders of other republics.
- During 1990 and 1991, the Soviet Union's economic and political crises deepened, with individual republics such as Russia (led by Yeltsin) increasingly taking their own economic decisions.
- In August 1991, conservative hardliners attempted a coup against Gorbachev, but this quickly collapsed. Gorbachev then resigned as general-secretary.
- Russia, Belorussia and Ukraine then formed the Commonwealth of Independent States (CIS), and Gorbachev resigned as president of the Soviet Union in December 1991. This marked the end of the USSR.

Figure 8.1: Unrest in Lithuania, 1990.

8.1 What happened with Gorbachev's economic policies, 1990–91?

By the end of 1989, it was possible to detect three main economic strategies within the ranks of Soviet leaders and reformers:

1 a 'conservative' approach, that is, one that aimed to keep things as they had been, with strong central planning and no concessions to capitalism

2 a strategy put forward by those radical socialists who wanted to preserve a mix, so, a system that would keep state ownership, but under workers' self-management; people would be able to lease state property but not own it

3 a strategy that aimed to introduce market-based reforms (and even full capitalism); confusingly its proponents were often called 'radicals' too.

According to Marcel Drach, professor of economics at Paris Dauphine University, there had been three possible 'models' for the reform of the Soviet economy in the 1980s. These were:

• a decentralised model, as in Hungary
• a dual model (a rationalised state sector), as in East Germany
• and a 'coercive' model, as in Czechoslovakia.

He believed that Gorbachev, after trying the second model, had eventually decided on the Hungarian approach. This would give businesses greater autonomy and also make them self-financing.

Problems of *perestroika*, 1990–91

However, by 1990, many observers (both supporters and opponents), had begun to feel that Gorbachev had no real plan in mind. Instead, they thought he just swung pragmatically from one option to another, adjusting his position according to circumstances.

As the implications of Gorbachev's economic reforms became clearer, the reforms increasingly ran into a series of obstacles which raised serious doubts as to whether these changes could be successfully implemented.

Unemployment and living standards

The most obvious of these obstacles was perhaps the impact on living standards that resulted from the changes. Gorbachev's attempts at reform were limited by the great difficulty in introducing changes which would lead to unemployment. At the time he was in power, unemployment was a huge problem in the seven most important states in the West – standing at about 20 million. Opinion polls in countries such as Britain regularly showed that most people regarded unemployment as a serious problem. Yet no major party, whether on the right or the left, ever promised a statutory right to work. Mainly, this is because such a legal right to employment is unrealistic under capitalism: it is incompatible with the idea of a 'free' market. Such socio-economic power factors place limits on what politicians can achieve in any system.

Though the great bulk of the Soviet economy was under public ownership in the USSR, its political leaders did not have the ability to do exactly what they wanted. While Gorbachev and his supporters wanted to speed up economic growth, improve economic efficiency, and modernise the country on every level, there were enormous socio-structural constraints. For example, creating unemployment and ending state subsidisation of prices for food, housing, gas, electricity and transport were likely to cause mass unrest (as in Hungary in 1956, Czechoslovakia in 1968 and Poland in 1981). Just as any attempt to undermine the basis of economic security of private capitalists would risk causing an economic crisis in the West, so any attempt to remove the economic security of workers in the USSR risked provoking a serious political crisis.

Gorbachev's 'market' elements *did* lead to increased prices and unemployment – both a real shock to most Soviet citizens. By 1990, though wages for some had increased, 25% of citizens were below the poverty line, and shortages often increased.

Significant signs of labour unrest (for example by railway workers) thus occurred in the final two years of the USSR's existence. Although some things did actually improve, these received little publicity. Instead, most workers just felt that their living conditions had worsened. Old people, too, were increasingly affected by rising prices which ate up much of their pensions – while the previously subsidised services now cost more.

So the earliest impact of many of Gorbachev's economic reforms was austerity for many workers, who saw their living standards decline. Not surprisingly, this did not encourage them to make greater efforts for increased productivity. For many ordinary people, it seemed that the system that had worked for them before 1985 was now being destroyed by *perestroika*. Such unrest and instability led to an economic slowdown and then decline. In 1990 there was a 4% fall in production, and in 1991 a fall of 15%.

SOURCE 8.1

	1986–91	1986	1987	1988	1989	1990	1991
National income produced	4.2	2.3	1.6	4.4	2.4	–4.0	–15.0
Industrial output	4.6	4.4	3.8	3.9	1.7	–1.2	–7.8
Agricultural output	2.7	5.3	–0.6	1.7	1.3	–2.3	–7.0

Soviet economic growth, 1986-91 (official data, %)

White, S., 1993, **After Gorbachev**, *Cambridge, Cambridge University Press, p. 121.*

This unhappiness about the way things were going was felt not just by ordinary people, but also by some intellectuals. One example was Gavril Popov, a professor of management at Moscow University, who argued against bureaucratic top-down initiatives, in favour of political reform which would allow those 'below' to push for economic reform. He was one of many who saw the political problems as being more crucial to reform than the economic issues. All this was the exact opposite of what Gorbachev had wanted, and the prospect of working-class discontent was increasingly used by Gorbachev's conservative opponents to oppose or frustrate his reforms.

Other factors

Political factors also contributed to the growing economic collapse. For example, the CPSU lost much of its power to force enterprises to implement the reforms which Gorbachev had decided on. This enabled managers to ignore those reforms that they didn't like; or to wait for state help where they found the new rules difficult. These political factors will be discussed in the next section. The main point is that Gorbachev's political reforms had reduced and undermined party and state control of the economy, so that it was increasingly difficult for Gorbachev's government to take strong or meaningful action to solve the problems.

Another factor identified by many historians was Gorbachev's indecision at times, and the fact that he and his team were not primarily trained economists. However, the banking crisis that took place in the capitalist world in 2008 suggests that they might not have done any better if they had been!

Figure 8.2: Gorbachev as an indecisive 'Humpty Dumpty', sitting on a crumbling Soviet wall.

QUESTION

What is the message of the cartoon in Figure 8.2?

Events in the various Soviet republics caused additional problems.
Many of the countries began to introduce customs barriers to protect
their own economies. This disrupted trade and led to unemployment
and worker unrest – which only added to the problems. Enterprises
also continued to lie about production figures – and even switched to
other goods which they thought might be more profitable. Thus the
government had no full picture of what was happening in the economy.
Furthermore the collapse of the Eastern European regimes during 1988
and 1989 meant the loss of the former Comecon trading partners. On
top of all this was the rising cost of trying to maintain some kind of
military parity with the US which was deliberately 'upping the game' at
a time when the Soviet economy could least afford it. By 1991, the all-
union government's revenue was only 15% of what it had planned for.

Socialism or a market economy?

By 1990, it was clear that the Soviet economy was experiencing a
major crisis. In December 1989, the Congress of People's Deputies had
voted for the Abalkin Programme. This report had been drawn up by a
committee – headed by Leonid Abalkin – which Gorbachev had set up.
The programme called for the gradual privatisation of state property to
create a market economy, with the state only retaining control of raw
materials, fuel and defence. But Gorbachev and his government did not
want to go down this route.

Instead, in May 1990, Ryzhkov presented a new economic plan to
the Supreme Soviet, calling for transition to a state-regulated 'market'
economy, in three stages, to be achieved by 1995. Central planning
would be gradually reduced – the plan also claimed that the falling
living standards would be reversed by 1993.

One group of reformers, including Boris Yeltsin, began to press for an
end to this halfway house by pushing ahead with the introduction of a
total market economy. With Gorbachev's approval, a team of economists
was set up under Stanislav Shatalin. In August 1990, the Shatalin Plan
recommended moving to a full market economy in 500 days and giving
most economic powers to the Soviet republics. However, the problem

was that to carry out any meaningful reforms a strong state with popular support was needed – and this did not exist. All this was a step too far for Gorbachev and Ryzhkov, and the Shatalin Plan was rejected on 1 September 1990.

Instead, Gorbachev received the approval of the Supreme Soviet for a compromise package the following month. This proposed four main steps:

1   the commercialisation of state enterprises

2   relaxation of state price controls (though with social security measures to help those workers 'adversely affected' – made unemployed)

3   changes to the housing market

4   the rouble to be fully convertible with foreign currencies (to be able to trade with other countries).

Even this compromise caused much dissension and argument. More importantly, as will be seen in the next section, the political situation was becoming increasingly difficult. So, even where it was accepted that more far-reaching reforms were necessary, there was the problem of actually being able to deliver them.

QUESTION

Why was the Shatalin Plan so radical, and why did Gorbachev reject it? What was the main difference between the Shatalin Plan and Gorbachev's proposed 'commercialisation' of state enterprises?

Two significant events occurred in January 1991. Firstly, as some price controls were removed, inflation became a growing problem, and the rouble collapsed. All high-denomination banknotes were then withdrawn at short notice, so that the government could issue new ones, in an attempt to stop inflation. However, this gave people little time to exchange their notes for lower-value ones. Many citizens kept all their money in cash – consequently, many lost their savings.

Also in January 1991, the Supreme Soviet of the Russian Federation (the biggest and wealthiest of the 15 republics that made up the USSR) passed a law legalising private property ownership. This in practice ended the legal basis of a planned and socially owned economy, since private enterprises could now be set up. The Russian Federation then began to take over all the oil, mining and gas enterprises in the republic, which technically belonged to the whole of the Soviet Union. This seriously undermined the Soviet economy as a whole, and was a major contributory factor in the collapse of the Soviet Union less than 12 months later.

Historians and Gorbachev's chances of success

For many Russians, it seemed that *perestroika* had pushed a reasonably functioning economy to the point of crisis and even collapse. Some historians have argued that Gorbachev's plans to have a modern and efficient economy, operating many market aspects, yet still under party-state control, was impossible. For instance, D. Volkogonov has argued that Gorbachev was attempting to change a system which could not be changed – instead of *perestroika* (restructuring), *novostroika* (a new structure) was needed.

Theory of Knowledge

History and the role of individuals

Many historians focus on the significance of 'great persons' in history – but the Russian writer Leo Tolstoy (1828–1910) saw Napoleon as essentially the instrument of underlying historical currents and trends, rather than being in control of events. How far does this view help us understand whether Gorbachev had any realistic chance of reforming the Soviet Union's economy?

KEY CONCEPTS ACTIVITY

Significance: Carry out some additional research on the problems Gorbachev faced in trying to implement his economic reforms. Then write a short paragraph to explain which one you think was most important.

8

8.2 What happened with Gorbachev's attempts to democratise the Soviet political system?

As had been agreed in 1988, elections to create two-tier systems, similar to those for the Congress of People's Deputies which had been elected in March–April 1989, took place in the republics in March 1990. Several political groups were formed in advance of the elections: the Democratic Russia Election Bloc, which was formed in January 1990, defeated several communist candidates. Other political groups included the Democratic Party (wanting a decentralised voluntary union of republics), the Democratic Reform Movement (set up in 1991 by Shevardnadze and Yakovlev, and other Gorbachev supporters), and more right-wing groups such as the Christian Democrats and the Liberal Democratic Party (led by Vladimir Zhirinovsky, an extreme Russian nationalist). Several of these right-wing groups were anti-Semitic.

In Russia, meanwhile, the success of the Democratic Russia Election Bloc – which, among other things, campaigned against one-party rule – played a significant part in the decision, in February 1990, of the Soviet parliament to amend Article 6 of the Soviet Constitution by removing the reference to the Communist Party of the Soviet Union (CPSU) as 'the leading and guiding force' of Soviet society. By mid-1991, however, only two parties had registered with the Ministry of Justice, which by then was the requirement – one of these was the CPSU. Most of the small groups – there were over 500 such 'parties' at republican level – lacked the resources to be effective in elections.

QUESTION
Why were hardline conservative communists opposed to the decision to amend Article 6 of the Soviet Constitution?

Executive presidency

As the conflicts between the Congress of People's Deputies, the USSR Supreme Soviet and the USSR Council of Ministers continued, Gorbachev began to implement another of his plans – the creation of an executive presidency. This was established in March 1990. The hope was that a strong executive presidency would be able to push through the reforms and keep the USSR together. The president would have the power to veto legislation (though the Supreme Soviet could overrule this) and to appoint the prime minister and other top government posts (though again these had to be confirmed by the Supreme Soviet). The president would also have the power to dismiss the government and dissolve the Supreme Soviet, and to get the Congress to elect a new Soviet. He could also declare a state of emergency.

Though, initially, it was proposed that the president should be elected by the whole country, in the end it was decided to have this done by the Congress. On 15 March 1990, Gorbachev was elected – unopposed – as the first executive President of the Soviet Union. He also kept his post as General-Secretary of the CPSU.

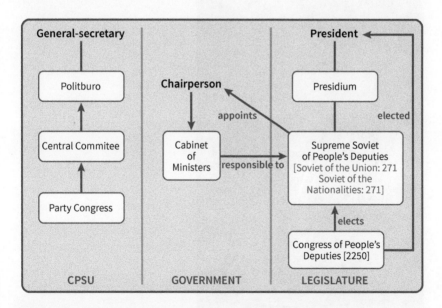

Figure 8.3: Gorbachev's political structure 1989–91. Gorbachev was elected by the Congress of People's Deputies in 1990 but it was planned that, in future, the president would be directly elected by the people. Adapted from Lane, D. 1992. *Soviet Society Under Perestroika*, London. Routledge. pp. 58–61.

As part of the new presidency, there were also other bodies – a Council of the Federation made up of heads of the Republics to oversee inter-Republican relations; and a Presidential Council responsible for foreign policy. In September 1990, the Council of Ministers became a Cabinet, responsible to the president but headed by a prime minister. There was also a president-appointed Security Council responsible for defence and internal security. Gorbachev then abolished the Presidential Council, and used the Council of the Federation to make most of the important state decisions.

Though Gorbachev had great power on paper – even more than Stalin had had – in practice, his position was much weaker. While there is no evidence that most Soviet citizens – as opposed to a few prominent dissidents – were demanding greater democracy before 1985, once Gorbachev began his reforms there were soon calls for a real multi-party system. The longer the reforms continued, the more confident people became in voicing their criticisms.

Figure 8.4: Gorbachev as Soviet president, 1991.

Reforming the CPSU

Mainly as a result of lack of direction, or incomplete democratisation, the CPSU continued to lose members – in 1990, over 3 million members left. This was a worrying trend, considering that it had always played such a leading role in the Soviet Union. After 1989, Gorbachev continued with his attempts to reform the party.

In August 1991, a new programme for the CPSU was drafted, mainly by Gorbachev – this made virtually no mention of communism, and instead talked more about socialism. In many ways it was like a social democratic programme rather than one for communists. This too would play a part in the attempted coup against Gorbachev later that month. As had already become clear, the separation of party and state had weakened Gorbachev's position, as he was now General-Secretary of a weakened CPSU, while the new state structures had yet to establish their authority. In a way, Gorbachev was cutting the ground away from under his own feet.

Nationalism and the Union, 1990–91

By the end of 1989, when Gorbachev had given up the Soviet Union's influence over the Eastern European states, it seemed to many Soviet republics that complete independence might be a way of escaping from the Soviet Union's growing economic crisis. Yet, given the amount of subsidies they received from the centre, this was not a very practical solution. This was later discovered by many of these republics which, after the collapse of the Soviet Union at the end of 1991, experienced serious economic problems.

However, an important point was that it was really only the CPSU which could give any kind of real coherence to the reality of all-union institutions, whether party or state; yet its leading role was abolished in February 1990.

In March 1990, the newly elected Lithuanian Supreme Soviet voted to secede from the USSR. Gorbachev reacted strongly and Soviet troops were sent in, resulting in some deaths. Then an even more serious threat to the existence of the USSR came in May 1990, when the Russian Supreme Soviet voted for sovereignty.

8 The Soviet Union and Post-Soviet Russia (1924–2000)

The new Union Treaty

This existing Union Treaty, which joined the 15 Soviet republics together to form the USSR, had been drawn up by Stalin. It had given prominence to the Russian Federation and was more centralised than Lenin had wanted. This had been one of the issues over which, in the last years of his life, Lenin had opposed Stalin. Gorbachev accepted the need for reform and wanted a new Union Treaty, which would establish a looser federation, designed to give more power to the Soviet Union's republics. However, in April 1990, the Supreme Soviet passed a law saying there ought to be a minimum two-year waiting period before any application for secession could be approved. This was because of issues such as Soviet enterprises and the question of nuclear weapons. The issue was further complicated by ethnic groups within the various republics also wanting to secede. For instance, in 1990, violence between Ossetians and Georgians broke out in Georgia, and continued into 1991.

During June and July 1990, the 28th Party Congress approved Gorbachev's proposals for a less centralised federal system. A first draft of a new Union Treaty was approved and published by the Supreme Soviet in November 1990; and a drafting committee was set up in January 1991 to make revisions. This led Lithuania to agree to suspend its declaration of independence until the treaty had been amended and ratified. But then the other two Baltic republics, Estonia and Latvia, declared their 1940 annexations illegal; while Moldavia (incorporated into the USSR after the Second World War) was also experiencing growing nationalist unrest, spearheaded by the Moldavian Popular Front which, in November 1989, had forced the resignation of the unpopular CPSU secretary.

However, six of the fifteen Soviet republics – Estonia, Latvia, Lithuania, Moldavia, Georgia and Armenia – refused to participate in the drafting process, as they wanted greater autonomy or even full independence. A new draft was approved by the Supreme Soviet in March, and Gorbachev then held a referendum on the future of the USSR. All nine republics which had participated in the drafting of the new treaty voted overwhelmingly in favour of maintaining a federal system – the other six republics boycotted the referendum, as they were already moving towards complete independence. Nonetheless, Gorbachev proposed going ahead with the signing of the treaty with these nine – Yeltsin

agreed, but only on condition that Gorbachev agree to presidential elections in Russia, as in all the other republics.

Yeltsin's actions in Russia

Despite the growing signs of nationalist tensions on the edges of the USSR, it was events in the Russian Federation under Yeltsin which pushed many republics into wanting to break completely away from central Soviet control. At first, Yeltsin had been a supporter of Gorbachev, but increasingly he had moved to supporting a fully marketised economy. In January 1990, Yeltsin helped form the Democratic Russia group to fight the forthcoming March 1990 elections to the Russian Congress of People's Deputies. Following these elections, Yeltsin was elected chairman of the Supreme Soviet of the Russian Federation in May 1990.

At the 28th Congress of the CPSU in June 1990, the arguments between those who wanted a market economy and those who didn't, were intense – and Yeltsin publicly resigned from the party. While Gorbachev seemed to move away from some of these more extreme calls, other reformers resigned – Yakovlev from the Central Committee, and then Shevardnadze from his post of Foreign Minister. Yeltsin now saw Russia, by far the biggest and wealthiest of the republics, as a useful power base. He then formed an alliance with Gorbachev's opponents in Ukraine and Belorussia to undo the Union. Gorbachev tried hard to hold it together and, initially, the US supported Gorbachev's approach as it preferred to deal with one government.

Figure 8.5: Yeltsin (right) confronting Gorbachev (left), 1991.

In an attempt to further strengthen his position, Yeltsin had called for a
Russian presidency. This was supported by a majority of Russian voters
and, in June 1991, he was elected as the first president of the Russian
Soviet Federative Socialist Republic. He then increasingly undermined
Gorbachev's position: from then on, a sort of dual power existed
between the Soviet and Russian leaderships.

> QUESTION
>
> **Why were developments in Russia in 1990 and 1991 so important
> for the future of the entire Soviet Union?**

In July 1991, Yeltsin banned members of parties from holding office
in state organisations such as the KGB and the army – this was mainly
aimed at members of the CPSU. He also signed an agreement with
Lithuania in which the Russian Federation and Lithuania recognised
each other's sovereignty.

Various nationalist groups began to emerge in Russia, with often quite
different aims and policies. There were those who thought Russia
would do better on its own, while others wanted to impose Russian
dominance on the other republics. Soyuz ('Union'), led by Ligachev and
others, wanted to keep the Soviet Union together; while the Russian
Orthodox Constitutional Monarchists, which had been founded in May
1990, wanted the traditional Russian empire restored. In July, Yakovlev
and Shevardnadze were among those forming the New Democratic
Movement.

A return to authoritarianism?

The changes towards a presidential system led to executive confusion
– and fears that Gorbachev, having earlier seemed to be moving to
a parliamentary democracy, was now trying to shift back to a more
authoritarian one. One of these critics was Yeltsin, who accused him of
trying to establish an 'absolutist and authoritarian' regime.

SOURCE 8.2

There were, in fact, considerable limitations upon the powers of the new [Soviet] President, extensive though they undoubtedly were. He could be impeached by a two-thirds vote of the Congress of People's Deputies; his ministerial nominations required the approval of the Supreme Soviet, which could force the resignation of the Cabinet as a whole if it voted accordingly; and he had himself to report annually to the Congress of People's Deputies upon the exercise of his responsibilities. Explaining his position to a gathering of miners in April 1991, Gorbachev pointed out that he had voluntarily surrendered the extraordinary powers of the General Secretary of the CPSU, powers which at that time were greater than those of any other world leader. Would he have done so if he had been seeking unlimited personal authority?

White, S., 1993, **After Gorbachev,** *Cambridge, Cambridge University Press, p.67.*

A further development to support the argument that Gorbachev was trying to become more authoritarian was the new Law on Press Freedom of June 1990. Although it allowed freedom of information and expression, the Press Law insisted that all public media had to be registered with the authorities. In addition, it made it a crime to 'abuse' free speech and to spread information which 'did not correspond with reality' – known as 'unreal' reporting. A month before, in May 1990, a law had been passed giving up to six years in prison for 'insulting the president'. Later on, Gorbachev brought back the State Radio and Television Committee to exert influence on a media which was increasingly attacking him and his policies.

Gorbachev's attitude towards *glasnost* seemed at best inconsistent – in many ways, he seemed to be going back on his earlier *glasnost* reforms.

Gorbachev's weakening position was clear in December 1990, when there were calls for him to resign as president. In fact, while by early 1991, Gorbachev's political reforms had succeeded in dismantling most of the political system established by Stalin, they had not managed to put in its place a system based on a combination of Leninism and democracy – in other words, a system of central party control based on the sovereignty of the people. In April 1991, the Central Committee requested that he resign as General-Secretary. Though he survived these calls, he was increasingly ignored by the republics – especially when they declared that their laws took precedence over those of the USSR.

8.3 Why did the Soviet Union collapse in 1991?

All these various political and economic upheavals came to a head in August 1991 when those political and military leaders strongly opposed to Gorbachev attempted to stage a coup against him. As well as growing concerns over developments in Eastern Europe, and other aspects of Gorbachev's foreign policy (see 7.3), they were particularly worried about the draft Union Treaty, which planned to remove the word 'Socialist' from the country's name, to make it the 'Union of Soviet Sovereign Republics'. They feared this new Union Treaty would shift power to the republics, and lead to the eventual break-up of the USSR and the end of the Soviet socialist system. They were also opposed to Yeltsin's increasing adoption of policies for a transition to a complete market economy.

From coup to collapse

It soon became apparent that the hardliners were plotting. On 18 August, while on holiday in the Crimea, Gorbachev was placed under house arrest by a small group of conservative hardliners, calling themselves the 'State Emergency Committee'. This consisted of eight Kremlin leaders, officially led by Gennadi Yanaev (vice-president), and included several who had been appointed by Gorbachev: Vladimir Kryuchkov (chairman of the KGB), Dimitri Yazov (Minister of Defence), Valentin Pavlov (prime minister), and Boris Pugo (Minister of Internal Affairs). These assumed power in Moscow, but Gorbachev refused to resign, or to declare a state of emergency which could then have led to the arrest and suppression of 'free' marketeers and those wanting to break away from the Union. Consequently, the plotters declared a state of emergency themselves, and issued several decrees: including cancellation of the Union Treaty. Several newspapers which had strongly supported *glasnost* were banned, and tanks moved to strategic points in Moscow.

When this became public, there were protests and demonstrations. These became large, and Yeltsin soon placed himself at the head of the protesters in Moscow to 'protect' the Russian parliament (known as the White House) from the plotters.

QUESTION

Assess the values and limitations of Figure 8.6 for finding out about Yeltsin's role in opposing the August 1991 coup.

Figure 8.6: Yeltsin (standing, left, with raised fist) in Moscow in August 1991, opposing the attempted coup, with the Russian 'White House' in the background.

The Soviet Union and Post-Soviet Russia (1924–2000)

As President of Russia, Yeltsin then issued a decree accusing the plotters of treason. He also called for a general strike – but this did not happen, and some observers dispute the size of the protests, claiming that most citizens did not get involved. In fact, there is some debate about whether Yeltsin, instead of attempting to lead the protests, simply waited to see how things would turn out.

As protests, barricades and demonstrations grew in both Moscow and especially in Leningrad, the plotters began to waver. The majority of the army and security forces decided not to back the coup – and the numbers turning out onto the streets meant the plotters eventually decided not to use force to crush the protests. Instead, on 21 August, the plotters gave up and fled. The Supreme Soviet then cancelled the decrees issued by the plotters.

When Gorbachev returned to Moscow, he continued with discussions about the new Union Treaty. He then filled the posts formerly held by the plotters mainly with conservatives who had not opposed the coup. Yeltsin was angry, and made strong speeches, forcing Gorbachev to sack the Soviet government, as, although most members had not been involved in the coup, they had not opposed it either. Yeltsin then banned the Russian Communist Party on 23 August; and Gorbachev was forced to accept that the Russian government, headed by Yeltsin, now had equal status to the Soviet one. On 24 August, Gorbachev resigned as General-Secretary of the CPSU, but remained as president of the Soviet Union. On 29 August, the Supreme Soviet banned the CPSU from the entire USSR.

Yeltsin then began moves to establish the power of Russia. This led many republican leaders to fear that he intended to take over all Soviet assets, making Russia the dominant power. It forced many more nationalists to see breaking away from the Soviet Union as the only way to protect their powers – especially when Yeltsin took control of the Soviet budget and promised to defend all Russians living in the various republics. In December, Ukraine voted to leave the Union, dashing any hopes for a looser federation. The Soviet Union was then effectively ended when Russia, Belorussia and Ukraine formed the Commonwealth of Independent States (CIS). The CIS would have no parliament or presidency – though it did agree to have unitary control of nuclear weapons, which was something the US wanted. Perhaps significantly, it informed George Bush, the US president, of this before it contacted Gorbachev. On 25 December, Gorbachev announced his resignation as president of the USSR. This marked the formal end of the Soviet Union.

Figure 8.7: Yeltsin and the leaders of the Ukrainian and Belorussian republics, after the signing of the agreement to establish the CIS.

Gorbachev's responsibility

Historians continue to debate the causes of the crisis, the eventual collapse of the Soviet Union – and the reasons why Gorbachev's reform project failed. Many argue that the deep-seated and long-standing economic and political weaknesses within the Soviet Union made successful reform highly unlikely. These weaknesses included, as has been seen, bureaucratic control of the economy which then resulted in much inefficiency and waste, and rates of productivity significantly lower than those achieved in the West. Its undemocratic political system alienated important – if not large – sections of Soviet society, and it has been argued that Gorbachev's attempts at reform came too late to save a system that was by 1985 already doomed.

One analysis – made without the benefit of hindsight – was offered over two years before the collapse of the USSR, by Ernest Mandel. He was a Marxist who, for a time, was an economics lecturer at the Free University of Brussels. In 1989, he saw four possible outcomes for the Gorbachev project:

- successful reform by 'revolution from above'
- a radicalisation of leading members of the CPSU, leading to a 'Moscow Spring' similar to developments in Czechoslovakia in 1968

- the conservative elements of the *nomenklatura* successfully stopping the democratisation and reform project
- the possibility of a new working-class political revolution.

SOURCE 8.3

Where is the Soviet Union headed under Gorbachev? What are the possible outcomes of the process that has begun in that country? If pressure from the masses... is adequate to neutralize the obstruction and sabotage of the more conservative layers of the bureaucracy; if the apparatus is progressively modernized and rejuvenated; if capitalist credits are made available; if Gorbachev's reforms are allowed to continue... then perestroika will begin to deliver fruits after a period of time and the living standards of the people will improve. In such a case the Gorbachev experience will succeed. Of the four possible scenarios that we outline here, we consider this one the least likely. It underestimates the resistance to reform and the social and political contradictions which are an obstacle to any 'reformist' solution.

Mandel, E., 1989, **Beyond Perestroika**, *London, Verso, pp. xv–xvi.*

However, this optimistic analysis left out a fifth possibility – the total collapse of the Soviet system and of the Soviet Union itself. Arguably, it was Gorbachev's weakening of the CPSU (which was the main element keeping the USSR together and functioning), before there was anything to replace it, which was the biggest cause of the collapse.

Historians are divided on how to assess Gorbachev's responsibility for the collapse. Some – such as C. Merridale – argue that Gorbachev's ultimate failure, which seriously undermined his chances of success, was mainly due to his refusal to give his whole-hearted backing to reform-minded people within and outside the CPSU, and to his lack of a coherent reform programme. This was despite the fact that, according to historians such as D. Maples and A. Brown, he was a genuine – if somewhat cautious – reformer. However, this view of him as a genuine reformer is disputed by other historians, such as R. Service and D. Volkogonov, who see him as essentially a Leninist whose commitment to reform was limited.

However, earlier US policies – especially in maintaining and deepening the nuclear arms race – significantly contributed to the increasing distortion and ultimate collapse of the Soviet Union's economic and political structures. One impact of this Cold War expenditure was to divert resources from modernising industrial technology and producing consumer goods. It can therefore be argued that the main reason for the collapse was the much greater economic and military strength of the USA, compared with the relatively weak Soviet economy. In particular, the USA's refusal to abandon its SDI project presented real problems for Gorbachev and other Soviet leaders, who realised that the Soviet economy would crack if they attempted to achieve parity.

US officials knew about the Soviet Union's economic weaknesses, and used this knowledge at the Malta Summit in December 1989. For instance, Gorbachev had initially been told he would receive much needed US loans to help solve the USSR's growing economic crisis if he signed the Conventional Forces in Europe Treaty, to reduce the deployment of troops in Europe. However, although Gorbachev signed this in November 1990, many of these funds were then held back during 1990 and 1991, and he was told that further funds would not be forthcoming unless he promised to move the USSR towards becoming a capitalist market economy, and agreed to the reunification of Germany.

At the time, the KGB claimed to have evidence that the US was attempting to bring about the disintegration of the Soviet Union. In fact, as early as 1970, Zbigniew Brzezinski (who later became the national security adviser to US president Jimmy Carter) had suggested five possible futures for the Soviet Union, given the context of the Cold War. One of those futures was 'adaptation' – in other words, becoming closer to Western economic and political models. Another was 'disintegration' – or collapse and break-up. Both these aims (getting the USSR to adapt to Western capitalism, and encouraging its collapse) were pursued by US governments during the Cold War – and especially during the Second Cold War which began in 1979. While, in 1991, Bush initially opposed disintegration – and was thus prepared, at first, to accept the coup attempt against Gorbachev – his administration then rapidly changed tack and made contact with Yeltsin.

ACTIVITY

Carry out some additional research on Yeltsin's actions in the period 1989–91. What do you think his main motives were?

Paper 3 exam practice

Question

Discuss Gorbachev's responsibility for the collapse of the Soviet Union in December 1991. **[15 marks]**

Skill

Using your own knowledge analytically and combining it with awareness of historical debate

Examiner's tips

Always remember that historical knowledge and analysis should be the core of your answer – details of historical debate are desirable extras. However, where it is relevant, the integration of relevant knowledge about historical debates or interpretations, with reference to individual historians, will help push your answer up into the higher bands.

Assuming that you have read the question carefully, drawn up a plan, worked out your line of argument and approach, and written your introductory paragraph, you should be able to avoid both irrelevant material and simple narrative. Your task now is to follow your plan by writing a series of linked paragraphs which contain relevant analysis, precise supporting own knowledge and, where relevant, brief references to historical debate interpretations.

For this question, you will need to:

- give a *brief* explanation of the problems facing the Soviet Union in 1985
- offer a brief résumé of Gorbachev's main aims (*perestroika, glasnost* and *demokratizatsiya*)
- outline the actions taken by Gorbachev after 1985, especially in relation to economic and political developments
- examine the results of his various actions and policies
- provide a consistently analytical examination of the **relative** significance of Gorbachev's decisions – against a **range** of 'other factors'.

Such a topic, which has been the subject of some historical debate, will also give you the chance to refer to different historians' views.

Common mistakes

Some students, aware of an existing historical debate – and that extra marks can be gained by showing this – sometimes just simply write things like: 'Historian x says…, and historian y says…' However, they make no attempt to **evaluate** the different views (for example, has one historian had access to more or better information than another, perhaps because he or she was writing at a later date?); nor is this information **integrated** into their answer by being pinned to the question. Another weak use of historical debate is to write things like: 'Historian x is biased because she is American.' Such basic comments will not be given credit – what is needed is explicit understanding of historians' views, and / or the application of precise own knowledge to evaluate the strengths / weaknesses of these views. Remember to refer to the simplified Paper 3 mark scheme in Chapter 10.

Sample paragraphs containing analysis and historical debate

Given that he was in power in the six years leading up to 1991, Gorbachev's responsibility for the collapse of the Soviet Union at the end of 1991, is likely to be considerable. However, it would be unfair to put all the blame on him and his policies. There were various reasons why his attempts at reform failed and the Soviet Union collapsed. These reasons include various long-standing internal economic and political weaknesses, the existence of a powerful group of conservative bureaucrats – the nomenklatura – opposed to reform, and increasing nationalist tensions between the various Soviet republics. The USSR's undemocratic political system is also important, as it alienated many sections of Soviet society. It has been argued that all these problems made successful reform highly unlikely – and even that Gorbachev's attempts at reform came too late to save a system that was by 1985 already doomed.

Certainly, this view is supported by such historians as D. Volkogonov, who has argued that Gorbachev was attempting to reform a system that could not be reformed. He argued that, instead of perestroika, Gorbachev should have aimed for complete novostroika (restructuring) – this, arguably, is what the Chinese Communist Party seems to have done since 1976. This view is in part supported by C. Merridale, who stressed that Gorbachev failed to give full support to serious reformers in the Soviet Union who wanted more fundamental changes and, instead, followed an incoherent reform programme which ultimately undermined his chances of success. Although historian R. Service also sees Gorbachev as someone who was not fully committed to far-reaching reform, this is partly disputed by historians such as D. Maples and A. Brown, who have described Gorbachev as a genuine – if rather cautious – reformer.

EXAMINER'S COMMENT

This is a good example of one way of using historians' views. The main focus of the answer is properly concerned with using precise own knowledge to address the demands of the question. The candidate has also provided some brief but relevant knowledge of historical debate which is smoothly integrated into the answer; however, there is no attempt yet at evaluating these views.

However, as well as these internal problems, there are also important external factors involved in the ultimate collapse of the Soviet Union. In particular, it is possible to argue that the earlier Cold War policies pursued by the US – especially in maintaining and deepening the nuclear arms race – contributed to the increasing burdens on and distortions of the Soviet Union's economy. Thus possibly the main reason for the collapse of the Soviet Union was not the problems of the USSR or Gorbachev's reforms – or lack of reforms – but the much greater military and economic strength of the USA.

In fact, as early as 1970, Brzezinski – a strongly anti-Communist Cold War 'warrior', who later became national security adviser to US president Jimmy Carter – had suggested that, of several possible futures for the Soviet Union, one was collapse and break-up. These were aims pursued by US governments during the Cold War – and especially during the Second Cold War which began in 1979. In the last years of the Soviet Union, the KGB claimed to have evidence that the USA was attempting to bring about the disintegration of the USSR by economic pressures. Although George Kennan – in many ways the architect of US policy during the Cold War – claimed in 1992 that the US did not have the power to bring about changes within the Soviet Union, the whole of the USA's policy of containment was based in part on the idea that this would help undermine the Soviet system…

[There then follows evaluation of the problems of the Soviet Union, and the effects of Gorbachev's attempts at reform, supported by precise own knowledge.]

One explanation of the collapse of the Soviet Union, which is directly related to Gorbachev's responsibility, is that which says his intention was never to reform the Soviet Union. Instead, it is argued that he deliberately aimed to bring about that collapse. This, for instance, is the view of M. McGwire. However, most historians accept that his attempts at reform were genuine, and certainly he stated many times that he wanted to return the Soviet Union, and the CPSU itself, to a more modern version of 'democratic centralism' which had existed immediately after the Bolshevik Revolution in November 1917. This can be supported, for instance, by his creation of a more democratically elected Congress of People's Deputies in 1989, the steps to separate party and state, and his willingness to give more powers and freedoms to the various Soviet republics via the new Union Treaty of 1991. In fact, it is possible to argue that, instead of Gorbachev being to blame – whether unintentionally or deliberately – for the final collapse of the Soviet Union, it was rather the increasingly disruptive role played by Yeltsin as president of Russia. In particular, his actions to further the interests of the Russian Federation led the other republics to consider that they needed to break away in order to protect their interests from Russian ambitions…

EXAMINER'S COMMENT

In addition to a brief reference to the views of another historian, this paragraph – like the others – has evidence analysis supported by good own knowledge.

Activity

In this chapter, the focus is on writing an answer which is analytical, and well-supported by precise own knowledge, and one which – where relevant – refers to historical interpretations / debates. So, using the information from this chapter, and any other sources of information available to you, try to answer **one** of the following Practice Paper 3 questions using these skills.

8

Paper 3 practice questions

1 'It was the growing problems of Gorbachev's *perestroika* reforms after 1989 which led to the break-up of the Soviet Union in 1991.' To what extent do you agree with this statement?

2 Discuss the significance of Gorbachev's reforms to the CPSU.

3 Examine the consequences of Gorbachev's introduction of an executive presidency.

4 Compare and contrast the roles of Gorbachev and Yeltsin in the period 1990–91 in relation to the collapse of the Soviet Union.

5 Evaluate the role of nationalism in the eventual break-up of the Soviet Union in 1991.

6 'By 1991, the collapse of communism in the Soviet Union was inevitable.' To what extent do you agree with this statement?

Yeltsin and Post-Soviet Russia, 1992–2000

9

Introduction

Much of what happened in the former Soviet republics after December 1991 gives some insight into the depth of the economic problems Gorbachev was attempting to reform and overcome. This is particularly true of Russia – the largest and the most important of the states which made up the CIS. After the break-up of the Soviet Union in December 1991, Yeltsin remained president of the new state of Russia (also known as the Russian Federation) until the end of 1999.

During that period, Yeltsin pushed through Russia's transformation into a 'free' market economy, based on a massive privatisation programme (at very low prices) of state assets, and increased prices for consumers. This resulted in a small group of oligarchs getting possession of state property, and becoming billionaires in the process. For many Russians, though, the result was high unemployment, unpaid wages and pensions, and real poverty. In addition, mainly because of his highly unpopular economic policies, Yeltsin ruled in a way which often undermined the democratic institutions set up by Gorbachev's political reforms before 1991. In fact, he increasingly ruled Russia in a dictatorial way, and was as guilty of nepotism and corruption as the old-style communists of the Soviet Union had been.

TIMELINE

1992 **Jan:** Start of Yeltsin's economic 'shock therapy'

     Feb: Rutskoi accuses Yeltsin of 'economic genocide'; Zyuganov forms the Communist Party of the Russian Federation (CPRF)

1993 **20 Mar:** Yeltsin announces state of emergency and assumes special powers

     26 Mar: Congress of People's Deputies (CPD) tries to dismiss Yeltsin

     21 Sept: Yeltsin decides to disband the Supreme Soviet and the CPD, and to rule by decree until new elections in December

     22 Sept: Supreme Soviet dismisses Yeltsin; Rutskoi elected acting president

     4 Oct: Yeltsin sends in army against parliament

     Dec: Elections result in more anti-Yeltsin than pro-Yeltsin deputies

1995 Dec: Parliamentary elections see the CPRF become the main opposition to Yeltsin's government

1996 Feb: Yeltsin announces he will seek re-election as president

Jul: Yeltsin defeats Zyuganov in the final round of voting

1999 May: Parliament again tries to dismiss Yeltsin

Aug: Yeltsin appoints Putin as prime minister

31 Dec: Yeltsin resigns as Russian president; Putin takes over

KEY QUESTIONS

• What were the main aspects of Yeltsin's rule in Russia, 1992–96?
• How did Yeltsin maintain his rule from 1996 to 2000?
• Has the 'spectre of communism' been laid to rest?

Overview

• After 1991, Yeltsin introduced a rapid privatisation of former Soviet industries in Russia, leading to unemployment and poverty.
• This economic 'shock therapy' – overseen by Western financial and business advisers (known as the 'Chicago Boys') led to considerable unemployment and poverty for millions of Russians.
• As part of his economic programme, state-owned enterprises were sold off cheaply – resulting in the emergence of many billionaire Russian oligarchs.
• These developments led to growing political opposition; in February 1992, the Communist Party of the Russian Federation was formed, and rapidly became the main parliamentary opposition to Yeltsin's economic policies.
• This political opposition increasingly led Yeltsin to rule in an autocratic way. In March 1993, he assumed emergency powers.
• This led to an unsuccessful attempt by the elected Congress of People's Deputies (CPD) to dismiss him as president.

- In September 1993, Yeltsin announced his decision to disband the Supreme Soviet and CPD, and to rule by decree until new elections in December 1993.
- The Supreme Soviet then voted 636:2 to dismiss him; so, on 4 October, Yeltsin ordered the army to shell the Russian parliament.
- In the December 1993 elections, more anti-Yeltsin deputies were elected than pro-Yeltsin ones. In the December 1995 elections, the CPRF became the main parliamentary opposition.
- However, Yeltsin won a second term of office in the presidential election in July 1996; but resigned in December 1999. He was succeeded by Vladimir Putin.

9.1 What were the main aspects of Yeltsin's rule in Russia, 1992–96?

Yeltsin, taking advice from the US and Western financial institutions, undertook to transform Russia's economy into a neo-liberal 'free market' capitalist economy. This was to be achieved by abolishing subsidies and price controls, and implementing a rapid and massive programme of privatising state industries.

Economic 'shock therapy'

This was essentially the implementation of the ideas of Friedrich Hayek and Milton Friedman who, from the 1960s, had advocated economic policies (such as monetarism and 'rolling back' the welfare state) for 'free market' or unrestrained capitalism. The ideas of this 'Chicago School' (so-called because Milton Friedman taught at the University of Chicago for over 30 years) were first applied in the military dictatorships of Chile and Argentina in the 1970s, and were later adopted by the Reagan and Thatcher governments in the US and the UK in the 1980s respectively.

The economic policies implemented under Yeltsin were similar to those which had been applied in the former Eastern European satellite states after 1989. However the application of these economic policies in Russia and the other former Soviet republics has been described by several commentators as 'All shock, no therapy'. Such people include the economist J. K. Galbraith, who wrote about the impact of these 'neo-liberal' economic policies in an article entitled 'Shock without therapy', published on 25 August 2002, in the monthly US journal *The American Prospect*.

These economic policies saw the rapid emergence of several billionaire Russian oligarchs, alongside an estimated 140 million Russians falling below the official poverty line. According to the British medical journal *The Lancet*, the result of such policies in Yeltsin's Russia was a 12.8% increase in the male death rate in just two years, due to increased unemployment and consequent rising alcoholism. By the mid-1990s, male life expectancy in Russia had dropped to 59 years – and it continued to fall.

Figure 9.1: This cartoon, published in 1996, was by an American cartoonist, and was commenting on life in Yeltsin's post-Soviet Russia, after the implementation of his economic 'shock therapy' programme.

9 The Soviet Union and Post-Soviet Russia (1924–2000)

What is the message of the cartoon in Figure 9.1? Look carefully both at what is drawn, and what words appear in the cartoon. Also – don't forget to look at the attribution information.

Several commentators have seen such developments as suggesting that no one economic system has all the right answers, and showing that there were no easy solutions to the particular problems of the Soviet economy with which Gorbachev attempted to cope. For instance, according to D. Lane, the under-utilisation of industrial capital in the US during the 1970s was about 20%; while in the early 1980s, there were over 8 million unemployed and a further 5 million under-employed. Such views have been more widely voiced since the 2008 banking crisis and its worldwide impact.

SOURCE 9.1

The most common explanation [of the problems of the Soviet economy] in the West today is a very simple one: planning does not work and you must have a market. This simple thesis is then given an ideological colouring: the market equals capitalism and it works; the plan equals socialism and it does not work. This is an entirely worthless argument at the level of general principles. Perfect markets would be fine and perfect planning would be fine, but neither are feasible in the present world. The neo-liberal case is based on an obvious double-standard. It compares a non-existent perfect market with the actually-existing Soviet planning mechanism. As the Polish economist W. Brus has often pointed out, in the East people exaggerate the qualities of markets because they haven't experienced it. The fact is that both planning and markets possess benefits and deficiencies. What is clearly required is to practically combine the advantages of each while minimising their costs.

Ali, T., 1988, Revolution from Above: Where is the Soviet Union Going?, *London, Hutchinson, pp. 70–1.*

Theory of Knowledge

History and bias

History is often seen as being more prone to bias than the natural sciences – especially when this involves consideration of political and economic theories and systems. Is it possible, for instance, for Western historians and economists to make objective judgements about the desirability of Yeltsin's 'free market' policies for the Russian economy? Or are they likely to just look for evidence which supports the cultural, economic and political values which dominate their own societies?

DISCUSSION POINT

Supporters of monetarism and 'free market' capitalism often argue that 'rolling back the state', and leaving decisions to the market instead, increases individual freedom. Do you think individuals' interests are best served by elected governments or by privately owned firms?

Economic policies and the 'Chicago Boys'

This rapid move towards the creation of a capitalist economy in Russia was to a large extent overseen by Jeffrey Sachs, who had been responsible for similar economic 'shock therapy' transformations in Bolivia and Poland, and who had begun advising Yeltsin before the collapse of the USSR. One result of these policies was the rapid emergence of several billionaire Russian 'oligarchs'. In effect, Yeltsin's privatisation schemes had put most of the nation's wealth into these people's pockets.

SOURCE 9.2

In practice, most Soviet enterprises were privatized for less than 1 per cent of their market price – the economists of the late 1980s were over-optimistic. When, in 1993, after a coup d'état, the parliament building was taken over by the government, it was decided to protect it by putting up a fence. The cost of erecting this fence was far greater than the revenues raised for the State budget through privatizing most of its property. Only three Russian companies were sold for a sum that exceeded the cost of the fence.

Kargarlitsky, B., 2009, **Back in the USSR***, London, Seagull Books, p.6.*

However, Yeltsin's Russian advisers (often referred to as the 'Chicago Boys') were split over the speed with which these changes should be implemented. In fact, some of Yeltsin's advisers wanted him to hold an election to get the voting public's support for these controversial economic reforms. However, Yeltsin's deputy, Yegor Gaidar, and Anatoly Chubais, Yeltsin's deputy for economic policy, both argued for rapid implementation – and, along with the Western advisers, opposed holding new elections.

In fact, even before the end of 1991, Yeltsin had already agreed to take the direction insisted on by the US Treasury Department, the International Monetary Fund, and the World Bank. Following the events in Eastern Europe in 1988 and 1989, these organisations were pushing for economic 'shock therapy' policies – to bring about a rapid transition to capitalism – to be implemented before people could organise much opposition to its effects on their living standards. Indeed they even seemed to favour the use of force to push them through.

SOURCE 9.3

So what happened at the G7 meeting in 1991 was totally unexpected. The nearly unanimous message that Gorbachev received... was that, if he did not embrace radical economic shock therapy immediately, they would sever the rope and let him fall. 'Their suggestions as to tempo and methods of transition were astonishing,' Gorbachev wrote of the event. Poland had just completed its first round of shock therapy under the IMF's and Jeffrey Sachs's tutelage, and the consensus among [Western leaders] was that the Soviet Union had to follow Poland's lead on an even faster timetable... What happened next – the dissolution of the Soviet Union, Gorbachev's eclipse by Yeltsin, and the tumultuous course of economic shock therapy in Russia – is a well-documented chapter of contemporary history. It is, however, a story... [of] one of the greatest crimes committed against a democracy in modern history... in order to push through a Chicago School economic program, that peaceful and hopeful process that Gorbachev began had to be violently interrupted, then radically reversed. Gorbachev knew that the only way to impose the kind of shock therapy being advocated by the G7 and the IMF was with force – as did many in the West pushing for these policies.... The Economist... [urged] Gorbachev to model himself after [Chile's Pinochet] one of the Cold War's most notorious killers... [Boris Yeltsin] was more than willing to play the role of a Russian Pinochet.

Klein. N., 2007, **The Shock Doctrine***, London, Penguin, pp. 219–21.*

Less than a week after the Soviet Union had collapsed, Yeltsin began a full-blooded economic 'shock therapy' programme. On 2 January 1992, Yeltsin allowed Gaidar, as first deputy prime minister, to introduce more policies recommended by Sachs – resulting in rapidly rising unemployment. At the same time, price controls, including those on basic foodstuffs, were lifted, and harsh austerity measures were taken to cut welfare spending just at a time when more people were in greater need of it.

These measures brought about a deep economic depression in early 1992, and drastically reduced the living standards of much of the population. In January alone, prices rose by 245%. Many Russians still in work often found their wages were not paid; pensioners often went without their pensions; and tens of millions of Russians were plunged into poverty. Beggars and homeless people appeared on the streets.

The Soviet Union and Post-Soviet Russia (1924–2000)

According to some economists, Russia suffered an economic downturn more severe than the United States and Germany had experienced in the Great Depression of the 1930s. Industrial production in 1992 was 18% down on 1991 levels, while food production dropped by 9%.

Figure 9.2: A homeless woman and her child in St Petersburg, 1993.

> QUESTION
>
> What are the values and limitations of a photograph like Figure 9.2 for understanding the impact of Yeltsin's economic policies after 1991?

Not surprisingly, many Russian politicians began to attack Yeltsin's 'shock therapy' programme. In February 1992, Russia's vice-president, Alexsandr Rutskoi, accused Yeltsin of presiding over 'economic genocide'. Nonetheless, Yeltsin's economic programme continued. In 1993, Russia's GDP fell by 12% compared with 1992 levels. By 1994, inflation was still in three figures, industrial output continued to decline, and free healthcare was for most just a memory. Yeltsin's reforms had succeeded in one way, however – the old Soviet economic system had been virtually destroyed.

SOURCE 9.4

To describe the changes in Russia in the late twentieth century as 'progress' is something the tongue simply cannot manage. In the course of ten years the country suffered an unprecedented economic collapse – one of the most profound peacetime declines in all of modern history, matched or exceeded only by the decline in other fragments of the former Soviet Union. In 1999 it was calculated that in the best of circumstances, simply to regain the level of 1990, the last 'pre-Yeltsin' year, would take at least a decade. Between 1991 and 1998 overall agricultural and industrial production fell by half. Even in the relatively prosperous oil industry, production was down by 44 per cent... Most tellingly, the population experienced a sharp fall, the result both of increased death rates and of declining numbers of births. During the period of the Civil War, from 1918 to 1920, the Russian population fell by 2.8 million. During the years of Yeltsin's 'first presidency' alone, from 1992 to 1996, the decline was 3.4 million. Economists are united in describing the course of events as 'regression'.

Kargarlitsky, B., 2002, **Russia Under Yeltsin and Putin: Neo-liberal Autocracy**, *London, Pluto Press, pp. 2–3.*

Yeltsin's political 'coup', 1993

The growing arguments in 1992 over the impact of the 'shock therapy' policies led to the growth of a political opposition which tried to halt his economic programme. This eventually led to a serious constitutional crisis in 1993, between Yeltsin and the Russian parliament, which had been elected in 1990. During 1992, the speaker of the Russian Supreme Soviet, Ruslan Khasbulatov, became an increasingly vocal critic of the pace of Yeltsin's economic reforms – and of Yeltsin's increasing tendency to ignore parliament. This soon became a political contest between Yeltsin on one side, and the Supreme Soviet of Russia and the Congress of People's Deputies on the other.

Growing opposition

Yeltsin's ban of the CPSU in November 1991 – just one month before the collapse of the Soviet Union itself – had been eventually overturned by the Constitutional Court. In February 1993, the Communist Party of the Russian Federation (CPRF) was formed by Gennady Zyuganov.

He had been one of the leaders of the CPSU and had strongly opposed many of Gorbachev's *perestroika* and *glasnost* reforms. The founding Congress of the CPRF was attended by delegates representing over 450000 members of the former Russian Communist Party who had decided to reconstitute themselves after the ban was lifted. During Yeltsin's mounting confrontations with the Russian parliament in 1993, the CPRF became increasingly influential. They then decided to participate in the National Salvation Front (NSF), a communist-nationalist grouping which was opposed to 'shock therapy' and further concessions to the West and which, instead, wanted to revive the Soviet Union. This grouping had about 30% of the deputies in Russia's parliament.

The Pinochet option

Continued disputes led Yeltsin, on 20 March 1993, to say he would declare a state of emergency, allowing him to assume 'special powers' to push through his economic policies. On 26 March, the Congress of People's Deputies tried, unsuccessfully, to dismiss him as president by a vote in parliament. During the summer of 1993, a situation of dual power developed in Russia, between the Supreme Soviet and Yeltsin.

SOURCE 9.5

On Saturday evening, March 20, 1993, regular broadcasting on Russian television was interrupted, and it was reported that President Yeltsin would make an address to the people of Russia... He announced that he had just signed a decree placing Russia under 'special administrative rule,' a condition in which the Supreme Soviet and Congress of People's Deputies would be subordinated to the president and would not have the right to cancel his decrees or to pass laws contradicting them.

Yeltsin's action was in violation of specific clauses of the constitution. It was a new attempt to carry out a coup d'etat from above and to change by decree the relations between the two branches of government.

Medvedev, R., 2000, **Post-Soviet Russia: A Journey Through the Yeltsin Era**, New York, Columbia University Press, pp. 96–7.

On 21 September 1993, Yeltsin – in what was referred to as the 'Pinochet option' (so-called after the military dictator of Chile) – announced his intention to disband the Supreme Soviet and the

Congress of People's Deputies, and to rule by decree until the election of a new parliament in December, and a referendum on a new constitution. The next day, the Supreme Soviet voted 636:2 to dismiss Yeltsin as president, as he had broken the constitution. Vice-President Rutskoi was then elected as the acting president.

Yeltsin's actions in September – along with his economic policies – resulted in mass popular unrest, which encouraged his parliamentary opponents. Tens of thousands of anti-Yeltsin demonstrators marched in Moscow in what seemed to be a copy of events in Eastern Europe in 1988 and 1989. Faced with this massive popular resistance, Yeltsin invoked the support of Russia's military to use force to overcome his opponents, and carried out his earlier threat to dissolve the Russian parliament.

On 4 October, after the parliament had refused to disperse, Yeltsin ordered the army to shell the parliament. Over 500 members of the parliament and their supporters were killed, and over 1000 were injured. Rutskoi and Khasbulatov, along with over 1000 others, were arrested. Yeltsin then scrapped the constitution, temporarily banned opposition parties, censored the media – and stepped up the pace of his economic policies. These actions were backed by the US, and some other Western states.

Yeltsin's decision to use military force to stop the criticism and opposition he was facing in the Russian parliament – was ironic, considering how he had 'protected' the Russian parliament in August 1991, during the attempted coup against Gorbachev.

ACTIVITY

Compare Yeltsin's actions in October 1993 with those of August 1991. Why do you think his actions were so different?

The December 1993 elections

In the parliamentary elections of December 1993, Yeltsin's party faced a resounding defeat at the hands of the NSF opposition parties. These elections were to create a new Federal Assembly, made up of a State Duma and a Council of the Federation. However, despite an obvious reporting bias in favour of Gaidar's Russia's Choice party (backed by

Yeltsin), Yeltsin's supporters were outnumbered by the huge number of anti-Yeltsin candidates elected. Most of these were either from Gennadi Zyuganov's new conservative CPRF, or from extreme nationalist parties – in particular, Vladimir Zhirinovski's Liberal Democratic Party. Although Zyuganov had succeeded in establishing the CPRF as the leading force on the left, he had not yet managed to defeat the nationalists and secure communist leadership of the opposition to Yeltsin's programme. In fact, the extreme nationalist LDP won 23% of the vote, compared with 12% for the CPRF and 8% for the CPRF's ally, the Agrarians.

The December elections thus confronted Yeltsin with a new parliament containing a strong anti-neo-liberal majority, implacably opposed to his economic programme. His response to this expression of the voters' choices was to draw up a new constitution to give the president much stronger powers. The results of the 1993 elections, however, did lead Yeltsin, at first, to slow down the pace of privatisation and, in January 1994, Gaidar resigned from the government. But, by 1995, Russia's growing foreign debt was causing even greater economic problems – according to the World Bank, 74 million Russians were below the poverty line. Thus, just prior to the December 1995 elections, opinion polls put Yeltsin's approval rating at 5%.

The 1995 elections

The parliamentary elections in December 1995 saw the CPRF become the dominant opposition to Yeltsin. This improvement in the fortunes of the CPRF was down to its determined opposition to Yeltsin, its promotion of a patriotic alliance to 'save Russia', and its backing for increasing trade union protests and resistance. The 'patriotic' aspect of Zyuganov's politics, however, was criticised by other communist and left groups within Russia, because of the way in which he used nationalist ideas. Several CPRF leaders were soon accused of promoting increasingly extreme forms of Russian nationalism. Nonetheless, the CPRF's support almost doubled, to 22%, while the LDP's dropped to 11%, and Yeltsin's party, Our Home is Russia, only won 10%.

The CPRF was able to use its call for a patriotic alliance to build a strong broad-based movement to oppose the privatisation of the Russian economy and the dismantling of Russian society. In January 1996, a survey conducted by Moscow's Bureau of Applied Sociological

Research had Yeltsin's ratings on all questions significantly lower than those for Gennady Zyuganov. Some of its results are shown below:

Survey questions	Yeltsin (%)	Zyuganov (%)
1 Who, after becoming president, could most quickly stop inflation?	8.4	24.8
2 Who could most quickly improve the economy?	7.9	21.8
3 Who could most quickly improve health care?	8.1	30.6
4 Who could most quickly solve the crime problem?	6.0	16.0
5 Who could most quickly stop the war in Chechnya?	6.1	15.4

Table 9.1: The Russian public's opinion on various political issues in January 1996. Based on: Medvedev, R., 2000, **Post-Soviet Russia: A Journey Through the Yeltsin Era**, New York, Columbia University Press, pp. 215–6.

In that same 1996 survey, only 15% of respondents believed they were living better than before *perestroika*, while 14% stated they had experienced no significant change in their living standards. However, 68% said they were either living 'worse' or 'much worse'. Perhaps most significantly, when asked whether they approved of the social and economic policies implemented by Yeltsin since the beginning of 1992, an overwhelming majority – 66%! – replied in the negative. By mid-February 1996, Zyuganov's personal ratings ranged between 20 and 22% – twice as high as Yeltsin's.

Faced with such significant opposition, Yeltsin decided he needed support from Russia's business elites in his bid to be re-elected president in early 1996. He thus planned a new wave of privatisation of Russia's most valuable state enterprises, by giving them shares in return for 'loans'. In effect, Yeltsin sold off valuable public assets, at unrealistically low valuations, to a small but powerful group of tycoons in industry, energy, banking, telecommunications, and – significantly – the media. By mid-1996, these oligarchs owned most of Russia's major firms.

The 1996 presidential election

In February 1996, Yeltsin publicly announced his intention to seek re-election. By then, the Communist Party had been gaining increased support, and had done well in the parliamentary elections in December 1995, attracting support from those who now looked back fondly at the time when the Soviet state had provided security, employment and social welfare. Yeltsin's opinion poll ratings were so low that some of his advisers suggested he should cancel the elections and rule as dictator. As noted by R. Service, Yeltsin's previous actions had shown that his commitment to democracy was, at best, less than solid.

SOURCE 9.6

When Yeltsin began his campaign his ratings stood near zero. He had presided over five years of 'shock therapy', unfulfilled promises, constantly rising prices, the hoodwinking of small investors, a declining standard of living, overnight enrichment for tens of thousands accompanied by impoverishment for tens of millions, destruction of the educational system, health care, and science and technology in general, rampant crime of all kinds, a falling birth rate and a rising death rate, the war in Chechnya, the degradation of the army, the decline of industry and agriculture, the weakening of all forms of social protection, unemployment, homeless children, refugees, strikes, and ecological disasters. The list could go on and on.

Medvedev, R., 2000, **Post-Soviet Russia***, New York, Columbia University Press, p. 215.*

By the time of the election, it was obvious that Russian politics had become seriously polarised, with it clearly established that the main opposition to Yeltsin's neo-liberal policies came from Zyuganov, the leader of the Communist Party, who had a big lead in the early opinion polls.

However, Anatoly Chubais then became Yeltsin's campaign manager: he effectively used the privatisation measures to gain the support of important financial and media oligarchs to finance Yeltsin's campaign, and to give positive coverage on television and in leading newspapers. In particular, television ran a series of films and documentaries which stressed the horrors of communism, claiming that Zyuganov was a modern Stalin. In return, Chubais enabled these oligarchs to acquire majority stakes in some of Russia's most valuable state-owned assets. Chubais also warned that a victory for Zyuganov would take Russia back to totalitarianism.

Despite all this, in the first round of the presidential elections, Yeltsin's vote was only 3% higher than Zyuganov's. By the time of the second round, it was clear that the election had become a straight contest between Yeltsin and Zyuganov. For a while, it really looked like Zyuganov might win. As the final election neared, it became obvious that Russia's financial system was on the verge of a total meltdown. The government's income had collapsed because of declining industrial output: this meant wages were increasingly not paid, while government borrowing sent interest rates through the roof: for instance, the rate for six-month bonds was 200%.

However, Yeltsin's chances of winning were increased by a timely announcement by the IMF of their intention to grant Russia a $10 billion loan – though this was dependent on carrying out total privatisation of state enterprises. The promise of these loans from the West allowed Yeltsin to begin paying some of the overdue wages and pensions before the elections. In addition, Yeltsin also promised to drop some of his more unpopular economic reforms, and increased welfare spending.

Thus, in the final round of voting in July, Yeltsin won 54% of the vote to Zyuganov's 41%. Almost 5% of the electorate voted against both candidates. Significantly, perhaps, some commentators doubted whether Yeltsin would have stood down as president if he had lost the election.

KEY CONCEPTS QUESTION

Causes and significance: What were the main reasons for Yeltsin's victory in 1996? Which one do you think was most important?

9.2 How did Yeltsin maintain his rule from 1996 to 2000?

After 1996, allegations of corruption increased – some claimed that, although Russia had received US$40 billion in loans from the IMF and other international lending organisations since 1991, most of the money had been stolen by Yeltsin's friends and backers.

Russian politics and economics, 1996–2000

Political crises

The late 1990s saw the beginnings of a significant shift in Russian politics. A financial collapse came in the context of a serious Asian financial crisis, which led investors to become nervous about the situation in Russia. In August 1998, Russia was forced to devalue the rouble, and to default on the country's domestic debt. The devaluation sent the prices of food and consumer-goods imports – on which Russian cities were now largely dependent, given the collapse of domestic production – up by 40%. As a result, living standards fell dramatically. In addition, almost all private banks were technically bankrupt.

Not surprisingly, this led to a serious political crisis, which saw Yeltsin – whose regime was severely weakened by this crisis – forced to appoint Yevgeny Primakov as prime minister, instead of Yeltsin's choice, Viktor Chernomrydin. Primakov was the choice favoured by the CPRF and was an indication of that party's growing influence. Primakov took immediate steps to deal with the financial crisis, and to break with Yeltsin's openly pro-Western policies. The latter included shifting Russia's foreign policy towards greater independence – this included establishing better relations with China.

SOURCE 9.7

Only the Russian parliamentary election of March 1990 and the presidential election of June 1991, in which Yeltsin was elected Russia's first president, were genuinely open competitions. The December 1993 parliamentary election and referendum on the new constitution established a pattern in which the electoral process was suborned by a force standing outside the competition. In 1996 the regime managed to organise Yeltsin's re-election, and in late 1999 the succession passed to a nominee of the regime, Putin. The electoral process underwent a dual adaptation: while formally conducted within the framework of law and electoral pluralism, the regime used elections (that were typically hard-fought) to legitimate its own power rather than subjecting that power to the openness of outcomes that is the characteristic feature of a free and fair political competition.

Sakwa, R., 2011, **The Crisis of Russian Democracy,** *Cambridge, Cambridge University Press, p. x.*

Continuing opposition

The post-1991 political experience in Russia (like the post-1989 experiences in the countries of Eastern Europe) was very different from that which had been assumed by many Western observers. In particular, the CPRF remained the largest opposition party in Russia throughout the late 1990s, with a significant level of popular support. In addition, various other parties and organisations calling themselves 'communist' also emerged in post-Soviet Russia.

	Communist	National-patriotic	Centrist	Liberal-democratic
Dec 1993	21	24	26	29
Dec 1995	33	21	23	21
Dec 1999	28	7	44	15

Table 9.2: Voting support by part groupings, 1993–1999. Adapted from: White, S., 2011, **Understanding Russian politics,** Cambridge, Cambridge University Press, p. 55.

Given the massive social and economic decline resulting from Yeltsin's 'shock therapy' reforms, it was to be expected that parties linked to those 'reformers' mostly closely tied to the West, privatisation and 'shock therapy' would find little popular or mass support. At the end of November 1998, the National Public Opinion Centre carried out a survey which showed that Yegor Gaidar's party, Russia's Choice, had the support of just 1% of the population. Even right-wing politicians began to claim that they, too, were opposed to the free market and the West, in recognition of the fact that to be seen to hold such a position was vital if they were to stand any chance of being elected.

SOURCE 9.8

The revival of support for a communist successor party in Russia was not surprising when seen in the context of the social and economic consequences of the dissolution of the Soviet Union and the reintroduction of capitalism from the end of 1991. The economic reform which began formally in Russia with price liberalisation in January 1992 produced the greatest peacetime industrial collapse of any economy in history. Moreover, the role of Western institutions in formulating the key stages of the reform process was well understood in Russia and helped shape popular attitudes towards the West. This was reinforced by the backing of Western governments for President Boris Yeltsin, even when his tanks were storming Russia's elected parliament in October 1993. The tragic effects of the economic reforms on Russian society are well-documented, although not commonly appreciated in Western society.

Hudson, K., 2012, **The New European Left: A Socialism for the Twenty-First Century?**, Basingstoke, Palgrave Macmillan p. 19.

The Russian economy

Russia's economic problems continued, and the living standards of ordinary people remained low. In May 1999, Yeltsin's opponents in the State Duma tried, unsuccessfully, to remove him by parliamentary vote. It was in this context that **Vladimir Putin** began to emerge as the champion of a stronger, more independent and confident Russia. In August, Yeltsin fired his prime minister – he was replaced by Putin. On 31 December 1999, Yeltsin announced his resignation. He also revealed that Putin was now the acting president – and that presidential elections would take place in March 2000. By then, one third of Russia's population was living below the poverty line of $38 per month; more than 80% of farms had gone bankrupt, and over 70 000 factories had been closed down.

Vladimir Putin (b. 1952):

Putin's rise was a serious challenge to the influence of the CPRF, as he did much to quickly restore the standing of Russia in international affairs, and simultaneously was able to strengthen the Russian economy via strong economic management and rising oil prices. Nonetheless, the CPRF has maintained its position as the largest opposition party in Russia, and has come second in every presidential election since the collapse of the Soviet Union at the end of 1991.

SOURCE 9.9

One of the most obvious consequences of the transition to an economy based largely on private ownership was a rapidly widening gap in earnings, and accordingly in living standards. In 1991, the USSR's last year, the best-paid fifth of the population took 31 per cent of all money incomes, and the least well paid 12 per cent. By the end of the decade, the richest fifth took half as much again (among them, nearly half of all earned income), but the poorest fifth only two-thirds as much as they had received at the end of the Soviet period. Differences of this kind are conveniently expressed in terms of the 'decile ratio', which relates the earnings of the most prosperous 10 per cent to those of the least prosperous 10 per cent. In 1990 it stood at 4.4: by the end of the decade it had jumped to 13.9.

White, S., 2011, **Understanding Russian Politics**, Cambridge, Cambridge University Press, p. 165.

According to a United Nations Development Programme (UNDP) report published in 1997, Yeltsin's reforms had had an extremely negative impact on the lives of most ordinary Russians.

SOURCE 9.10

The attempted 'shock therapy' reforms launched in January 1992 ushered in a period of economic decline of unprecedented proportions... Partial price liberalisation in January 1992 unleashed an inflationary process in which consumer and producer prices rose by over 2,500 per cent in less than a year. The resulting dislocation and fall in personal incomes were reinforced by the gradual reduction in subsidies for rent, transport, and other necessities of life.

United Nations Development Programme (UNDP), 1997, **Human Development UnderTransition: Europe and CIS***, New York, p. 180.*

Under Yeltsin, Russia experienced 'hyper-stagflation' (a mixture of high inflation, low economic growth and high unemployment) as a result of the 'liberalisation' of the economy. Russia's GDP decreased continuously following the collapse of the Soviet Union. In 1994, it declined by 20%, and industrial output declined by 4.7% in 1995. By then, industrial output had decreased by 53% since 1989. National income fell by over 40% between 1991 and 1996. As a result, living standards declined sharply. Before 1991, it was estimated that 10% of the population were living in poverty – by 1997, and using the previously accepted poverty line of $38 per month, the percentage had risen to an incredible 90%. Even using a very different poverty threshold of $50 per month, the figure was still estimated to be between 25 and 34%. In part, this was the result of the fact that, from 1990 to 1994, the price index for paid services like housing, transport and domestic utilities such as gas and electricity rose by over 6000%.

SOURCE 9.11

The debate whether or not liberalisation of trade and investment is the best way to reduce inequality, boost employment and help the poor is the most keenly contested corner of the argument between the proponents and opponents of economic globalisation... However, wage inequality has increased in almost all... countries that have undertaken rapid trade liberalisation... By the beginning of 1999, there were some 150 million people unemployed worldwide and up to 1 billion under-employed – a third of the world's labour force. Not since the Depression of the 1930s have things been so bad... by 2003 the global unemployment total had reached 180 million...

In 1997, the UN Conference on Trade and Development (UNCTAD) concluded that this dramatic increase in global inequality... is being caused by economic globalisation. By 2002, UNCTAD was of the opinion that further rounds of globalisation had done little to improve the situation....

Indeed, there is no better illustration of the dangers of following the misconceived prescriptions of economic globalisation than the devastating situation in Russia. Ten years after liberalisation of the Russian economy began in 1989, the UNDP reported that inequality had doubled, wages had fallen by almost half, and male life expectancy had declined by more than four years to 60 years.

Woodin, M. and Lucas, C., 2004, **Green Alternatives to Globalisation**, *London, Pluto Press, pp. 46–47 and 55.*

Thus the vast majority of Russia's people faced real hardship – this was reflected in, among other indicators, by a significant decrease in life expectancy; and by a significant increase in heart, digestive and infectious diseases. Wages were often late in being paid – and, in many cases, were not paid at all. Among other things, all this resulted in dramatic increases in unemployment and homelessness. According to R. Sakwa, by the late 1990s, Russia had moved so far away from the relative egalitarianism of the Soviet Union that it had been transformed into a society with Latin American structures of property and income inequalities.

Expectations of high levels of investment from Western countries were not fulfilled. In fact, from 1991 to 1998, there was an annual outflow of capital from Russia which greatly exceeded the total inflow of capital in the form of investment, foreign aid, IMF credits and other loans. Much of this capital outflow was of the huge funds accumulated by Russian oligarchs and gangsters who had amassed massive fortunes during the deeply criminalised way in which privatisation of state assets had been carried out.

The results of Yeltsin's 'reforms'

By 1999, many observers drew up 'balance sheets' to assess the outcome of the reform programme pushed for by Western states and institutions and implemented by Yeltsin. While there had been a massive change in ownership of economic assets, there appeared to have been little in the way of evidence of an increase in entrepreneurial initiative which, according to its critics, had been suffocated under the old Soviet system. Under that pre-1991 system, growth had always been an important 'success indicator'. Although there had been some growth under Yeltsin, most of this had been negative. This was the result of the series of contractions experienced by the economy during the 1990s. This outcome was the complete opposite to what Yeltsin and his Western advisers had promised. These had stated that there would be a short-term fall in output, while a 'restructuring' took place to align resources with 'market demand' – which would then quickly lead to significant and consistent growth.

As Figure 9.3 shows, the reality was very different. Although there had been a fall in national income under the last years of Gorbachev, ten years of 'market reform' had clearly not reversed it. In fact, in cumulative terms, the fall in national income which took place during the early years of the Yeltsin-Gaidar reforms was unprecedented: greater than the Great Depression that had taken place in the West at the end of the 1920s, and greater than Russia had experienced during the First World War, the Civil War, or even the hugely destructive Great Patriotic War. This decline, according to official figures, was at last halted and even reversed – by just 0.4% – in 1997. However, there was little confidence in these official statistics – especially when, in 1998, a group of senior officials at the statistical office were arrested and charged with taking bribes.

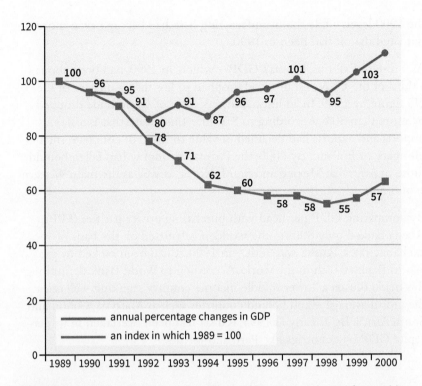

Figure 9.3: Russia's economic performance, 1989–2000. Adapted from White, S., 2011, **Understanding Russian Politics**, Cambridge, Cambridge University Press, p. 138.

In addition, as pointed out by S. White, figures relating to physical indicators, such as electricity consumption – which are less open to manipulation, suggest that, in fact, there was a *fall* of between 3% and 4% in that year. The collapse of the currency which took place in 1998 led to a further contraction. As a result, by the time Yeltsin resigned, Russia's Gross Domestic Product (one way economists estimate a country's economy and wealth) was not much higher than it had been in the last year of communist rule.

The decline in the heavy industries of the old Soviet era was massive: between 1990 and 1999, coal, oil, gas and steel production all fell by about 30 to 35%. However, the decline in light industry's production of modern consumer goods was catastrophic – an overall fall of 85%. This was even more marked as regards advanced technology products, such as personal computers (90%), cameras (96%) and video recorders (over 99%). In addition, capital investment collapsed to less than 25% of the 1990 level; while the manufacturing base had become even more outdated than it had been in 1990.

As a result of all this, Russia's GDP – which, in 1990, had been about a third of the USA's GDP – had dropped to less than a quarter of the US figure by 1999. In addition, Russia's share of world trade dropped by more than 50%. According to S. White, this meant that Russia's imports and exports had declined in value to those of countries such as Hungary or Finland. By 2000, the Russian economy had fallen behind those of Australia, Mexico and South Korea, as well as the main Western economies.

By comparing GDP per head with purchasing power parities (PPP), Russia ranked only 80th in the world; if calculated on the basis of exchange rates, Russia was 98th – in 1990, it had been ranked by the World Bank as 16th in the world. According to World Bank definitions, this made Russia a 'lower middle income country', ranking well *below* the global average – and behind countries such as Malaysia, Gabon and South Africa. By as early as 1995, Russia had been overtaken in its per-capita GDP by countries like Peru and Jordan.

9.3 Has the 'spectre of communism' been laid to rest?

During 1989 and 1991, all the communist regimes in Eastern Europe, and then that of the Soviet Union itself, collapsed, following unsuccessful attempts to cope with the various economic and political crises they faced. In addition, from 1989, these states – often advised by US economists – quickly restored capitalist economies. These developments prompted Francis Fukuyama – then a US official – to announce that the 'end of history' had arrived. By this, he meant the final victory of 'liberal' capitalism over Marxism and communist (or other radical) movements based on this political philosophy.

'I CAN'T BELIEVE MY EYES!'

Figure 9.4: In this cartoon, Gorbachev leads a funeral procession burying communism, as Lenin, Stalin and Marx look down from 'Communist Paradise' above.

QUESTION

What is the message of the cartoon in figure 9.4? How does the cartoonist put this message across?

Certainly, after 1991, communism remained the official ideology of only a handful of states. Apart from China (which also soon started applying capitalist economic policies), the only other states to retain it were North Korea, Cuba and Vietnam, and of these, the latter two (once aid from the Soviet Union ceased) also began moving towards market-based economic reforms. By 2000, history's verdict on communism as a general political and economic theory seemed to be that – in practice – it had conspicuously failed.

9 The Soviet Union and Post-Soviet Russia (1924–2000)

The opening words of Marx's and Engels' *The Communist Manifesto*, first published in 1848, are: 'A spectre is haunting Europe – the spectre of communism.' Given the visible collapse by 1991 of most states claiming to be communist, this 'spectre' would appear to have been laid to rest. Certainly, the failure of attempts in the Soviet Union and Eastern Europe to construct socialism led to a 'retreat from Marxism' in the first decades after the collapse of these communist regimes.

Yet Marx's analysis had claimed that capitalist globalisation was bound to lead to periodic and serious economic crises – some of which could lead to its demise. And indeed the 2008 financial crash and the global economic crisis of 2011 (the worst since the 1930s), along with the ecological crises associated with the unrestricted drive for profit, suggest that Fukuyama's claim that capitalism was secure and that Marxism had been permanently consigned to the 'dustbin of history' might prove to be a rather premature judgement. Thus Marx's theories might still have some relevance for the 21st century.

Unregulated 'free' capitalist economies have proved to be as flawed as the 'actually existing' socialism of the former European communist regimes. This has left the 'Chicago School' economists – with their claims about the self-regulating 'rationality' of the global market, and their predictions that their 'market fundamentalism' would deliver tremendous economic growth *and* 'liberty' for *all* private individuals – with an ideology as untenable as the 'Marxism-Leninism' of the European communist regimes before 1991.

Thus historians such as E. Hobsbawm have argued that the events of 1989–91 and afterwards do not necessarily mark the end of Marxism or communism. They have pointed out that Marxist theory and communist practice arose from conditions of poverty, the destruction of war, and strong desires for liberty, fairness and equality. Some commentators have suggested that a newer, more liberal and libertarian, version of communism might emerge which will challenge both capitalist globalisation and the Stalinist versions of Marxism and communism which had marked the political forms of rule in the various 'communist' regimes of the Soviet Union and Eastern Europe.

SOURCE 9.12

The risk of a sharp shift of politics to a nationalist or confessional [religious] demagogic radical right is probably greatest in the formerly communist European countries... And yet, something has changed for the better. We have rediscovered that capitalism is not the answer, but the question... Since the 1970s the [capitalist] system... reverted to the extreme, one might even say pathological version of the policy of laissez-faire... that finally imploded in 2007–8. For almost twenty years after the end of the Soviet system, [capitalism's] ideologists believed that they had achieved 'the end of history', 'an unabashed victory of economic and political liberalism' (Fukuyama)... None of this is tenable any longer... Once again it is evident that even between major crises, 'the market' has no answer to the major problem confronting the twenty-first century: that unlimited and increasingly high-tech economic growth in the pursuit of unsustainable profit produces global wealth, but at the cost of an increasingly dispensable factor of production, human labour, and, one might add, of the globe's natural resources. Economic and political liberalism, singly or in combination, cannot provide the solution to the problems of the twenty-first century. Once again the time has come to take Marx seriously.

Hobsbawm, E., 2009, **How to Change the World: Tales of Marx and Marxism**, *London, Little, Brown, pp. 417–9.*

While many people in the developed world enjoy important freedoms and good living conditions, this is hardly true for millions of others. In fact, in some developed Western states since 2008, governments have imposed varying degrees of austerity cuts. In countries such as Greece and Spain, the poverty caused by these measures has led to the emergence of radical left-of-centre political movements, such as Syriza in Greece and Podemos in Spain. In 2015, Syriza became the largest party in the Greek parliament and headed a coalition government committed to ending austerity. However, despite winning a referendum to oppose further austerity, the government then decided to accept cuts being demanded by the European Union.

SOURCE 9.13

We have to take the long view of the historical process... For as long as contemporary capitalism, a system based on exploitation and inequality and recurring crises, not to mention its impact on the fragile economy of the planet, continues to exist, the possibility of anti-capitalist movements taking power cannot be ruled out... The duels between the possessors and the dispossessed continue, taking new forms.

Ali, T., 2009, **The Idea of Communism***, London, Seagull Books, pp. 112–14.*

Other commentators have observed that Marxism – in its original form – was in large part an extension of the 1789 French Revolution's ideals of 'liberty, equality and fraternity', as interpreted by the radical socialist Francois-Noel 'Gracchus' Babeuf (1760-97) and his 1796 'Conspiracy of Equals'. Movements calling for the full implementation of these ideals continue to emerge around the globe in the 21st century. Thus it may be rather too early for historians to proclaim the death and funeral of communism.

Paper 3 exam practice

Question

Examine the reasons for Yeltsin's decision to disperse the Congress of People's Deputies in 1993. **[15 marks]**

Skill

Writing a conclusion to your essay

Examiner's tips

Provided you have carried out all the steps recommended so far, it should be relatively easy to write one or two concluding paragraphs.

For this question, you will need to cover the following possible reasons:

- the economic and political problems that Yeltsin inherited in 1992
- the impact of his 'shock therapy' policies on the Russian economy and the people
- the lack of support from ordinary people because of the impact of his policies
- the extent of opposition he faced from the elected Congress of People's Deputies from 1992 to 1993 – including from the newly-established CPRF.

This question requires you to consider a **range** of different reasons and factors, and to support your analysis with **precise and specific** supporting knowledge – so avoid generalisations.

Also, such a question, which is asking for an evaluation or analysis of several reasons, implicitly expects you to come to some kind of **judgement** about which reason(s) was/were most important.

Common mistakes

Sometimes, candidates simply re-hash in their conclusion what they have written earlier – making the examiner read the same things twice! Generally, concluding paragraphs should be relatively short: the aim should be to come to a judgement or conclusion which is clearly based on what has already been written. If possible, a short but relevant quotation is a good way to round off an argument. Remember to refer to the simplified Paper 3 mark scheme in Chapter 10.

Sample student conclusion

As I have shown, it is difficult to come to a single conclusion about why Yeltsin decided to close down – by military force – the Congress of People's Deputies in October 1993. While the impact of his 'reforms' led to great poverty and suffering for millions of Russians, I don't think this was a major consideration in itself. However, he was certainly worried by the various opinion polls which showed him, and his economic policies, to be deeply unpopular with the majority of Russian citizens. More important, I think, was the advice of the Western 'Chicago Boys' – and some Western political leaders – who advised that, in order to carry through the economic policies they were recommending, it might be necessary to assume dictatorial powers, in order to override the growing popular opposition to his economic policies by adopting emergency powers and, if necessary, imposing them with military force.

However, the main reason for his decision was that the strong opposition coming from the elected Supreme Soviet and the Congress of People's Deputies, which contained a large number of deputies from the newly-formed Communist Party of the Russian Federation. In the run-up to October 1993, there were attempts by the Russian parliament to remove him as president via votes of no confidence – as allowed by the constitution in force at that time. I think it was this – in conjunction with the advice from the 'Chicago Boys' – that ultimately led him to have recourse to military action and the assumption of emergency powers until he could draw up a new constitution which would give him, as president, greater powers. It was this combination of reasons which ultimately lay behind his decision to go for the 'Pinochet option'.

EXAMINER'S COMMENT

This is a good conclusion as it briefly pulls together the main threads of the argument (without simply repeating or summarising them), and then also makes a clear judgement. In addition, there is an intelligent final comment which rounds off the whole conclusion – and no doubt the core of the essay – in a memorable way.

Activity

In this chapter, the focus is on writing a useful conclusion. So, using the information from this chapter, and any other sources of information available to you, write concluding paragraphs for **at least two** of the following Practice Paper 3 questions. Remember – to do this, you will need to do full plans for the questions you choose.

Paper 3 practice questions

1   To what extent were Yeltsin's economic policies after 1992 essentially those put forward by Western economic and financial advisers?

2   Discuss the main results of Yeltsin's economic policies on the Russian economy in the period 1992–2000.

3   'Yeltsin attempted to establish an autocratic political system after 1992.' To what extent do you agree with this statement?

4   Examine the impact of Yeltsin's economic policies on the lives of Russian citizens after 1992.

5   Evaluate the reasons for the growth of opposition to Yeltsin's governments in the period 1992–99.

10 | Exam Practice

Introduction

You have now completed your study of the main events and developments in the Soviet Union and post-Soviet Russia during the period 1924–2000. You have also had the chance to examine the various historical debates and differing historical interpretations which surround some of these developments.

In the previous chapters, you have encountered examples of Paper 3-type essay questions, with examiner's tips. You have also had some basic practice in answering such questions. In this chapter, these tips and skills will be developed in more depth. Longer examples of possible student answers are provided, accompanied by examiner's comments which should increase your understanding of what examiners are looking for when they mark your essays. Following each question and answer, you will find tasks to give you further practice in the skills needed to gain the higher marks in this exam.

IB History Paper 3 exam questions and skills

If you are following HL Option 4 – *History of Europe* – you will have studied in depth **three** of the eighteen sections available for this HL Option. *The Soviet Union and post-Soviet Russia 1924–2000* is one of those sections. For Paper 3, two questions are set from each of the 18 sections, giving 36 questions in total; you have to answer **three** of these.

Each question has a specific mark scheme. However the 'generic' mark scheme in the *IB History Guide* gives you a general idea of what examiners are looking for in order to be able to put answers into the higher bands. In particular, you will need to acquire reasonably precise historical knowledge so that you can address issues such as cause and effect, change and continuity, and so that you can explain historical developments in a clear, coherent, well-supported and relevant way. You will also need to understand relevant historical debates and interpretations; refer to these and critically evaluate them.

Essay planning

Make sure you read each question *carefully*, noting all the important key or 'command' words – you might find it useful to highlight them on your question paper. You can then produce a rough plan (for example a spider diagram) of *each* of the three essays you intend to attempt, *before* you start to write your answers: that way, you will soon know whether you have enough own knowledge to answer them adequately. Next, refer back to the wording of each question – this will help you see whether or not you are responding to *all* its various demands / aspects. In addition, if you run short of time towards the end of your exam, you will at least be able to jot down in note form – and in a clear and structured way – the key issues / points you would have gone on to address. It is thus far better to do the planning at the *start* of the exam.

Relevance to the question

Remember, too, to keep your answers relevant and focused on the question – don't go outside the dates mentioned in the question, or write answers on subjects not identified in that question. Also, don't just *describe* the events or developments – sometimes, students just focus on one key word, date or individual, and then write down everything they know about it. Instead, select your own knowledge carefully, and pin the relevant information to the key features raised by the question. Finally, if the question asks for 'reasons' and 'effects', 'continuity and change', 'successes and failures', or 'nature and development', make sure you deal with *all* the parts of the question. Otherwise, you will limit yourself to half marks at best.

Examiner's tips

For Paper 3 answers, examiners are looking for well-structured arguments which:

- are consistently relevant / linked to the question
- offer clear / precise analysis / evaluation
- are supported by the deployment of accurate, precise and relevant own knowledge
- offer a balanced judgement
- refer to different historical debates / interpretations or to relevant historians and, where relevant, offer some critical evaluation of these.

Simplified mark scheme

Band		Marks
1	**Consistently clear understanding of and focus** on the question, with **all main aspects addressed.** Answer is **fully analytical, balanced** and **well-structured/organised.** Own knowledge is **detailed, accurate and relevant**, with events placed **in their historical context.** There is **developed critical analysis**, and **sound understanding of historical concepts.** Examples used are **relevant**, and used effectively **to support analysis/evaluation.** The answer also integrates **evaluation of different historical debates/perspectives.** All/almost all of the main points are **substantiated**, and the answer reaches a **clear/reasoned/consistent judgement/conclusion.**	13–15
2	**Clear understanding of the question**, and most of its **main aspects are addressed.** Answer is mostly **well-structured and developed**, though, with **some repetition/lack of clarity** in places. Supporting **own knowledge mostly relevant/accurate**, and events are placed **in their historical context.** The answer is **mainly analytical**, with relevant examples **used to support critical analysis/evaluation.** There is **some understanding/evaluation of historical concepts and debates/perspectives.** Most of the main points **are substantiated**, and the answer offers a **consistent conclusion.**	10–12
3	**Demands of the question are understood** – but some aspects **not fully developed/addressed.** **Mostly relevant/accurate supporting own knowledge**, and events generally placed **in their historical context. Some attempts at analysis/evaluation but these are limited/not sustained/inconsistent.**	7–9
4	**Some understanding** of the question. **Some relevant own knowledge**, with some factors identified – but with **limited explanation. Some attempts at analysis**, but answer **lacks clarity/coherence, and is mainly description/narrative.**	4–6
5	**Limited understanding of/focus on** the question. **Short/generalised** answer, with very **little accurate/relevant own knowledge.** Some **unsupported assertions**, with **no real analysis.**	0–3

Student answers

The extracts from student answers which follow will have brief examiner comments throughout, and a longer overall comment at the end. Those parts of student answers which are particularly strong and well-focused (such as demonstrations of precise and relevant own knowledge, or examination of historical interpretations) will be highlighted in red. Errors/confusions/irrelevance/loss of focus will be highlighted in blue. In this way, you should find it easier to follow why marks were awarded or withheld.

Question 1

'Khrushchev fell from power in 1964 because he had attempted to do too much, too soon.' To what extent do you agree with this statement? **[15 marks]**

Figure 10.1: Nikita Khrushchev and Fidel Castro on the rostrum of V.I. Lenin Mausoleum, 1962.

Skills

- factual knowledge and understanding
- structured, analytical and **balanced** argument
- awareness/understanding/evaluation of historical interpretations
- clear and balanced judgement

Examiner's tips

Look carefully at the wording of this question, which asks you to consider the view that Khrushchev's overthrow in 1964 was the result of his attempting too many reforms, at too quick a pace. This means you would need to show *both* how the statement is true *and* how it is not true. Thus, remember, it is perfectly all right for you to challenge the view – as long as you support your arguments with relevant and precise own knowledge. All aspects of the question will need to be addressed in order to achieve high marks. And remember – don't just describe what Khrushchev did: what's needed is explicit analysis and explanation of his policies and actions, *and* how these do or do not explain his fall. So try to consider other factors which might explain his *fall*.

Student answer

Khrushchev came to power in the mid-1950s, following the death of Stalin in 1953. At first, there was a collective leadership, with the main people being Malenkov, Molotov, Bulganin and Khrushchev. However, by 1955, Khrushchev had already begun to establish himself as the dominant figure. By 1958, this was completed – in that year, Khrushchev, like Stalin, combined both the post of first-secretary of the party and prime minister of the government. He held this dominant position until his fall in 1964. In the six years in which he held such power, he tried to push through various reforms – these included de-Stalinisation, and attempts to improve the Soviet economy. Many of these reforms were disliked by other leading communists, and by the bureaucrats who administered the state and the economy. The reforms, their speed, and their outcomes were all factors behind his fall. To a large extent, this was because they were so different from Stalin's policies and methods of rule.

10

The Soviet Union and Post-Soviet Russia (1924–2000)

EXAMINER'S COMMENT

This is a clear and well-focused introduction, showing accurate knowledge of the topic, and a good understanding of several of the general factors contributing to Khrushchev's overthrow in 1964.

To understand why Khrushchev's reforms were so disliked, it is necessary to understand what Stalin's methods of rule and policies had been. Many of the top people in the Soviet Union – like Khrushchev himself – had been in important positions under Stalin. This meant they were used to a certain way of working.

One of the main features of Stalin's rule was fear. All communists – especially those at the top – were afraid that Stalin might purge them. This was based on what Stalin had done in the 1930s. Following Kirov's assassination in 1934, Stalin launched what became known as the 'Great Purge and the Great Terror'. Leading Communists (who had worked closely with Lenin in the years before and after 1917) were accused of plotting against Stalin and the Soviet Union. Following a series of 'Show Trials', these people (such as Zinoviev, Kamenev and Bukharin) were found guilty and executed. Many of them pleaded guilty to the charges – often as a result of sleep deprivation and beatings during their interrogations by the secret police, or because of threats too their families if they did not 'confess'. These purges were extended to the military – most of the top generals were executed. After the Second World War, though the numbers involved were much smaller, Stalin continued to purge and execute people.

EXAMINER'S COMMENT

Although there is some accurate own knowledge, this is mostly background material, and so is not explicitly linked to the demands of the question. While making a brief reference or two to the historical context preceding Khrushchev's period in control is a sound idea, it is not wise to give too much information on this. What is needed is precise own knowledge of what Khrushchev attempted to do between 1955 and 1964, and how this may have contributed to his fall. The amount of detail provided about Stalin's purges suggests that this answer might easily slip into irrelevant narrative.

In fact, there are several different theories about why these purges took place, and why Stalin was able to come out as the top leader of the Soviet Communist

Party, even though no one had ever thought he would succeed. One theory – the totalitarian one – sees them as the result of Stalin's desire to remain as top leader. Others, such as Tucker, however, think they were mainly the result of Stalin suffering from some sort of mental illness. However, various revisionist theories say they were a response to genuine threats to his position. Finally, historians such as Rittersporn see them mainly as resulting from local officials who were more extreme than Stalin wanted to be.

EXAMINER'S COMMENT

This paragraph shows awareness of an aspect of historical debate, although these different interpretations are merely mentioned, with no attempt to evaluate them. However, the overriding point is that all this information is largely irrelevant – and so will not score any marks. The candidate is thus wasting time, when he/she should be writing about Khrushchev's rule. It is possible that this candidate had revised Stalin very well – but had been unprepared to answer any question on another leader. Remember – it is important to study all the bullet points set down in the IB History Guide, as each section will have only two questions set on it.

When Khrushchev came to power, he had two main aims – to alter the methods of rule associated with Stalin, and to alter aspects of the Soviet economy. Stalin's main policies were based on his policy of 'Socialism in One Country'. In fact, this had been an important part in Stalin's rise to power in the struggle for power between him and Trotsky, which took place in the four years following Lenin's death in 1924. Lenin in fact had tried to get Stalin dismissed from his posts – especially as General-Secretary of the Communist Party, but Stalin had been able to get the party not to act on Lenin's wishes. Once in power, Stalin then put this policy of 'Socialism in One Country' into practice – his main policies for this were the forced collectivisation of agriculture and the Five-Year Plans.

EXAMINER'S COMMENT

Again, there is accurate own knowledge in this paragraph – but this is not what the question requires. Despite an opening sentence which suggests the correct focus might now be applied, the candidate instead produces another irrelevant section.

[There then follow several more paragraphs giving detailed and accurate accounts of Stalin's economic policies.]

Thus, when Khrushchev took control, he was determined to alter things. First of all, he decided to stop the terror which had existed under Stalin – in fact, though, this was not just his policy. All the leaders after 1953 wanted to avoid going back to the years of fear and terror. That is why Beria, the head of the KGB, was quickly arrested and executed. After 1953, top communists who lost support in power struggles were simply removed from their posts.

However, Khrushchev did initiate a policy which was his own – de-Stalinisation. This was an attempt to release people from the gulags, and to allow more freedom to writers and artists. One book that resulted was Solzhenitsyn's One Day in the Life of Ivan Denisovich, which Khrushchev insisted was published in 1962 – even though it was a novel about life in a forced labour camp. He also made a 'secret' speech at the 20th Party Congress in 1956, attacking Stalin for his brutality and mistakes. However, this was leaked, and caused unrest in Poland and especially in Hungary, where a revolt broke out.

He also introduced various economic policies – such as his 'Virgin Lands' scheme. These were intended to increase both agricultural and industrial production. However, these were very often changed half-way through, and so caused much confusion.

EXAMINER'S COMMENT

At last, there is some relevant focus on the demands of the question – and what own knowledge there is, is relevant and mostly accurate, and sometimes precise. However, there is little development of Khrushchev's attempts at de-Stalinisation, and there is no precise knowledge of the various economic policies. Once again, this suggests that Khrushchev's rule had not been well revised.

So, in conclusion, I think the view expressed in the question is correct. Given what had happened under Stalin, who only died in 1953, he should have moved more slowly. If he had, he might not have toppled in 1964.

EXAMINER'S COMMENT

There is then a brief conclusion, which makes a valid judgement.
Unfortunately, this is neither a supported judgement (because
most of the detailed information given has been about the Stalin
era), nor a balanced one (there has been no consideration of 'other
factors' or explanations which might explain Khrushchev's fall –
such as his various foreign policy actions).

Overall examiner comments

There is plentiful and accurate own knowledge – unfortunately, it
is *mostly irrelevant*. While there are some hints of analysis, it is mostly
descriptive. The bulk of the answer is thus not really focused on the
demands of the question. However, there are brief sections which *are*
relevant, so the answer is thus probably just good enough to be awarded
a mark in Band 4 (4-6 marks). What was needed was an answer which
focused on Khrushchev's various policies, and which showed their
impact – and how other communists leaders felt about them. The
candidate also needed to demonstrate consideration of other aspects
of Khrushchev's policies which were not a question of 'too much, too
soon' – for instance, foreign policy events such as the Cuban Missile
Crisis. Also, though there was some awareness of (irrelevant) historical
debate, it was not evaluative.

ACTIVITY

Look again at the simplified mark scheme, and the student
answer above. Now draw up a plan focused on the demands of
the question. Then try to write several paragraphs which will be
good enough to get into Band 1, and so obtain the full 15 marks.
As well as making sure you address *all* aspects of the question, try
to integrate into your answer some references *and* evaluation of
relevant historians / historical interpretations.

10

Question 2

Compare and contrast the domestic policies of Stalin and Gorbachev.
[15 marks]

Skills

- factual knowledge and understanding
- structured, analytical and balanced argument
- awareness/understanding/evaluation of historical interpretations

Examiner's tips

Look carefully at the wording of this question, which asks you to
compare and contrast the domestic policies of Stalin and Gorbachev.
Questions like this show how important it is to study *all* the bullet
points in the sections you study. If you only select a few of the named
individuals for detailed study, you could seriously limit your options
in the exam. To answer questions like this in the most effective way,
it is best to structure your answer so that the comparisons / contrasts
are brought out *explicitly*. In other words, draw up a rough plan with
headings for 'comparisons' and 'contrasts' – then jot down where aspects
of their policies were similar under 'comparisons'; and where / how
they were different under 'contrasts'. And remember – don't just *describe*
what their policies were: what's needed is *explicit focus* on similarities *and*
differences.

Figure 10.2: Gorbachev, the General Secretary of the Soviet Communist Party, meets workers of the Volga factory in 1986 in Kuibyshev, USSR.

Student answer

Although Stalin and Gorbachev were very different on most issues, there was at least one area in domestic affairs where they were similar – and this is that they both wanted to maintain some kind of socialist society in the Soviet Union. To show this, I shall examine Stalin's policies first, and then look at Gorbachev's domestic policies.

EXAMINER'S COMMENT

This introduction starts in a generally promising way. However, the final sentence in this paragraph is very worrying – this is because such an approach will almost certainly result in a narrative of the two sets of policies with, at best, only some kind of implicit comparison/contrast. As has been seen in previous answers, a narrative account without clear focus on the demands of the questions unlikely to get beyond Band 4 (6 marks).

Stalin's main domestic policies can be divided into two areas – political policies designed to maintain his power, and economic and social ones intended to transform the Soviet Union into a modern and industrialised socialist state. The main political policies he followed to establish and maintain his power were a combination of terror and propaganda. Although he was in a powerful position by 1928, his power was not fully secure. Many communists were concerned about aspects of his economic policies – such as the problems caused by forced collectivisation. This lack of total power is shown by the fact that in 1932, there was the Ryutin Affair – several leading communists signed a document which, as well as criticising forced collectivisation and calling for the return of expelled oppositionists, also called for Stalin's dismissal. Although Stalin managed to get these people expelled from the Central Committee, the Politburo refused to back his call for Ryutin's execution.

EXAMINER'S COMMENT

This paragraph contains a lot of very precise information – and is clearly the result of solid revision. However, it is mainly background material – there is little on his actual policies.

This episode made Stalin feel insecure. His bid for total power came just two years later, in 1934. The previous year, 1933, had seen another call for Stalin's dismissal – this time from Smirnov, a leading communist. At the 17th Party Congress in 1934, there appears to have been an attempt to persuade Kirov – a popular Politburo member and the party boss of Leningrad – to stand against Stalin. Although he refused, this Congress abolished the post of General-Secretary (held by Stalin) – in theory, this meant he was now no more important than the other three secretaries of the CPSU. Later that year, Kirov was assassinated – this gave Stalin the excuse to begin a purge of the party, in what was his first policy designed to establish his control. He used the NKVD, headed by Yagoda, to have hundreds of party members shot, while thousands – including leading communists such as Zinoviev and Kamenev – were arrested and imprisoned. While this purge came to a halt in 1935, the following year saw the start of what became known as the 'Great Purge.'

EXAMINER'S COMMENT

Again, there is a lot of accurate own knowledge – this time, some of it is relevant, as it deals with Stalin's use of purges. However, so far, this answer seems to be turning into a descriptive account of what Stalin did – there has as yet been no attempt to address the key issue of similarities / differences. This is the danger with such a 'one by one' approach to questions like this.

Stalin's 'Great Purge' began in 1936 with the first of three 'Show Trials' – there were others in 1937 and 1938. As a result of these Show Trials, most of the leading communists – who might have been rivals – were executed. He then extended the purges to the leaders of the armed forces – by then, the Great Purge had become the 'Great Terror'. As the threat of war increased, following Hitler's appointment as chancellor of Germany in 1933, Stalin feared the military leaders might use war as an opportunity to overthrow him. In all, it is estimated that almost 505 of the officer corps were executed or imprisoned. The Great Terror came to an end in 1939 – by then, Stalin was left with almost total power.

However, as well as purges and terror, Stalin also used the political policy of propaganda to secure his position. He was increasingly compared to Lenin in a very favourable way – his early differences with Lenin (and especially Lenin's call, just before he died, to have Stalin dismissed from his posts) were never mentioned. Soon, a 'cult of personality' was developed – and statues and posters of Stalin appeared in public places and factories. Streets and towns were also named after him. In addition, newspaper articles, poems and films all praised his great leadership.

EXAMINER'S COMMENT

Again, there is plenty of accurate own knowledge, some of which supports the political policies Stalin followed. However – as in the previous paragraphs – no comparisons/contrasts with Gorbachev's political style and policies have been made.

[There then follow several paragraphs on Stalin's main economic and social polcies – touching on forced collectivism, industrialisation, policies towards women, young people and religion. However, there is absolutely nothing on Gorbachev's domestic policies.]

Stalin's policies – both political, and social and economic – were thus very brutal, and involved the death and suffering of millions. However, although he created a police state, he did make the Soviet Union strong – by the time of his death, the Soviet Union had become a regional (if not a global) superpower. It also had a buffer zone made up of several East European 'satellite' states. This is very different from Gorbachev – whose approach was much more democratic and tolerant. Yet, under his policies, the Soviet Union became increasingly weak – it lost its East European buffer zone in 1988–9, and eventually collapsed in

1991. Thus his policies were very different from Stalin's – and had very different results.

Overall examiner comments

Though there is precise and accurate own knowledge, the essay is basically a narrative of Stalin's domestic policies. If the candidate had written about Gorbachev in the same way, then the answer would have been awarded Band 4 (6 marks) – even though it hasn't really addressed the demands of the question.

However, because it *only* deals with Stalin, it can only be awarded Band 5 – which would be 3 marks at most. To reach Band 3 and higher, the answer would need some **explicit and well-structured treatment of comparisons and contrasts, with consistent analysis of *both* similarities and differences.**

ACTIVITY

Look again at the simplified mark scheme, and the student answer above. Now draw up a plan, with a structure focused on the demands of the question. Then try to write your own answer, making sure you consistently make comparisons and contrasts – so that the answer can get into Band 1 and obtain the full 15 marks.

Question 3

Examine the reasons why, and the extent to which, the USSR experienced stagnation during the period 1964-85. **[15 marks]**

Skills

- factual knowledge and understanding
- structured, analytical and balanced argument
- awareness/understanding/evaluation of historical interpretations

Examiner's tips

Look carefully at the wording of this question, which requires **two** aspects to be addressed: reasons for stagnation, and the extent to which the term 'stagnation' is a valid one when looking at the Soviet Union during the 21-year period identified in the question. Both aspects of the question – reasons *and* extent – will need to be addressed if high marks are to be achieved. And remember – don't just describe what happened: what's needed is explicit analysis and explanation, with precise supporting own knowledge. There are also some relevant historical debates which could be made part of the answer.

Student answer

The period between the fall of Khrushchev and the coming to power of Gorbachev is seen by most historians as one of stagnation – both political and economic. The reasons for this stagnation are various – however, four factors were especially important: the opposition from many managers and bureaucrats to any reforms which disrupted the working patterns they were used to; the fear that reducing state control would lead to capitalism; corruption at all levels of the system; and the impact of the nuclear arms race on the Soviet economy. However, it is important to realise that stagnation wasn't a constant factor during this period – certainly, up till the mid-1970s, the USSR was still able to achieve reasonable results.

The Soviet Union and Post-Soviet Russia (1924–2000)

EXAMINER'S COMMENT

This is a clear and well-focused introduction, showing a good appreciation of all the demands of the question, and indicating an analytical approach is likely to be followed. This is a good start.

In many ways, it is difficult to justify the use of the term 'stagnation' when looking at the USSR in the mid-1960s. For instance, it was during the period 1964–74 that the USSR – though with only half the GDP of the US – was able to catch up with the US in terms of nuclear weaponry in many areas. Such an achievement doesn't suggest stagnation. By 1964, the USSR had scored a number of 'firsts' in the space race – the first orbiting satellite and the first man in space.

The economic and political system which had delivered these successes was a centralised one controlled by an undemocratic state – as it was this system which had industrialised an essentially backward agricultural economy, and made it strong enough to survive and then defeat the armed might of Nazi Germany, there seemed to be little reason for making major changes. Yet there were inefficiencies – and it was Khrushchev's various attempts to introduce economic and political reforms to overcome these which had played a big part in his downfall in 1964.

EXAMINER'S COMMENT

There is some accurate supporting own knowledge, explicitly linked to the question's issue of stagnation – but, so far, there has been little examination of the evidence of stagnation.

There are really two aspects to the question of stagnation in the USSR during this period – one is political stagnation, the other is economic. As regards political stagnation, this was mainly the result of Stalin's establishment of a strict central control during the 1930s. This had continued until his death in 1953 – one result was that political leaders and economic managers had become too afraid to initiate reforms in case they got into trouble. Khrushchev had tried to overcome some of this by his policy of de-Stalinisation – but though this was limited and controlled from the centre, it had helped spark off unrest in the East European satellite states (especially in Hungary). This had frightened many Soviet leaders, and so made them more cautious about political reform. Consequently, when Brezhnev and Kosygin replaced him in 1964, they tended to take a more conservative approach – although they made no attempt to go back to Stalin's brutal methods. Khrushchev's reforms had also upset many party bureaucrats, and his successors were keen to get them 'on side' by promising them that there would be no major shake-up under their leadership. While this assured them of support, it did nothing to modernise the system. As a result, there was political stagnation when the demands of managing a modern industrial society in the mid-twentieth century needed a more dynamic and responsive system.

EXAMINER'S COMMENT

Again, this is a well-focused paragraph, with some initial analysis of why there was political stagnation. So far, though, there is limited precise supporting own knowledge.

This political stagnation can be seen in the fact that under Brezhnev – who by 1970 was clearly the most dominant leader – the average age of the Politburo rose from 58 to 68; the situation was similar in both the Central Committee and the government. As a general policy, if anyone died or was sacked, they were replaced by someone old rather than by someone young. This is why the Brezhnev leadership was sometimes referred to as a gerontocracy. By sticking with older officials, the push for significant reform was reduced.

This political conservativism and stagnation was also caused by the 'nomenklatura' system – this was a list of 'reliable' party and administrative people. As all top- and middle-ranking appointments to party and state were made from this list, the temptation was not to cause problems to ensure you stayed on the list. This, too, led to conservatism.

An additional sign of these problems of stagnation was that the annual increase in Communist Party membership dropped to lower levels under Brezhnev compared to the situation under Khrushchev: from about 7% a year to only 2%. Many Soviet citizens were disillusioned by the signs of widespread corruption – this corruption even applied to Brezhnev's own family.

EXAMINER'S COMMENT

Very relevant paragraphs, focused on how the political conservatism and thus stagnation arose from aspects of the way the Communist Party was run, and from widespread corruption. The approach is still mainly analytical, and focused on the demands of the question.

[There then follow several paragraphs – with detailed supporting own knowledge – analysing economic stagnation and the reasons for this. There are also sections assessing the relative degree of stagnation. However, there is no mention or evaluation of different historians' views.]

In conclusion, there were clear signs of stagnation in the USSR during this period – and they were becoming more serious by the time Gorbachev took over in 1985. However, this was not true for all parts of that period – especially, in the period up to 1974, the Soviet Union was still dynamic enough to achieve certain successes.

Despite this, the low levels of labour productivity, and the increasing slowdown in economic growth, were serious signs of stagnation – and eventual collapse.

EXAMINER'S COMMENT
The conclusion is brief but well-focused, and ends a well-focused and analytical argument.

Overall examiner comments

This is a good, well-focused and analytical answer, with some precise and accurate own knowledge to support the points made. The answer is thus certainly good enough to be awarded a mark in Band 3 – and possibly at the lower end of Band 2. To reach the top of Band 2, and to get into Band 1, the candidate needed to provide some reference to historians' views / historical interpretations, and some critical evaluation of these interpretations.

ACTIVITY

Look again at the simplified mark scheme, and the student answer above. Now try to write your own answer to the question, and attempt to make it good enough to get into Band 1 and so obtain the full 15 marks. In particular, make sure you are aware of the main historical debates about this topic – and incorporate some critical evaluation of them in your answer.

Index

Abalkin Programme 245
absenteeism from work 179
Abyssinia 75
Afghanistan 162, 182, 186–8,
    189, 226–7
Aganbegyan, Abel (b. 1932)
    198, 199, 200, 203
agriculture *see also*
    collectivization
    under Brezhnev 176–7
    collectivisation's impact
        on 63–4
    under Gorbachev 202–3,
        205
    'grain crisis' 53
    under Khrushchev 129,
        138
    kolkhozes (co-operative
        farms) 59, 99, 176–7, 202
    New Economic Policy
        (NEP) 57 and
    Sovkhozes (state-run
        farms) 99, 203
    under Stalin 49–50,
        57–61, 89, 100
Akhmatova, Anna 135
alcoholism 179
Ali, T. 211, 272, 296
Andropov, Yuri (1914-84)
    162, 169–70, 177–9, 189
Anti-Comintern Pact (1937)
    75
Argentina 270
arms, manufacture of *see*
    defence industry
arts, the *see* culture and the
    arts
austerity programmes 19,
    243, 295
Austria 76
authoritarianism 254–6

Babeuf, Francois-Noel
    'Gracchus' (1760-97) 296
Baikal-Amur Magistral
    (BAM) railway 176

Balkan Federation 116
Baltic states 74, 79, 91, 93,
    168, 223, 224, 252
Barsov, A. 64
Baruch, Bernard 18
Bazhanov, Boris (1900-83)
    30
Belorussia 93, 240, 258
Beria, Lavrenti (1899-1953)
    70, 129, 131
Berlin, Treaty of (1930) 74
Berlin Blockade and Airlift
    (1948-49) 118
Berlin Crisis 150–1
Berlin Wall 129, 151, 230
bias 106, 166, 273
birth rates 277
Biryukova, Alexandra
    215–16
Bizonia 117–18
Bolshevik Revolution
    (1917) 16, 23, 25
Bonner, Elena 167
Brezhnev, Leonid (1906-
    1982)
    agriculture under 176–7
    background 136
    corruption under 164–5
    culture and the arts
        under 166
    death of 162, 169
    Eastern Europe under
        184–6
    economic policies under
        172–8
    Five-Year Plans 173,
        175–6
    Foreign policy under
        180–1, 183–8
    industry under 173–6
    Khrushchev and 136
    living standards under
        172, 177–8
    neo-Stalinism 165–9
    rise to power 163–4
    Sovietisation and 223

as successor to
    Khrushchev 155
Brezhnev Doctrine (1968)
    185, 197, 229
'Brezhnev Mafia' 164
Britain
    alliance with Soviet
        Union 75–6, 78, 81,
        88–9, 100–3
    declaration of war against
        Germany 80
    Munich Agreement
        (1938) 77
    NATO (North Atlantic
        Treaty Organisation)
        (1949) 119
    neo-liberalism in 19
    Percentages Agreement
        (1944) 102–3
    post-war Germany and
        117–18
    Potsdam Conference
        (1945) 89, 106–7
    Second World War and
        101
    support of right-wing
        groups 76
    Tehran Conference
        (1943) 88–9, 102
    Yalta Conference (1945)
        89, 103–6
Brown, A. 260
Brussels Treaty Organisation
    (BTO) 119
Brzezinski, Zbigniew 261
Bukharin, Nikolai 24, 27, 33,
    34, 38–40, 51, 52, 53, 57,
    58, 64, 67–8, 69
Bukovski, Vladimir 168
Bulganin, Nikolai 131, 132,
    149, 154
Bulgaria 113, 116
Bush, George 258, 261

C. Ward 91
calendar 23

The Soviet Union and Post-Soviet Russia (1924–2000)

Canada 119
Capitalism
  vs. communism 12
  definition of 18
  Gorbachev's reforms
  and 203
  historians on 294–5
  New Economic Policy
  (NEP) and 26, 43
  under Yeltsin 273
Carr, E. H. 41
Castro, Fidel 152
Caucasus 63
censorship 134, 171, 279
Chernenko, Konstantin 169,
  171–2, 178–80, 189
Chernobyl nuclear plant
  211–12
Chernomrydin, Viktor 284
Chicago School 19, 270
Chile 270
China 76, 129, 149, 152–3,
  183, 284
Chubais, Anatoly 274, 282
Churchill, Winston 73, 94,
  102, 112, 116
CIS see Commonwealth of
  Independent States (CIS)
Civil War, Russian (1918–
  21) 25, 73
Cohen, Stephen 41, 214
Cold War see also Second
  Cold War
  Afghanistan and 226–7
  defence spending and
  99–100, 162
  definition of 17–18
  economy and 180–1
  Grand Alliance collapse
  and 89, 101
  nuclear arms race 110,
  119–20, 121, 260–1
collectivisation 49–50, 57–
  61, 63–4, 100, 138
Comecon (Council for
  Mutual Economic
  Assistance) 89, 119, 185
Cominform (Communist
  Information Bureau) 89,
  115, 116, 120
Comintern (Communist
  International) 34, 73, 115
Committee for State

Security (KGB) see KGB
  (Committee for State
  Security)
Commonwealth of
  Independent States (CIS)
  240, 258
communism see also Russian
  Communist Party (RCP)
  China-Soviet split 153
  collapse of 230–3, 245,
  292–4
  definition and
  explanation of 12–14
  historians on 294
  Khrushchev on 136
  War Communism 25–6
Communist Manifesto, The
  (Marx & Engels) 12, 294
Communist Party of the
  Russian Federation
  (CPRF) 269, 277–8, 280,
  287
Communist Party of the
  Soviet Union (CPSU) see
  also Russian Communist
  Party (RCP)
  19th Party Conference
  218–20
  27th Congress 215–18
  crisis within 209–10
  name change to, from
  Russian Communist
  Party (RCP) 99
  reforms, under
  Gorbachev 204, 222–3,
  251
  Yeltsin and 277–8
Conference on Security and
  Cooperation in Europe
  (CSCE) 167, 183, 184
Congress of People's
  Deputies (CPD) 218–19,
  220–1, 269, 270
Conquest, Robert 41, 63
consumer goods 141, 143,
  173, 175, 177–8, 180–1,
  188, 291
Conventional Forces in
  Europe Treaty (1990) 261
'conveyor system' 67
Cooper, J. 63
'cordon sanitaire'
  (containment policy) 73

corruption 164–5, 169–70,
  171, 211, 224, 268, 283–4
CPRF see Communist
  Party of the Russian
  Federation (CPRF)
CPSU see Communist Party
  of the Soviet Union
  (CPSU)
Cuban Missile Crisis (1962)
  129, 152
cult of personality 97
culture and the arts
  under Brezhnev 166
  under Gorbachev 212
  under Khrushchev 134–5
  under Stalin 98
Czechoslovakia 75, 76, 77,
  113–14, 162, 183, 184,
  230

Daniels, R. 43, 214
Das Kapital (Marx) 12
Davies, R. W. 63
deaths see mortality rates
defence industry 56, 99–100,
  162, 180–1, 260–1 see
  also industry; nuclear
  arms race
demokratizatsiya
  (democratisation) 195,
  197, 208–9, 213–14,
  216–20, 248–56
demonstrations see also
  dissidents
  coup against Gorbachev
  257–8
  in East Germany 144,
  150
  in Eastern Europe 197,
  230
  in Georgia 224
  in Hungary 146
  labour unrest 206, 242
  nationalism and 168–9
  in Poland 186
  in Red Square (1965)
  165
  against Yeltsin 279
de-Stalinisation 128, 129,
  132–7, 145, 154
détente 166, 183–4, 186, 188
Deutscher, I. 33, 40, 42, 67,
  72, 214

dissidents 135, 165–9, 170, 213 *see also* demonstrations
Doctor Zhivago (Pasternak) 135
Drach, Marcel 241
Dubcek, Alexander (1921-92) 184–5

Eastern Europe *see also specific countries*
under Brezhnev 184–6
as 'buffer zone' 80, 89, 108, 109, 121, 182, 184, 228
collapse of communism in 230–3, 245
demonstrations in 197
de-Stalinisation of 145
under Gorbachev 227–33
under Khrushchev 144–8
neo-liberalism in 231–2
Percentages Agreement (1944) 102–3, 105, 111, 116
as 'satellite states' 115
Sovietisation of 120–1, 145, 223–4
under Stalin 89, 91, 108–23
'velvet revolutions' 230–3
economic determinism 56
economic policies *see also* Five-Year Plans
under Andropov 177–9
under Brezhnev 172–8
under Chernenko 178–80
under Gorbachev 195, 197, 198–206, 228, 241–7
under Khrushchev 137–44
New Economic Policy (NEP) 26
'shock therapy' 19, 232, 269, 270–7, 286, 288
under Stalin 51–64, 99–100
under Yeltsin 268, 269, 270–7, 280–1, 283–4, 286–90

economy, the
Cold War and 180–1
collapse of 242–3, 288–92
growth rate, under Gorbachev 198–9
impact of Great Patriotic War on 96
reconstruction of, after war 99–100
reform models 241
socialism vs. market economy 245–7, 253
education 30, 143, 171
Ehrenburg, Ilya, *The Thaw* 134
Eisenhower, Dwight D. 149
Elections
in Bulgaria 113
in Czechoslovakia 113–14
under Gorbachev 216–17, 220–2, 248
in Hungary 113
in Poland 112
rigged, in Eastern Europe 113–14, 120
in Romania 113
under Yeltsin 270, 279–83
Ellman, M. 63
embargoes 73
employment
absenteeism from work 179
labour shortage 176
minimum wage 143
productivity incentives and 209–10
wage differentials 177
working conditions 143, 206
Engels, Friedrich (1820-95) 12, 294
Estonia 74, 79, 252 *see also* Baltic states
ethics 133
ethnic tensions 224, 252
Ezhov, Nikolai (1895-1940) 68, 70

Fainsod, M. 71
famines *see* food shortages

farming *see* agriculture; *kolkhozes* (co-operative farms); *sovkhozes* (state-run farms)
Fatherland Front, Bulgaria 113
financial crisis (2008) 272, 294
financial crisis (2011) 294
Finland 74, 79, 91, 223
First World War (1914-18) 25
Fitzpatrick, S. 43
Five-Year Plans 49–50, 52–6, 62, 89, 99, 139–40, 173, 175–6, 199
food prices, subsidised 144, 176, 177, 178, 180, 198, 242, 288
food shortages 38–9, 50, 54, 57, 59, 63, 188, 206
forced labour camps see gulags (forced labour camps)
foreign policy
under Andropov 189
under Brezhnev 180–1, 183–8
under Chernenko 189
under Gorbachev 195, 197, 226–33
under Khrushchev 129, 144–54
under Stalin 72–82, 87, 89, 100–23
France
alliance with Soviet Union 74, 75–6, 81
declaration of war against Germany 80
defeat of 91
invasion of 101
Munich Agreement (1938) 77
post-war Germany and 118
support of right-wing groups 76
Franco-Soviet Non-Aggression Pact (1932) 74
Franco-Soviet Pact (1935) 76

'free market' system 18
Friedman, Milton 19, 270
Friendship, Alliance and
    Mutual Assistance, Treaty
    of (1950) 153
Fukuyama, Francis 292

Gaddis, John 107, 150
Gaidar, Yegor 274, 275, 280,
    286
Galbraith, J. K. 271
Gamarnik, Yan 69
Gargarin, Yuri 141
Geneva Conference (1988)
    227
Georgia 28, 223, 224, 252
Germany
    Anschluss with Austria 76
    Berlin Wall 129
    currency reform 118
    division of 104, 118,
    149–51
    expansionist aggression
    of 74–5
    industrial revival of
    117–18
    invasion of
    Czechoslovakia 77–8
    invasion of Poland 80
    invasion of USSR
    (Operation Barbarossa,
    1941) 88, 91–3
    Khrushchev and 149–51
    Nazi-Soviet Non-
    Aggression Pact (1939)
    50, 76–81, 82
    as post-war threat to
    USSR 117–18
    reunification 230
    and Spanish Civil War 75
    surrender of 94
    Treaty of Berlin (1930)
    74
    Treaty of Rapallo (1922)
    74, 81
Getty, J. Arch 72
GKO (State Committee of
    Defence) 89, 92–3, 97
glasnost (openness) 71, 195,
    197, 208, 211–13
globalisation 19
Gorbachev, Mikhail (b.1931)
    abandonment of

Brezhnev Doctrine
    (1968) 229
agriculture under 202–3,
    205
background 171
collapse of Soviet Union
    and 233
coup against 256–9
culture and the arts
    under 212
demokratizatsiya
    (democratisation) 195,
    197, 208–9, 213–14,
    216–20, 248–56
Eastern Europe under
    227–33
economic policies under
    195, 197, 198–206, 228,
    241–7
economic 'shock therapy'
    and 275
elections under 216–17,
    220–2
foreign policy under 195,
    197, 226–33
glasnost (openness) 71,
    195, 197, 208, 211–13
historians on 214, 231–2,
    247, 259–60
industry under 203
living standards under
    206, 242–3
perestroika (restructuring)
    195, 197, 201–3, 210,
    241–3, 247
political reforms under
    207–25, 243–5, 248–56
resignation of 240, 258–9
rise to power 171–2
Trotsky's ideas and 195
Yeltsin and 253–4
Gosplan (State General
    Planning Commission)
    52, 56, 139
Gottwald, Klement 114
'grain crisis' 53, 58
grain procurement 38, 57,
    58–9
Grand Alliance 88–9, 100–3,
    111
Great Depression 74
Great Patriotic War (1941-
    45) 87, 90–6 see also

Second World War
    Germany's surrender 94
    historians on 95
    impact of 96
    Kursk, battle for 95
    Leningrad, siege of 95
    mortality rates 96
    Operation Barbarossa
    (1941) 91–3
    Operation Uranus (1942)
    94
    'scorched earth' policy
    93, 96
    Stalingrad, battle for 94
    US Lend-Lease
    agreement 94
'great person' theory 247
Great Purge 50, 66–9
Great Terror 50, 69–72, 133
Greece 295
Grishin, Viktor 200, 208
Gromyko, Andrei 208
Gulag Archipelago, The
    (Solzhenitsyn) 166
gulags (forced labour camps)
    63, 69, 70, 135

Halliday, F. 181
Haslam, J. 81
Hayek, Friedrich 19, 270
Helsinki Accord (1975) 167,
    168
Hiroshima 107
history, materialist concept
    of 12
Hitler, Adolf 8, 50, 75
Hobsbawm, Eric 232, 294–5
Hough, J. F. 71, 214
housing shortages 54
Hudson, K. 286
human rights 166–7
Hungarian Revolt (1956)
    129, 145–8
Hungary 111, 113, 178, 186,
    230
Hunter, H. 64
Husak, Gustav 185
hyper-stagflation 288

ideological explanations, of
    Stalin's defeat of rivals
    43–4
'ideological purity' 98

IMF *see* International
    Monetary Fund (IMF)
industrialisation 49, 50, 63–4
industry *see also* defence
    industry
    under Andropov 180
    under Brezhnev 173–6
    factory associations
        (*ob'edineniya*) 176
    in Germany 117–18
    under Gorbachev 203
    under Khrushchev 129,
        139–40, 141–3
    under Stalin 52–6, 62–3,
        89, 99
    under Yeltsin 288, 291
inevitability, concept of 111
inflation 246, 276
infrastructure 99
Intermediate Nuclear Forces
    (INF) Treaty (1987) 227
International Monetary
    Fund (IMF) 185, 283
Inter-Regional Deputies'
    Group 221
Iran 187
Iron Curtain, establishment
    of 112
Islamist fundamentalism 187
Italy 75, 77, 101

Japan 74, 75, 76, 88

Kadar, Janos 147
Kaganovitch, Lazar 64, 154
Kamenev, Lev 24, 26–7, 32,
    33, 34, 35, 36, 37, 39, 40,
    50, 52, 64, 66, 67 see also
    triumvirate
Kargarlitsky, Boris (b. 1958)
    222, 274, 277
Kazakhstan 223
Keep, J. 143
Kenez, P. 143
Kennedy, John F. 151, 152
Kennedy-Pipe, C. 81, 108
Keynes, John Maynard 18
KGB (Committee for State
    Security) 71, 261
KGP (Smallholders Party,
    Hungary) 113
Khalkin-Gol, Battle of 76
Khasbulatov, Ruslan 277,

279
Khrushchev, Nikita (1894–
    1971)
    agriculture under 129,
        138
    background 99
    Brezhnev and 136
    China and 152–3
    culture and the arts
        under 134–5
    de-Stalinisation 128, 129,
        132–7, 145, 154
    Eastern Europe under
        144–8
    economic policies under
        137–44
    Five-Year Plans 139–40
    foreign policy under 129,
        144–54
    German problem 149–51
    industry under 129,
        139–40, 141–3
    legal reforms 135
    living standards under
        135, 138, 143–4
    'peaceful co-existence'
        policy 148–9, 153
    political reforms under
        130–7
    resignation of 128, 129,
        154–5
    rise to power 131–2
    secret speech 128, 129,
        133–4, 137, 144, 148
    Stalin and 131
    as Stalin's successor 98,
        128
Kirov, Sergei 35, 50, 65–6
Klein, N. 275
kolkhozes (co-operative
    farms) 59, 99, 176–7, 202
Komsomol (Young
    Communists) 30, 59
Kosygin, Aleksei (1904–80)
    155, 162, 163, 173–4, 183
Kronstadt Rising (1921) 26
Krupskaya, Nadezhda
    (1869–1939) 29, 30, 32,
    34, 35, 36
kulaks (wealthy peasants) 38,
    43, 57, 58–9, 63
Kun, Bela 146
Kuromiya, Hiroaki 30, 58,

121
Kursk 95

Lancet, The (medical journal)
    271
Lane, D. 272
language 208, 224
Latvia 74, 79, 252 see also
    Baltic states
Law on Individual Labour
    Activity (1986) 203, 205
Law on Joint Enterprises
    (1986) 203
Law on Press Freedom
    (1990) 255
Law on State Enterprises
    (1988) 205
League of Nations 75
Left Opposition 31–2, 39, 51
legal reforms 135
Lenin, Vladimir Ilyich
    (1870-1924)
    background 16
    ban on factions 16, 26
    Bolshevik Revolution
        (1917) and 16
    death of 29–30
    democratic centralism
        and 15–16
    New Economic Policy
        (NEP) 16
    one-party state and 25–6
    Stalin and 23, 25, 28–9,
        32, 41, 223
    Testament and Postscript
        23, 28–9, 30, 32, 36, 133
    Trotsky and 16, 26, 27,
        29
    wife of 29–30, 32
Leningrad, siege of 95
Leningrad Affair 98
Leninism 15–16
Lewin, M. 42, 61, 92, 137,
    170, 174
life expectancy 271, 289
Ligachev, Yegor 200, 216,
    254
Lippmann, Walter 17
Lithuania 74, 79, 91, 240,
    251, 254 see also Baltic
    states
Litvinov, Maksim 75, 81
living standards

The Soviet Union and Post-Soviet Russia (1924–2000)

under Brezhnev 172,
177–8
under Gorbachev 206,
242–3
under Khrushchev 135,
138, 143–4
Malenkov and 132
under Stalin 54
under Yeltsin 275–6, 281,
284, 286–7, 288
Loth, W. 149
Lucas, C. 289

Machine-Tractor Stations
(MTS) 59, 138
Malenkov, Georgi (1902-88)
98, 129, 131, 132, 146,
154
Malta Summit (1989) 261
Mandel, Ernest 259–60
Mao Zedong 153
Maples, D. 260
market economy 245–7
Marshall Plan (1947) 89,
115, 119
Marx, Groucho (1890-1977)
82
Marx, Karl (1818-83) 12–13,
294
'permanent revolution'
16, 33
Marxism-Leninism 17
McCauley, M. 144
McGwire, M. 231
media *see also* culture and
the arts
glasnost (openness) and
212
Law on Press Freedom
(1990) 255
underground, by
dissidents 166
medical care 143, 206, 276
Medvedev, Roy (b. 1925) 72, '
95, 168, 170, 278, 282
Medvedev, Zhores 168
Merridale, C. 260
Mikolajczyk, Stanislaw 112
Military-Industrial Complex
226–7
Millar, J. 64
minimum wage 143
Moldavia 252

Molotov, Vyacheslav (1890-
1986) 56, 64, 81, 92, 98,
129, 131, 154
'monetarism' 19
Montefiore, S. S. 43
mortality rates
collectivisation 63
Great Patriotic War
(1941-45) 96
Great Terror 71–2
infants 143, 206
under Yeltsin 271, 277
MTS *see* Machine-Tractor
Stations (MTS)
Munich Agreement (1938)
77, 81, 101
Mussolini, Benito 75

Nagasaki 107
Nagy, Imre (1896-1958)
145–7
National Peasants, Romania
113
nationalism 168–9, 197, 209,
223–5, 251–3, 258
NATO (North Atlantic
Treaty Organisation)
(1949) 119–20
Nazi-Soviet Non-
Aggression Pact (1939)
50, 76–81, 82
neo-liberalism
definition of 18–19
in Eastern Europe 231–2
under Yeltsin 270
neo-Stalinism 165–9
NEP *see* New Economic
Policy (NEP)
nepotism 164–5, 268
New Economic Policy
(NEP)
abandonment of 53
adoption of 26
agriculture and 57
Bukharin and 38–40
Gorbachev and 195
Lenin's pragmatism and
16
smychka (alliance) 33, 58
Stalin and 43–4, 51–2
Trotsky and 34
NKVD (People's
Commisariat of Internal

Affairs) 50, 66, 67, 68,
92, 93
nomenklatura system 164–5,
200, 213
North Atlantic Treaty
Organisation (NATO)
(1949) 119–20
Nove, A. 62, 64
Novosibirsk Report 200
novostroika (new structure)
247
nuclear arms race 107, 110,
119–20, 121, 180–1, 183,
189, 226, 227, 260–1 *see
also* defence industry
nuclear disasters 211–12

OGPU *see* Unified State
Political Directorate
(OGPU)
oil crisis (1973-74) 175
oligarchs 268, 269, 271, 273,
281, 282, 290
*One Day in the Life of Ivan
Denisovich* (Solzhenitsyn)
135
one-party state 25–6
Operation Barbarossa (1941)
88, 91–3
Operation Uranus (1942) 94
Orlov, Yuri 167
Overy, R. 95

Pakistan 187
Paris Summit (1960) 149
Pasternak, Boris 135
Pavlov, Valentin 257
PDPA *see* People's
Democratic Party of
Afghanistan (PDPA)
'peaceful co-existence'
policy 148–9, 153
Peasants' Party, Poland 112
People's Commisariat of
Internal Affairs (NKVD)
see NKVD (People's
Commisariat of Internal
Affairs)
*People's Democratic Party of
Afghanistan (PDPA)* 187
Percentages Agreement
(1944) 102–3, 105, 111,
116

perestroika (restructuring)
195, 197, 201–3, 210,
241–3, 247
'permanent revolution,'
theory of 16, 33
'Phoney War' 91
Pinochet option 278–9
Podgorny, Nikolai 163, 164
Poland
demonstrations in 145,
162
division of 50, 79
elections in 112
Germany's invasion of 80
Grand Alliance
discussions on 102
protection of, from
Germany 78
reform in 230
refusal by, to Red Army
entry 77
Solidarity trade union
protests 186
Soviet control of 112
Soviet invasion of 91
Soviet pact with 74
Politburo 26, 34–5, 97, 99 *see
also* Russian Communist
Party (RCP)
political reforms
executive presidency
249–50, 255
under Gorbachev 207–
25, 243–5, 248–56
under Khrushchev 130–7
Popov, Gavril 243
post-Soviet era, economic
policies 18–19
Potsdam Conference (1945)
89, 106–7
poverty 268, 269, 271, 275–
6, 280, 287, 288, 289
Prague Spring (1968) 184–5
Pravda (newspaper) 38, 40
Presidium 99
Primakov, Yevgeny 284
private property ownership
246
privatization
Abalkin Programme 245
under Gorbachev 202–3,
205
of social services 19

under Yeltsin 268, 269,
270, 273–4, 281, 282,
283, 286, 290
Pugo, Boris 257
purges *see also* Great Purge;
Great Terror
effects of, on
industrialisation 56
in Red Army 69–70
under Stalin 25, 65–72,
89, 97, 98, 116, 133
of Titoists 116
Putin, Vladimir (b. 1952)
background 287
as successor to Yeltsin
270, 286–7

Rakosi, Matyas 145
Rapallo, Treaty of 74, 81
RCP *see* Russian
Communist Party (RCP)
Reagan, Ronald 19, 227,
270
'realpolitik' 82
Red Army, purges in 69–70
reform communism 137
reparations *see* war
reparations
Rhineland 75
Rigby, T. H. 71
Rittersporn, G. 72
Roberts, G. 81, 109, 151,
184
Romania 79, 111, 113, 186,
230
Romanov, Grigori 200, 208
Rome-Berlin Axis 75
Roosevelt, Franklin D. 89,
101, 103, 105, 118–19
RSDLP *see* Russian Social
Democratic Party
(RSDLP)
Russian Communist Party
(RCP) *see also* Politburo
Bolshevik Revolution
(1917) and 23
expulsions from 36–8
Left Opposition and
31–2
name change, to
Communist Party of the
Soviet Union (CPSU) 99
Politburo and 26

post-1945 98
Right, defeat of 38–40
split of, into Left, Centre,
and Right 34
Russian Social Democratic
Party (RSDLP) 16
Russian Socialist Federal
Soviet Republic
(RSFSR) 25, 32
Rutskoi, Alexsandr 275–6,
279
Ryutin, Martemyan 64–5
Ryutin Affair 65
Ryzhkov, Nikolai 200, 202,
216, 245

Sachs, Jeffrey 273
Sakharov, Andrei 165, 167,
168, 170, 213, 220
Sakwa, R. 285, 289
SALT (Strategic Arms
Limitations Treaty) 183,
184
Sapir, Jacques 198
'satellite states' *see* Eastern
Europe; *specific countries*
secession 252
Second Cold War 162, 181,
182, 184, 186, 188, 189,
227, 228 *see also* Cold
War
'second revolution, from
above' 61
Second World War *see also*
Great Patriotic War
(1941-45)
economic impact of 96
Grand Alliance 88–9,
100–3
mortality rates 96
Soviet neutrality (1939-
41) 88
secret police *see* KGB
(Committee for State
Security); NKVD
(People's Commisariat of
Internal Affairs)
security *see* foreign policy
Service, Robert 28, 30, 71,
78, 133, 140, 168, 188,
215, 232, 260, 282
Sewell, M. 73
Shatalin Plan 245

Shevardnadze, Eduard 248, 253, 254
'shock therapy' policies 19, 232, 269, 270–7, 286, 288
Shostakovich, Dmitri 135
show trials 67–9, 114 *see also* Great Purge
Sinyavsky, Andrei 166
Smallholders Party (KGP), Hungary 113
Smirnov, Ivan 65, 67
social services 18–19
social wage 178
'socialism in one country' 33, 34, 44
socio-cultural explanations, of Stalin's defeat of rivals 43
Solidarity trade union (Poland) 186
Solzhenitsyn, Alexander (1918-2008) 166, 168
Soviet Union, collapse of 233, 240, 246–7, 256–61
Sovietisation 120–1, 145, 223–5
sovkhozes (state-run farms) 99, 203
space programme 140–1, 189
Spain 295
Spanish Civil War (1936-39) 75, 76
'sphere of influence' 102, 103, 105, 106, 111, 119, 153, 182, 187
Stakhanov, Alexei 55
Stalin, Josef (1880-1953)
   agriculture under 49–50, 57–61, 89, 100
   background 25
   cult of personality 97
   culture and the arts under 98
   death of 128, 129
   defeat of rivals 41–4
   Eastern Europe under 89, 91, 108–23
   economic policies under 51–64, 99–100
   Five-Year Plans 52–6, 62, 89, 99
   foreign policy under

72–82, 87, 89, 100–23
   historians on 41–4, 61–4, 108
   industry under 52–6, 62–3, 89, 99
   Khrushchev and 131
   Lenin and 23, 25, 28–9, 32, 41, 223
   Marxism-Leninism and 17
   New Economic Policy (NEP) and 43–4, 51–2
   Politburo and 34–5, 97
   post-1924 power struggle 31–8
   post-1945 political control 97–9
   power consolidation by, 1929-1935 64–72
   pre-1924 position 24–31
   purges under 25, 53, 65–72, 89, 97, 98, 116, 133
   Right, defeat of, and 38–40
   'second revolution, from above' 61
   Second World War and 88–9
   'socialism in one country' 33, 44
   Trotsky and 33, 42
   Trotsky's assassination 27
   United Opposition and 35–8
Stalinism 17
Stavka (Soviet Military High Command) 89, 92, 97
Steininger, R. 149
'storming' method, in industrial production 63
Strategic Arms Limitation Treaty (START) (1988) 227
Strategic Arms Limitations Treaty (SALT) talks 183, 184
strikes *see* demonstrations
structuralist explanations, of Stalin's defeat of rivals 42–3
Sudetenland 76, 77
Supreme Soviet 219, 221, 246, 249, 270

Syrtsov, Sergey 64, 67

Taylor, A. J. P. 44, 81
Tehran Conference (1943) 88–9, 102
Tereshkova, Valentina 141
Thatcher, Margaret 19, 228, 270
thaw, the 129, 131–2, 135 *see also* de-Stalinisation
Thaw, The (Ehrenburg) 135
Tikhanov, Nikolai 169
Tito, Josip 116, 145
Tolstoy, Leo (1828-1910) 247
trade unions 18, 19, 178, 186, 206, 280
triumvirate 27, 29
Trizonia 118
Trotsky, Leon (1879-1940)
   assassination of 27
   background 27
   Bukharin and 38–40
   defeat of 24, 27
   deportation of 38, 39
   Gorbachev and 195
   historians on 42
   industrialisation and 51
   Left Opposition and 31–2
   Lenin and 16, 26, 27, 29
   'permanent revolution' and 33, 44
   Politburo and 35, 36–7
   Soviet regime as transitional society 203–4
   Stalin and 33, 42, 223
   on Stalin's rise to power 44
   United Opposition and 35–8
Trotskyism 32–4, 67, 68, 69, 72
Truman, Harry S. 89, 105–6, 110
Truman Doctrine (1947) 89, 115
Tucker, Robert C. 41, 61, 72, 81
Tukhachevsky, Mikhail 69
Turkey 152

Ukraine 63, 93, 211, 240,

258
Ulbricht, Walter 151
unemployment 242–3, 245,
    268, 269, 272, 275, 289
Unified State Political
    Directorate (OGPU) 66
Union of Soviet Socialist
    Republics (USSR),
    formation of 32
Union Treaty 252–3, 256,
    257, 258
unions see trade unions
United Nations 288
United Opposition 35–8,
    52, 53
Urals-Siberian method 57,
    58
US
    alliance with Soviet
        Union 74, 88–9, 100–3
    collapse of Soviet Union
        and 261
    Cuban Missile Crisis
        129, 152
    détente and 183
    Lend-Lease agreement
        with USSR 94, 99, 105
    Malta Summit (1989)
        261
    Marshall Plan (1947)
        89, 115
    Military-Industrial
        Complex 226–7
    NATO (North Atlantic
        Treaty Organisation)
        (1949) 119–20
    neo-liberalism in 19
    post-war Germany and
        117–18
    Potsdam Conference
        (1945) 89, 106–7
    relations with, under
        Khrushchev 148–9
    Second Cold War and
        181
    Soviet invasion of
        Afghanistan and 188
    Spanish Civil War (1936-
        39) and 76
    'Star Wars' (Strategic
        Defensive Initiative –
        SDI) project 227, 261
    Tehran Conference

(1943) 88–9, 102
    Truman Doctrine (1947)
        89, 115
    unemployment in 272
    Yalta Conference (1945)
        89, 103–6
uskorenie (accelerated
    growth) 201

'velvet revolutions' 230–3
Versailles, Treaty of 76
Vesenkha (Supreme
    Council of the National
    Economy) 52
'Virgin Lands' policy 138
Volkogonov, D. 247, 260

Walker, R. 225
War Communism 25–6
war reparations 89, 96, 99,
    104, 106, 112, 117, 119,
    144
war scares 52–3
Ward, C. 95
Warsaw Letter (1968) 185
Warsaw Pact (1955) 120,
    146, 185, 227–9
West, the, relations with,
    under Brezhnev 183–4
Wheatcroft, S. 63
White, S. 255, 287, 291, 292
Williamson, D. 147
'Winter War' (1939-40) 91
Wood, A. 105
Woodin, M. 289
work see employment
working conditions 143, 206
World War I see First World
    War (1914–18)
World War II see Second
    World War

Yakovlev, Alexander 200,
    212, 226, 248, 253, 254
Yalta Conference (1945) 89,
    103–6
Yanaev, Gennadi 256
Yazov, Dimitri 257
Yeltsin, Boris (1931-2007)
    background 201
    Bush and 261
    constitutional dissolution
        278–9

corruption under 283–4
    coup against Gorbachev
        and 257–8
    economic collapse under
        288–92
    economic policies under
        268, 269, 270–7, 280–1,
        283–4, 286–90
    elections under 279–83
    Gorbachev and 221
    industry under 288, 291
    living standards under
        275–6, 281, 284, 286–7,
        288
    as market economy
        supporter 245, 268
    opposition to 269, 270,
        277–8, 280–1, 285–6
    political crises 284–5
    politicking of, 1990-91
        253–4
    privatisation under 268,
        269, 270, 273–4, 281,
        282, 283, 286, 290
    resignation of 270, 286
    as Russian president 240,
        254, 268
    shelling of parliament
        279
    vs. Supreme Soviet
        278–9
Young Communists
    (Komsomol) 30
Yugoslavia 98, 116, 145, 149

Zaslavskaya, Tatiana (1927-
    2013) 200
Zhdanov, Andrei (1896-
    1949) 70, 98, 115
Zhirinovsky, Vladimir 248,
    280
Zhukov, Georgi 89, 93, 97,
    131, 154
Zinoviev, Grigory 24, 26–7,
    32, 33, 34, 35, 36, 37, 39,
    40, 50, 52, 64, 66, 67 see
    also triumvirate
Zyuganov, Gennady 277–8,
    280, 281, 282, 283

Acknowledgements

The authors and publishers acknowledge the following sources of copyright material and are grateful for the permissions granted. While every effort has been made, it has not always been possible to identify the sources of all the material used, or to trace all copyright holders. If any omissions are brought to our notice, we will be happy to include the appropriate acknowledgements on reprinting.

Figure 2.1 – ullsteinbild/TopFoto; Figure 2.2 – David King; Figure 2.3 – David King; Figure 2.4 – Fine Art Images/Heritage Images/ Getty Images; Figure 3.1 – Sovfoto/UIG via Getty Images; Figure 3.2 – RIA Novosti/Alamy; Figure 3.4 – David King; Figure 3.5 – David King; Figure 3.6 – TopFoto; Figure 4.1 – Hulton-Deutsch Collection/ CORBIS; Figure 4.2 – Mary Evans Picture Library/Alamy; Figure 4.3 – Ann Ronan Pictures/Print Collector/Getty Images; Figure 4.4 – Three Lions/Getty Images; Figure 4.5 – original published in Krokodil, #10, 1951, by cartoonist Boris Efimov, available via East View Information Services Pravda Digital Archive (DA-PRA); Figure 4.6 – David Low/Solo Syndication; Figure 4.7 – CTK/Alamy; Figure 5.1 – World History Archive/Alamy; Figure 5.2 – Keystone-France/ Gamma-Keystone/Getty Images; Figure 5.3 – RIA Novosti/Alamy; Figure 5.4 – Keystone-France/Gamma-Keystone/Getty Images; Figure 5.5 – ITAR-TASS Photo Agency/Alamy; Figure 6.1 – ITAR-TASS Photo Agency/Alamy; Figure 6.2 – Heritage Image Partnership Ltd/ Alamy; Figure 6.3 – Universal History Archive/Getty Images; Figure 6.5 – Mondadori Portfolio/Getty Images; Figure 7.2 – AP/Topfoto; Figure 7.3 – RIA Novosti/TopFoto; Figure 7.4 – SHONE/GAMMA/ Gamma-Rapho/Getty Images; Figure 7.5 – RIA Novosti/TopFoto; Figure 7.6 – AFP/Getty Images; Figure 7.8 – Jeff Koterba; Figure 8.1 – Vitaly Armand/AFP/Getty Images; Figure 8.2 – Punch; Figure 8.4 – World History Archive/Alamy; Figure 8.5 – PIKO/AFP/Getty Images; Figure 8.6 – Diane-Lu Hovasse/AFP/Getty Images; Figure 8.7 – RIA Novosti/Alamy; Figure 9.1 – David Horsey, seattlepi.com; Figure 9.2 – Steve Raymer/Corbis; Figure 9.4 – Library of Congress, Prints & Photographs Division, drawing by Edmund S. Valtman, [LC-USZ62-130438]; Figure 10.1 – ITAR-TASS Photo Agency / Alamy; Figure 10.2 – Keystone-France/Gamma-Keystone/Getty Images.